To Build Our Lives Together

Hist 96
Sp'05

To Build Our Lives Together

Community

Formation

in Black Atlanta,

1875–1906

ALLISON DORSEY

The University of Georgia Press • Athens and London

© 2004 by the University of Georgia Press

Athens, Georgia 30602

All rights reserved

Set in Minion by Bookcomp, Inc.

Printed and bound by Maple-Vail

The paper in this book meets the guidelines for

permanence and durability of the Committee on

Production Guidelines for Book Longevity of the

Council on Library Resources.

Printed in the United States of America

08   07   06   05   04   C   5   4   3   2   1

08   07   06   05   04   P   5   4   3   2   1

Library of Congress Cataloging-in-Publication Data

Dorsey, Allison, 1959–

To build our lives together : community formation in Black Atlanta,
1875–1906 / Allison Dorsey.

    p.   cm.

Includes bibliographical references (p.) and index.

ISBN 0-8203-2618-6 (hardcover : alk. paper) —

ISBN 0-8203-2619-4 (pbk. : alk. paper)

1. African Americans—Georgia—Atlanta—History.   2. Atlanta
(Ga.)—History.   3. Atlanta (Ga.)—Race relations—History.   I. Title.

F294.A89N435   2004

975.8'700496073—dc22

2003023677

British Library Cataloging-in-Publication Data available

With gratitude to my mother, Nellie Pearl, at whose knee
I learned the love of reading and of history.

CONTENTS

ILLUSTRATIONS

ACKNOWLEDGMENTS

The mythology of American individualism would have us believe that all accomplishments and successes are a result of our own independent efforts and actions. The fallacy of this ideology was never more apparent to me than when I began to try to document the amazing number of people whose assistance made this work possible. Indeed, dozens of people have offered their expertise, time, energy and support over the years. I begin by acknowledging the institutional support of Swarthmore College through which I received a Lindback Foundation Grant that supported necessary research travel and an Albertson Faculty Fellowship that funded academic leave such that I might devote time to writing.

A special thank you to Malcolm Call for long ago believing in this project, and to editor Nancy Grayson for seeing the project to fruition. Thanks as well to the anonymous readers whose criticisms and suggestions made the work richer and stronger.

Several librarians and archivists were of great assistance in completing the research for this project. The archivists and library staff at the Woodruff Library at Atlanta University, the Auburn Avenue Research Library, and the archivist at Spelman College were most helpful in guiding me through the materials in their collections. Similarly, the librarians at Emory University, in particular Curator of African American Collections Randall K. Burkett, offered immeasurable assistance in helping me track down some of Atlanta's nineteenth-century movers and shakers. The staff of the Amistad Collection at Tulane University and their counterparts at the Peabody Museum at Harvard University were more than cooperative in helping me to secure needed materials in the tiny window of opportunity allotted during my short research trips. Thank you to the Atlanta History Center staff and Carol Purdy of the DeKalb Historical Center for going the extra mile to track down an obscure reference, often in record time. I offer a very special thank you to all the library personnel who provided, with good cheer, professional, speedy aid on the "home front" at Swarthmore College. Thank you as well to former student Andrew Kinney for his research support, pouring over microfilm during long hot un-air conditioned days.

Beyond all the research assistance, I am grateful to several people who offered assistance in the writing phase of this project. Thank you to Victoria Vernon whose superior skills as a "ghost" editor and gentle nudging helped smooth out the prose of this work. All remaining errors of syntax, style, or substance are mine, and mine alone. A special thank you to Jane James, whose computer wizardry safeguarded this manuscript, with no lost data, through many incarnations. Thank you as well to Richard Blackett and Linda Reed who organized the Black History Workshop at the University of Houston. The workshop provided an excellent opportunity to share my work with, and receive much needed feedback from, other scholars, Beth Bates and Karen Ferguson among them, with an interest in black community studies.

Over the years many fellow academics have befriended and encouraged me to complete this work. To fellow Black Atlanta scholar Gregory Mixon, thank you for the many hours of conversation and debate. Thank you for the seemingly endless devotion to your craft and for pulling me along in your wake. Special notes of thanks to Leslie Harris with whom I have discussed this project since our days at the Martin Luther King Jr. Papers Project, to Doug Egerton, for reading and rereading this manuscript, and to Venus Green, for always reminding me of the value of my subject matter. To Felix Armfield, Martha Hodes, Richard Pierce, and Rick Valelly who also read parts of the manuscript, thank you for your critical feedback and suggestions. I must also acknowledge the friendship and support of Swarthmore College colleagues Bruce Dorsey, Keith Reeves, Charles James, and Cynthia Halpern whose commentary and insight have helped shaped my thinking about history and teaching.

The love and support of devoted and compassionate friends has aided me at every step of the long walk to complete this project. Adenike Sharpley, Natalie Roberts, Eve Sandberg, and Sabrina Ford have each been there to encourage me, make me laugh when I wanted to cry and most important, help me stay the course. Thank you. I also offer much gratitude to the 3R Coolfont Ladies, sisterfriends, who cheered me all the way to the deadline. And to the Council of Wise Women, aka the Sunday Afternoon Book Club, thank you for being a much needed source of alternative mental stimulation! Your passion for knowledge, your love of reading, insight, advice, and warm friendships remind me of the joy of learning. A heartfelt thanks to the members of Team 1. Here's to being "First amongst firsts!"

To my students: for more than a decade I have been privileged to work with talented, intelligent, enthusiastic young people who challenged me to expand my knowledge of the past and to constantly fine-tune my teaching skills. Thank you for the gentle criticism and the generous praise.

Ultimately, the love and kindness of several family members made this work possible. My sister Marion Frank has been steadfast in her support of my choice of an academic career. Her material assistance has been surpassed only by her spiritual support. Indeed, our many lengthy phone conversations were necessary restoratives. I must also acknowledge the contribution of Roberta Frank who, sadly, did not live to see this work completed. Aunt Robbie, who reminded me to always celebrate my successes and to offer assistance to those who came behind me, also cared for my family when both money and time were tight. Robbie, for all the cups of tea, holiday dinners, and slices of blueberry pie, laced with love and kindness, thank you.

Thank you as well to my sons Brandon and Ian. The work for this text, from completing the research for the dissertation to revising the manuscript for publication, has consumed the better part of your young lives. You showed immeasurable patience as your mother cloistered herself in archives, libraries, and offices, always "working" to complete the project. Thank you for being the necessary distractions of life, for serving as delightful reminders of all that is deeply rich and truly important. I look forward now to watching as you begin the next exciting stage of your lives.

Last but not least, I offer my love and appreciation to my single greatest cheerleader, closest friend, confidante, and the center of my family, my husband Brian Ward. For never wavering in your love and support, for your wise council and the gift of laughter, and for our two beautiful sons, thank you. Meet you at the Bellagio!

To Build Our Lives Together

INTRODUCTION

The present study focuses, as its title indicates, on the positive evolution of a community of African Americans in Atlanta. My subject here is the long, slow, and painstaking process of interwoven personal and communal actions and interactions through which Black Atlantans successfully constructed a community from the ashes of slavery and the Civil War. Atlanta was manifestly a city of the New, rather than the Old, South. The nature of antebellum urban development, the special disorganization and displacement caused by the war, and the relocation of freedmen and -women to the Gate City meant that blacks in Atlanta were comparatively few in number, dispersed in location, and had little common history of municipal community as Reconstruction began. They were, therefore, forced to start fresh in their shared project of making a place and life for themselves in the relatively raw conditions of postwar Atlanta. Such conditions offer historians ideal circumstances in which to study the creation of a black community in freedom and the adverse reactions that such a community provoked in white southerners. The race riot that brought national attention to the city in 1906 was, in part, an attempt to destroy the gains made by Black Atlantans in the decades leading up to the violence. However tragic, the story of the riot should neither surpass nor erase the memory of earlier efforts of men and women to build new lives for themselves and their people. It is my intent here to commemorate the efforts of the members of the African American community in Atlanta to create conditions in which they might prosper rather than to emphasize yet again the drama of the race riot.

My study of the city argues that the culture, traditions, and survival mechanisms that African Americans developed in slavery played a significant role in the culture and community institutions they created in the post–Civil War period. Blacks exited slavery with a belief structure, an ideology, of race-based cooperation that was at the core of identity for the African American community in freedom. The shared past of the freedmen and -women included both the terrors of slavery *and* the solidarity of the slave quarters. The active racism of southern whites in particular and American racialist thinking in general reinforced black notions of solidarity. What is more, given the fiscal reality of most African Americans, this ideology of intraracial cooperation, especially in the first three to four decades after the end of slavery, was not yet compromised by nascent intraracial class conflicts. Central to the physical and socioeconomic development of the black community in Atlanta, the ideology of racial solidarity became the foundation on which organizations and institutions would later be built. African Americans had been enslaved as a race, and they understood that they must rise in freedom as a race.

This racial solidarity was not, however, immune to contemporary social and political discourse about the mission of "civilizing" the newly freed. Slavery's end had a progressive and increasingly disruptive impact on the community networks and worldview. Yet the values and traditions laid down in the slave quarters did not simply fall away with the chains of bondage. Instead, below the surface of dialogue about the "civilization" and cultural regeneration of freed people, mouthed by both black elites and white liberals, lay a fundamental belief in and dedication to racial solidarity. Blacks' commitment to the vote, to education, to fair wages, and to equitable treatment as citizens was tied to commitment to their communities and "the race" at large.[1]

The goal of this study is to develop an understanding of the lives of black people who lived in the preeminent city of the New South in the first generation after the end of slavery. It addresses Black Atlantans' understanding of race, and the behavior stimulated and defined by it. This inquiry into the history of Atlanta's African American community, though not intended as the definitive treatment, does seek to suggest its richness and variety. I will emphasize here the core institutions of the community in Black Atlanta: the black churches, fraternal organizations, and social clubs that were at the forefront of the community's battle with a repressive southern society. The style and form of community organizations reveal both the structures of community evolution and something of the changing belief systems involved in the work of racial progress and uplift. Atlanta's black churches were centers of education, social services, and political activism for African Americans both during and after Reconstruction. As Robert McMath has observed, "Wherever Americans sought to establish ties of community in the nineteenth century, they built churches and Atlanta was no exception."[2] Fraternal organizations provided internal social welfare and support networks for the African American community, and simultaneously were sites of status competition and conflict. Social clubs and literary societies proved to be important locations for cultivating a new cultural ideology and new sets of social behaviors, especially among higher-status blacks.[3]

Only as we investigate the history of the community's formation, its growing size and strength, unity and relative independence, does a more complete picture of Black Atlanta emerge. Because Black Atlantans, routinely denied municipal services and benefits, access to financial institutions, and the rights of citizenship, had to do for themselves, they were partially able to elude some of the social controls imposed on blacks in less progressive communities. Consequently, their slight but increasing success as a community constituted an implicit threat to white power and authority, which provoked a violent reactionary response. Race riot, the bigger, bolder second cousin to lynching, was a new violent form of racial control in the post–Civil War American South. Emancipation had deprived southern whites of slavery, their most effective method of repressive control over African Americans. Lynching, the highly sexual torture and murder of individual black men and women, had a chilling but somewhat fleeting effect upon black consciousness and behavior. Riots, as Joel Williamson has argued, were most often "preceded by a long period of agitation on the white side." And, unlike lynching, "which singled out individual" blacks for maiming and murder, riot "broadened" the scope to allow more whites to extend violent control over "any and all blacks."[4] The violent outburst of riot was often resolved by the passage of repressive legal codes that provided white supremacist southerners with new tools with which to bludgeon African Americans. Atlanta was engulfed by this kind of violence for three days in the fall of 1906. The riot began in the downtown area and spread to encompass the black neighborhoods of Darktown and Brownsville. Black citizens experienced property destruction, physical terror, and murder at the hands of their white peers. Before the riot ended, at least twelve Atlantans were dead, hundreds of thousands of dollars' worth of property had been destroyed, and seventeen units of the Georgia State militia—amounting to more than six hundred soldiers—had been assigned to the city.

The local, national, and international press was fascinated by the violence in Atlanta, a city previously heralded for progressive race relations. The media determined that the Atlanta race riot was a dramatic and spontaneous response to incidents of interracial rape perpetrated by black men against white women. Front-page stories of assaults against helpless white females appeared in the local newspapers, including the *Atlanta Constitution* and *Journal*. These stories so inflamed the passions of white men, or so it was argued, that rage overruled reason, and, sadly, violence had ensued. Yet in the rush to judgment, reporters and critics failed to unearth the deeper causes of the disturbance. Although the idea of rape, rumors of rape, and even actual rapes may have been the spark, they were not the fuel that fed the firestorm of the riot.

The Atlanta race riot was a product of a manufactured frenzy concerning black degeneration, "intemperance," and crime that had been instigated in the 1880s and reinvigorated in the weeks preceding the riot by politicians, with considerable aid from the local press. More important, the riot was in large measure a visceral reaction on the part of the white population to the presence of a maturing black community with dynamic, forward-looking leadership. The existence of this African American community represented a multilayered challenge to the power white society possessed to maintain a racial status quo. As Tera Hunter has observed, "despite effective community mobilizations on many fronts—indeed, because of their effect—blacks were increasingly met with systematic encroachments on their civil and human rights."[5] The historical record of the last quarter of the nineteenth century clearly indicates how, at every turn, white racial radicals led the charge to limit the kinds of gains blacks identified as essential to their own progress and development as citizens and members of a community.

Citizens of Black Atlanta worked to organize their lives to maximize their liberty through the pursuit of education, employment, religious life, and social activities. The creation of a viable black community was of paramount importance to survival and for "racial progress." My use of the term "community," however, should suggest neither consummate solidarity nor perfect consensus. African Americans in nineteenth-century Atlanta did not share a utopian communality based on either their class or their racial category. But freedmen and -women did cultivate a sense of community based on the shared circumstances of their lives: past enslavement, poverty, and, later in the period, institutionalized segregation. Of course, such descriptives may conjure up images of life as it might exist in a prison rather than in a society marked by the interconnected spaces of fraternal, familial, and financial relationships. And indeed, historians must be mindful of Clarence Walker's admonition: "Community generated by oppression is no true community."[6] Still, African Americans in Atlanta sought to push beyond these shared negatives to create a viable community, and this work seeks to examine the ways in which they achieved this goal.

Community formation is a complex process. Communities are fixed and flexible, real and (as has been argued) "imagined," spaces.[7] "Fixed" categories, whether created by market forces, religious beliefs, sexual orientation, or national/racial ideologies, can generate lines of demarcation that outline potential communities. Such divisions are often reinforced externally by the beliefs, legal codes, and social customs of the external and dominant group. This partitioning is just one feature of community. Inside the lines, persons marked by gender, religion, or class create community while negotiating daily life in a shared space, with shared options and pleasures and often shared goals. This is the flexible facet of community. Human interaction—the development of patterns that become custom, common language styles, mutually remembered morality tales, and days of celebration—makes up the interior of community. The real and the imagined are the woof and warp of community, which is both an entity in and of itself and a site of opposition to other communities.

"Black Atlanta" refers here to a collection of black enclaves scattered across the city. Different enclaves might order the collective goals differently—lower-status blacks placing pursuit of viable employment above formal education, propertied blacks placing moral reformation and political access above social activity. Nonetheless, like the interlocking pattern of a honeycomb, diverse segments of the black population in Atlanta were linked through shared cultural fraternity and racial solidarity, forming a larger community—each group a multisided unit, separate and discrete, yet also interdependent, creating a variegated and dynamic whole.

The concept of racial solidarity was at the heart of community for blacks in Atlanta. Slavery was a raced experience; that is, only people marked as black and nonwhite were enslaved. "Slavery," as Eric Foner notes, "was a historical experience which would remain central to their [blacks'] conception of themselves and their place in history."[8] One must, therefore, come to the conclusion that one aspect of this conception was the development of a racial consciousness. Beyond their own internal awareness of themselves as raced, freedmen and -women understood that they were identified in the census, the newspapers, the courts, and tax records by race. They were distinguished from other citizens by the notation "negro," "colored," or "black" next to their names. Yet to say that African Americans organized and worked together because of their race is not to credit some biological factor dependent upon the melanin in their skin. Race in the context of this work refers to something more than physical makeup. Geneticists have discredited the concept of race as a biological determinant and physical marker, which is the way it was used in the late nineteenth and early twentieth centuries.[9] Similarly, social scientists, historians, and literary critics have challenged as fallacy the biological notion of race. Historian Barbara J. Fields, for example, has noted that those who continue "to believe in race as a physical attribute of individuals . . . might as well also believe that Santa Claus, the Easter Bunny and the tooth fairy are real and that the earth stands still while the sun moves."[10]

Although scholars no longer adhere to a concept of race as biological and "natural," it does not follow that concepts of race are invalid or without meaning. Race is "real" inasmuch as people attach meaning to the term, interpret the world around them through that meaning, and are motivated to action in relation to that interpretation. "Social constructions of identity," be they rooted in gender, class, or race, assume that human beings create meaning around a given point of identity. And nineteenth-century Americans did indeed attach specific meanings to racial difference—to blackness in particular.[11] White intellectuals, politicians, ministers, and businessmen rooted their evaluation of intelligence, of who should have access to the rights of citizenship, of who possessed a soul or deserved equal treatment in the marketplace using a construct of racial hierarchy. White Americans defined themselves in part through their racial ranking, which was at the top. African Americans, who had just escaped racebound slavery and lived in a racialist society, attached meaning and value to their raced selves.

The challenge, then, is to develop a working definition of race that avoids the criticism that it is "transhistorical." For my purposes, "race" refers to the combination of complexion, culture, and ancestry by which individuals and communities define themselves and, consequently, others. In accordance with Walker's comment that the "unifying factor in the aggregate experience of nineteenth-century Americans is race," I argue that African Americans (and other Americans) in the late nineteenth century understood themselves to be members of a race. Referring to themselves as "African," "Black," "Colored," or "Negro," these people believed that as individuals they belonged to an interconnected racial group. Race in this construct was as powerful an entity and as motivating a factor as class consciousness or gender identification. Indeed, race conditioned class and gender relations both internal and external to the group.[12]

The survival and success of the race as a whole was crucial to individual African Americans at the end of slavery and well into the twentieth century. The concept of "uplift" addressed in recent studies of African American history reflects this vision. Some of the best scholarship on the subject has both emphasized the "middle-class" origins of the concept of uplift and problematized the core premise of it. Kevin Gaines's work, *Uplifting the Race,* reveals the intellectual tightrope walked by black elites and other uplift workers who understood the challenge of advocating moral and social reform for the "lower classes" while championing basic human rights for all blacks within a racialist society. Evelyn Brooks Higginbotham has offered an important analysis of the complex negotiations carried out by Baptist women in their pursuit of racial justice and reform from within a construct of "respectability." Higginbotham's *Righteous Discontent* has had a significant impact upon my study of Black Atlanta. Her concept of the "politics of respectability," so essential to the struggle for equal access within the dynamic of race relations in the last quarter of the nineteenth century, features prominently in my discussion of high-status blacks in the city. If, as William H. Chafe has argued in his discussion of the Civil Rights movement in Greensboro, North Carolina, progressive race relations were marked on the white side by the "culture of civility," then the politics of respectability identified by Brooks Higginbotham is the necessary corollary on the black side.[13]

Glenda Gilmore's study of gender and politics in North Carolina and Stephanie Shaw's pioneering study of black professional women have also helped scholars discern the interwoven and sometimes conflicting patterns of the work of race uplift in the era of Jim Crow. Like Brooks Higginbotham, Gilmore, with whom I share an understanding of black "communitarianism" in the post–Civil

War era, stresses the dual nature of black women's uplift efforts. While black elite women understood themselves to be of a higher class than women of the masses and worried that "uneducated women" were "dangerously unprepared" to communicate proper racial politics, they also understood that it was their duty to uplift their poorer sisters for the benefit of the race. Stephanie Shaw also analyzes the concept of uplift. More important, she offers scholars a guide designed to help us retrace the process of indoctrination through which young black women came to understand that they must prioritize race over "egotism." Black institutions of higher learning, argues Shaw, simply layered lessons about "community responsibilities" over "earlier socialization in homes." Black women professionals could not escape an understanding that their own status and success in life were firmly attached to the fate of the race as a whole.[14]

There are, however, dangers implicit in the construct of uplift work. Analyses emphasizing the elite origins of the ideology tend to be importing back into time a certain present-day spin on the gulf between the "black middle class" and the "permanent underclass" of the inner city.[15] Discussion of this gulf today—rooted in philosophizing about the causes of poverty and drawing upon urban sociology and heavy doses of media hyperbole—often obscures the real historical and familial links between the human beings in these categories. Thus the much ballyhooed African American who has risen to prominence by way of the middle-class traditions of clean living, self-restraint, and hard work frequently has brothers, sisters, cousins, and friends who have not. Let us consider, for example, the visits of relatives who have "attained" the middle-class status of residency in affluent Prince George's County to mothers and cousins in inner-city Baltimore. In earlier decades, residents of Atlanta's "elite" Brownsville neighborhood undoubtedly experienced a similar angst upon visiting family and friends across the city in Darktown or in rural DeKalb or Fulton County. Such intimate family connections challenge more clinical notions of divisions within the black community. As historian Earl Lewis has noted, "class in the black community must be viewed as part of an intraracial discourse. Oftentimes, a middle-class existence hinged upon the community's agreement; as a consequence, most middle-class blacks lacked the luxury of removing themselves from their working-class relatives and neighbors."[16] In positing a more or less complete separation between middle- and lower-class blacks, the scholarship on racial uplift also tends to discount the impact of extended family networks on the black community's concept of racial solidarity. The title of Don Wallis's oral history of a black community in a twentieth-century midwestern town, *All We Had Was Each Other*, captures the essence of such feeling.

African Americans in Black Atlanta, whose memories of the trials of slavery and the betrayals of Reconstruction were fresh, shared such a sentiment.[17] Their experiences were not uniform and their solidarity was not perfect, but most Black Atlantans enjoyed both a common history of survival and common hopes for the future. The experiences of working in concert to gain access to education for themselves and their children, combining efforts toward material and "moral" progress for the race, and participating in social events (from attending lectures held at the Odd Fellows Hall to gathering in Darktown dives) created and defined community for black residents in Atlanta. This was a racial community to be protected from attacks from without and nurtured from within.

The material circumstances of the vast majority of freedmen and -women in Atlanta in the era of Reconstruction and immediately beyond do not reveal differences in economic position or education and values that would support the premise of intraracial class conflict. Upon the abolition of slavery the percentage of African Americans across the South who owned land, substantial livestock, or other "means of production" that might elevate their position was minute.[18] The vast majority owned only their skills as agricultural laborers, and for the first time they owned themselves and their progeny. Similarly, the percentage of the roughly four million freedmen and -women who were well educated or even literate was tiny. Hundreds of thousands sought education in the postwar period. They flocked to schools sponsored by aid societies or religious organizations, yet most were unable to secure basic schooling let alone advanced degrees. In truth, the lives of most freedmen and -women were not transformed by the core curriculum that dished out moral regeneration along with "readin', " "ritin', " and " 'rithmetic." Scholars must investigate how these structural factors—general poverty and lack of education—may have mitigated class aspirations and divisions within the black community in the immediate postwar era. Most African Americans, especially those who resided in the agricultural South, found that their reality was marked more by class similarity than by difference.

Formerly "free people of color" who had had access to education and economic advancement during slavery were concentrated in a few areas of the South. These southern "aristocrats of color," including mulattos and quadroons, who resided in major urban centers such as Charleston, South Carolina, and New Orleans, Louisiana, often assumed positions of leadership within the black community in the postwar period. They developed political relationships with influential white patrons and supposedly wielded power in closed "Brown Fellowship" societies.[19] Representing a small portion of the African American community, however, they were more the exception than the rule. Not all mixed-race children of the antebellum period could claim the status of free persons. Most whites who had fathered children by slave women maintained them in bondage rather than freeing them and providing them with an education or trade. Nor could all of those who were free depend upon "kinship networks" with affluent whites. Many free people of color were neither affluent nor well educated and found themselves living closer to the margins of slave society than white.[20] Those who were lettered and prosperous might draw lines of distinction that set them apart from their darker peers, but most had few options in the face of the stronger black/white color line except to act as members of the black community.[21]

More important, in the southern cities that blossomed following the Civil War—Atlanta, Memphis, Little Rock—there had been far fewer free people of color in the antebellum years than in cities of the Old South such as Charleston or New Orleans. Atlanta's free black population had not, in the antebellum era, developed an extensive social network or political base. Only one of the ministers who would become a political influence in Black Atlanta had already put down roots in the prewar years.[22] Many of the men and women who became leaders in the postwar community had been slaves with no formal education and certainly no background or experiences that would mark them as middle class.[23] In Atlanta, much of the rhetoric of uplift came from academics and social activists whose commitment to their race demanded a commitment to progress and success irrespective of their working-class origins.

I argue that social status rather than class in a strictly economic sense was the basis of stratification in the late nineteenth century. The vast majority of Black Atlantans between 1875 and 1906 should be classified as working class. It was a population that lived by daily labor rather than on "property income" or "as creditors in loan relationships."[24] Within this larger working-class category, African Americans affiliated with one another on the basis of "a common mode of life and . . . code of behavior."[25] The presence or absence of similar educational backgrounds, religious beliefs, club memberships, and political ideologies determined which Black Atlantans belonged to which status groups within the larger African American community. Status ranking determined Black Atlanta's "best," "rising," and "poor," whether or not the external white community recognized such differences.

The marginal gradations in wealth in early postwar Black Atlanta had increased by the twentieth century. The first two decades of the new century witnessed the development of a small black middle class in Atlanta. The development of this twentieth-century middle class was linked to the pursuit of higher social status, and it grew out of the diverse status affiliations already present in the nineteenth century. Historians, as noted by sociologist Randall Collins, may have misinterpreted Max Weber's theory of social stratification, placing status and class erroneously in opposition. "Status groups are not the antithesis of economic class but precisely the way in which stratified classes are able to emerge and maintain themselves. It is through the organization of status groups that classes become distinctive entities in the market, instead of parts of the endless . . . flux of labor with the tides of supply and demand."[26]

The status groups that developed in Black Atlanta in the post–Civil War period laid the groundwork for business successes in the African American community at the end of the nineteenth century. These successes in turn produced greater gradations in wealth and greater diversity of lifestyle, including increased access to higher education. These lifestyle changes, though always constrained by white racism, stimulated changes in black employment, in the development of financial institutions, and in business investment, and slowly a portion of the black community moved out of the working class and into the middle and upper classes.

Fraternal orders are an excellent example of this process; they provided both social services and status elevation for many black males in Atlanta during this period. Early-twentieth-century black insurance firms in Atlanta (and elsewhere) did not build their businesses from the top down. Rather, they bought out the insurance programs originally run by fraternal and church groups. Thus, the insurance programs of these fraternal orders were the basis for the development of a highly successful private insurance firm, the Atlanta Life Insurance Company, shortly after the turn of the century. Once their fraternal or church groups' insurance programs were bought out by private insurance companies, blacks in Atlanta continued to pay for group insurance from an entity run by and for African Americans. However, they now purchased a policy from a black insurance agent who was generating profit for a group of black middle-class stockholders. Black entrepreneurs appropriated the monopoly that fraternal and church groups had had on insurance within the black community. They quite literally capitalized upon the market created by status groups. The banking and real estate industries would similarly become linked in the African American community. The pursuit of status and the presence of status groups were therefore essential to the eventual development of Atlanta's black middle class.[27]

Status competition best describes the economic conflicts in the black community in post–Civil War Atlanta, but this status-seeking behavior had an additional component. The activities and rituals of the fraternal orders, the benevolent societies attached to black churches, and the social clubs connected with Atlanta's black colleges were not only mechanisms of stratification, but also new places for the creation of community and validation of culture. Much of the writing of historians of slavery has, since 1970, emphasized the ways in which enslaved African Americans nurtured a culture and ideology.[28] Enslaved Americans had their own worldview(s), their own internal set of values and beliefs that sustained them in the face of violence and oppression. Slave culture placed great emphasis upon extended and fictive kin networks; it encouraged group decision-making and community solidarity. Brenda Stevenson's recent work on slavery, for example, stresses the distinctiveness of the slave family and marriage patterns, as well as the development of a "community ethos" marked by an emphasis upon a "responsibility to help others."[29] Whittington B. Johnson's *Black Savannah* challenges traditional ideas about Savannah's race relations and details the efforts of that city's blacks to build and maintain community rooted in the black church. The ideology of slaves was not just a source of mutual support for blacks; it also encouraged them to see whites as untrustworthy and dangerous. Both Wilma King and Norrece Jones have written studies of slavery that question the romantic vision of paternalistic relations between masters and slaves by recasting the slave experience as one of a perpetual war in which blacks viewed whites as enemy "others" who posed a threat to the health of their community.[30]

The study that follows will similarly focus on African American initiative and social development within the black community. The first chapter of the text details black life in antebellum up-country Georgia. Newly born in the 1830s, Atlanta bore little resemblance to far older southern cities, a circumstance that significantly affected the formation of black community in it. Chapter 2 focuses on the reconstruction of the city in Sherman's wake and black efforts to embrace freedom. The story of the American Civil War in Atlanta is not retold in these pages. Rather, the purpose of this chapter is to focus the discussion on community growth and development over time. Chapter 3 chronicles the establishment of a separate and diverse black church life in the city and seeks to uncover the social theology of the churches as transmitted through church records and ministerial commentary. The analysis in chapter 4 of the battle for education shifts the focus from inside the African American community to one of the most contested spaces of black-white relations. Chapter 5 examines the activities of a sample of community associations with an eye toward understanding the social and civic activities of Black Atlantans of high and middling status. Chapter 6 analyzes political retrenchment in the state of Georgia and the city itself. The focus is on the way race figured in the prohibition battles of the 1880s and on African American efforts to claim and defend their rights of citizenship. Lastly, chapter 7 addresses the riot, specifically interpreting the violent attack on black lives, property, and rising social aspirations as something best understood within the context of a regional movement to disfranchise and otherwise politically restrain black voters.

Early-twentieth-century Black Atlanta was an exciting place. Six separate black institutions of higher education and more than a dozen independent black churches were situated in the "phoenix city" that had risen from the ashes after Sherman's triumphant march to the sea. Prominent black intellectuals, educators, and journalists—W. E. B. Du Bois, John Hope, and Ben Davis—all made the city their home. Historian, sociologist, novelist, activist, and radical intellectual William Edward Burghardt Du Bois lived in Atlanta from 1897 to 1920. Employed at Atlanta University, he both taught and practiced sociology, organizing several conferences on "the Negro condition." Du Bois arrived in Atlanta late in the period, vis-à-vis my discussion of the city, but the race relations in Atlanta helped inform perhaps his most famous work, *The Souls of Black Folk*. Du Bois would eventually position himself in opposition to Booker T. Washington's perhaps pragmatic but deadening proposition that African Americans set aside concerns for civil and political rights to focus on economic development. Du Bois was both academic compatriot and personal friend of John Hope, professor and later president of Atlanta Baptist College. Hope came to the city just a year after Du Bois, when he and his social worker wife Lugenia Burns Hope relocated from Nashville, Tennessee. A native Georgian, John Hope had been educated in northern institutions before returning to the South to teach. Described by his biographer as a "race" man, Hope was committed to developing and expanding liberal arts curriculum in black colleges and universities, in opposition to Washington's program of industrial education. Hope's early career in Atlanta was marked by a defiant stance on race relations that softened to a more moderate position in the last thirty years of his tenure at Atlanta Baptist, later Morehouse, College. Ben Davis, journalist, committed Republican activist, and "champion mulatto baiter," arrived in Atlanta after 1903. Editor of the *Atlanta Independent*, Ben Davis positioned himself as a Negro beyond prejudice, who believed it was time to "forgive and forget any wrong that our white neighbor may have done us by the institution of slavery" in order to focus on economic "boot strapping" and moral development. Davis shared with fellow Atlanta transplants, Du Bois and Hope, a commitment to racial uplift through education and moral reform, yet parted with the two activists in his often zealous support of Washington's agenda and his undue interest in the origins and complexions of high-status blacks.[31] These men were just three of the black leaders/activists who would struggle to maintain black access and agitation for racial equality in the phoenix city.

Atlanta became a diverse and multilayered city in the postwar period. Financial development produced some economic and social stratification among blacks. Fraternal orders, mutual aid societies, and women's clubs dotted the landscape. Black-owned dry goods stores, barbershops, restaurants, and saloons gave African Americans access to goods, services, and leisure activities. The shining New South city was, on the eve of World War I, a very different place from the sleepy crossroads it had been in the antebellum period. This is the story of the ways in which Black Atlanta contributed to that change.

CHAPTER ONE

An Island in the Up-country

African Americans in Early Atlanta

In order to appreciate the full magnitude of the task African Americans faced in building a community for themselves in post–Civil War Atlanta, the particular circumstances in which they lived and worked—stranded, as it were, on an island in up-country Georgia—must be explored. The origins and history of the city demonstrate that it shares few of the features of urban centers of the Old South, and within the confines of antebellum Atlanta, African Americans were scattered, few in number, and heavily controlled. Enslaved or free, African Americans in the city experienced life on the extreme margins of white society, oppressed by a rigid legal code, social exclusion, and white racism. The efforts of African Americans in this isolated up-country region to expand community relations by developing organized social networks were repeatedly blocked by white society, but nonetheless they struggled to build networks of family and church life to sustain their sense of self in the face of the oppression of slavery.

The experiences of African Americans in Atlanta prior to Sherman's incredible march to the sea set this community apart from many other southern urban communities. A "new" city in the Old South, Atlanta's racial backdrop was simpler, more starkly black and white, than that found in other urban landscapes. Atlanta was born in the 1830s and bore little resemblance to other southern centers that had come into existence in the rough-and-tumble of the colonial era or the high drama of the Revolutionary period. Neither bustling river nor seaport city, Atlanta began life as a stagecoach crossroads located in rural DeKalb County. Antebellum Atlanta was not a city typified by a large population of urban slaves engaged in "quasi-autonomous" relations with white society. Nor was there a large population of free people of color carving out a niche between black and white, slave and free.[1] Rather, Atlanta was a small city rooted in an upland economy marked by a lack of cotton production and a low slave-to-master ratio. Essentially rural in its culture and background, up-country Georgia offered none of the high-society life found among Charleston's brown men or at the quadroon balls of New Orleans.

DeKalb County made its U.S. Census debut in 1830. The population then numbered slightly more than 10,000 people: 8,388 whites, 1,666 enslaved African Americans, and a mere 18 free people of color. Part of the territory forfeited by the Creek Indians in 1821, the land that became DeKalb County was rough and wild in the 1830s, still very much a part of the nation's southwestern borderlands. The white population consisted of immigrants from the Carolinas and Virginia. Many were drawn to the state by government-granted parcels of land. For a nineteen-dollar fee, generous lots of land (202 acres) were distributed to men whose number came up in the state's 1821 land lottery. Others traveled to up-country Georgia with the militia to tend to the relocation of the Cherokee and stayed in search of precious metals in the wake of the discovery of gold in northern Georgia. Younger sons of plantation masters and war veterans alike headed west to build fortunes on the Georgia frontier.[2]

DeKalb County is situated in the upper Piedmont region typified by rugged terrain and cool temperatures that are less conducive to cotton production than the state's black belt. Further, unlike Augusta, the area lacked an efficient, affordable method for growers to transport raw cotton to market.[3] Up-country farmers therefore devoted the majority of their cultivated acres to a diversified agriculture of staple crops and livestock rather than to a cash crop of cotton. Wheat, oats, and Indian corn, along with swine, were the chief production items of the small and midsize farms that dominated the economy of the up-country. Whiskey distilleries rather than cotton-processing plants provided the bulk of "manufactures" in the county according to the 1840 census.

The Atlanta region distinguished itself from the lower Piedmont in that it was not plantation country. The production schedules and the capital limitations of most farmers did not support extensive slaveholding. Few Georgians in the up-country owned as many as ten slaves, and the vast majority of slaveholders had fewer than five.[4] Even though the cotton boom of the 1850s encouraged farmers to invest in cotton production to supplement their income, most did so by relying upon free white farm laborers rather than by purchasing additional slaves.

In this environment Atlanta—or White Hall, as it was first called—came into being in 1835. Charner Humphries, a recent émigré to Georgia and a successful farmer, purchased a plot of land situated at the junction of central roads in DeKalb County. On this site Humphries erected a small emporium and "watering hole," complete with a livestock pen and stable that faced his eight-room, two-story tavern.[5] Humphries' choice of location was a wise one. He must have been well aware that farmers were the economic force of the county, though perhaps none were as successful as he. Humphries was a man of considerable means. He owned eight slaves; his estate was valued at twenty thousand dollars;

and he increased his wealth by catering to his up-country peers. Drawn from a radius of some thirty-five miles, farmers traveled by wagon to the area to sell or trade their surplus livestock, produce, and distilled spirits for necessary dry goods and farm supplies.

The value of the White Hall settlement grew when in 1837 the area was designated as the end point for the Western and Atlantic Railroad. Merchants and other businessmen soon recognized the importance of up-country agricultural production to their economy.[6] The establishment of a permanent public market in the city in the late 1840s encouraged the growth of other businesses designed to meet the needs of the visiting farmers. Historian James M. Russell notes that both Washington Hall and the Atlanta Hotel, "fairly luxurious hotels for the area," were erected in 1846. General stores and drinking establishments also sprouted in the city. The completion of the railroad meant that goods could then be moved from the upper Piedmont to the coast faster and more cheaply. The up-country trade also supplied necessary food for local consumption as well as foodstuffs to trade to smaller towns in the immediate vicinity.[7]

DeKalb County's population had grown to sixteen thousand by 1850, the first year the city of Atlanta was designated as such by the U.S. Census. Atlanta housed some 2,572 residents. There were 493 slaves in the city, almost 20 percent of the total population. Females numbered slightly more than half of the slave population, outnumbering males by sixty-one.[8] The bulk of these slaves were employed in domestic labor and probably lived with or nearby their owners.[9] The growing service industry, specifically the two hotels in the city, employed another large group; each hotel owner had more than twenty slaves.[10] The railroad industry and traditional slave "professions" of blacksmith, wheelwright, and carpenter occupied the remaining slaves.

The slave population had increased to slightly over 20 percent of the total population of the city on the eve of the Civil War. There were 1,914 slaves and 7,615 free citizens in Atlanta in 1860. The gap between male and female slaves had also increased, female slaves outnumbering males by two hundred. Such disparity had, no doubt, a negative effect on slave family formation. The slave population was dispersed throughout the city rather than concentrated in a slave quarter or square, though the largest group (725) lived in the fifth ward. The remaining 1,189 lived in clusters, in descending order of size, in Atlanta's first, fourth, second, and third wards.[11]

Despite their relatively small number, the presence of slaves in the city intruded upon the consciousness of the city fathers. The city council moved to develop municipal policy regulating slaves as early as 1848. The city marshal was instructed to "by a locke from Smith which has two keys and also to fix sum rings and poles on the calaboose for the conviance of whipping nigras."[12]

Atlanta also made provisions for the death of slaves; the city set aside the east-ernmost portion of the municipal cemetery for their burial.[13] The increased trafficking in slaves in the city led officials to formalize guidelines for their sale, which became a source of municipal revenue in 1850 when Atlanta added a tax of one dollar on the sale of slaves within the city limits. This tax was increased by a dollar one year later, and an additional tax of thirty cents per one hundred dollars of slave property was added in 1852.[14]

Despite the fiscal boon to the city coffers, the institution of slavery offered challenges to whites in Atlanta and others in up-country Georgia. In the decade before the war, white Atlantans, like their peers in Augusta, were confronted by and struggled with the fissures in the southern fantasy of a republican society in which all white men, regardless of class, were potential equals united over and against the debased enslaved. J. William Harris, building upon the work of historians who have sought to explain the link between slaveholders and their white propertyless peers, argues that white elites in Augusta, Georgia, at-tempted to smooth over differences by cultivating "personal relationships" be-tween themselves and their poorer brethren. More important to the discussion of Atlanta, Harris, like Edmund Morgan, maintains that southerners adopted an ideology in which black slavery allowed for white political freedom. "This ideal, which white Southerners called republican, had as one important facet a strong commitment to an agrarian economy in which most white men were independent producers and in which most menial labor was performed by a degraded and dependent race that was excluded from the political commu-nity."[15] Harris goes on to argue that the republican ideal was not easily main-tained in the decades immediately preceding the Civil War. While there were several differences between the Augusta hinterlands and Atlanta, the two up-country cities shared the tensions of negotiating between white laborers and slaves. White elites in Atlanta recognized the dangers inherent in urban slave-holding and worked to build racial solidarity with their nonslaveholding peers. Anxiety about the inability to control black slaves in Atlanta resulted in the monitoring, regulation, and repression of all African Americans through the manipulation of municipal law and the cultivation of white antipathy across class lines.

Eleven slaves were arrested in July 1851 on the charge of plotting an insurrec-tion.[16] White lawmakers responded by swiftly passing legislation restricting and regulating slave movement and residency in the city. A city ordinance gave the "marshall, deputy marshall and night watchman" the power to arrest any slave found off the property of his owner or employer without a pass after the ring-ing of the ten o'clock evening bell.[17] The ordinance regulated the hiring out of slaves by their owners and prohibited slaves from "living out" in the city without the direct supervision of their master or employer. The law specifically forbade slaves to own their own homes or operate independent businesses, including restaurants and boardinghouses.[18] New legislation in 1853 banned blacks from entering retail liquor stores and prohibited the sale of alcohol to all African Americans under penalty of a fifty-dollar fine. Blacks were also restricted from selling beer, cake, fruit, or confections on the street. All these stipulations were to be applied universally to blacks whether enslaved or free.

Such legislation suggests that blacks in Atlanta, attempting to make some life for themselves beyond the restrictions of slavery, were indeed selling goods, hiring themselves out, and living out. The peddling of either produce grown in their own garden plots, or, as slaveowners always assumed was the case, items stolen from the master's own stores was a common practice among slaves. Historians of slavery continue to document the existence of a marketing network among slaves. Joseph P. Reidy, *From Slavery to Agrarian Capitalism,* notes that slaves, especially those "on plantations or in towns" in low-country Georgia expanded their "independent production" in the antebellum era. Slaves, continues Reidy, "made market transactions of their own authority, often despite express orders to the contrary." Similarly, Larry Hudson, in " 'All that Cash,' " writes that in the South Carolina low country "often young, female and quite 'ordinary' slaves were able to accumulate substantial amounts of property." While there is no evidence to suggest slaves in Atlanta were able to amass such wealth by peddling, nevertheless, the anxiety whites expressed via city council ordinances was undoubtedly linked to market activity by the city's slaves and free blacks.[19]

Baked goods, eggs, and fruits and vegetables were sold to poor white as well as fellow black residents. Slaves were often eager to "work outside" because they earned wages, which they used to buy some form of independence. Hired slaves earned cash to purchase items of food or clothing to supplement their rations or, as former slave Henry Wright noted, save toward securing their freedom. In the case of Wright's slave peers, trips from Buckhead or other surrounding areas to Atlanta gave black males, who often lived in social isolation, the opportunity to meet their brothers, and perhaps sisters, in bondage and form social connections. Hiring out, as J. William Harris notes of slaves in Augusta, gave blacks "a practical, if limited, freedom of movement."[20] The need to curb such "freedom" was, in large part, the goal of the 1853 and subsequent legislation, which aimed to reduce the independent action of slaves by increasing the master's supervision.[21]

Legislation tightening restrictions on slave laborers was also connected to efforts designed to sustain white racial solidarity. The actions of white city officials that focused on controlling slave labor grew, in part, out of their efforts to make common cause with white workingmen in Atlanta. Slave laborers were a source of irritation for white mechanics in Atlanta, as they were for white laborers in much of the South. White artisans complained that slave labor constituted unfair competition and sought relief from municipal leadership. The city attempted to outlaw the practice in 1855, but it continued despite changes in the law.[22] Buckhead farmers Philip and George House, owners of the aforementioned Henry Wright, continued to hire out their slaves despite the fifty-dollar fine for doing so imposed by the city council. Wright later reported that his master, George House, hired out his male slaves to white mechanics skilled in carpentry or masonry.[23] The hiring-out system benefited slaveowners in three ways. House, like most owners, appropriated a share of the wages paid to his hired slaves. Once skilled, the slaves in question saved their owners money by performing any necessary carpentry or masonry work on their respective farms or plantations. Finally, whenever masters had need of ready cash, skilled slaves sold at auction brought considerably higher prices.

White elites were reluctant to forego the benefits associated with the hiring-out system, and so slaveowners wrestled with the city council over the imposition of fines for allowing their slaves to live and hire out. Masters, taking advantage of a clause in the law that gave the mayor power to reverse the decision of the city council regarding such fines, consistently appealed to the mayor for redress. Persistent slaveholders were successful in having fines revoked in a number of cases. The judgment against J. J. Thrasher, owner of black barber Solomon Luckie, was reversed November 2, 1855, along with the judgment against Aaron Gage regarding his slave Dolly. In Gage's case, the city council actually refunded his ten-dollar fine! City officials who were either concerned about unregulated black hired labor or who sided with working-class whites on the issue of hiring out developed legislation to close this loophole. An ordinance passed in 1857 prohibited such case-by-case review. Nonetheless, conflict over the issue would continue until the Civil War.[24]

Tensions over the practice of hiring out reveal the cracks in the wall of racial solidarity as envisioned by the South's white elite. Neither land- nor slaveowners, working-class white men who objected to the practice of hiring out argued in defense of their own labor. While a white worker might acquire some labor savings "because he was able to place all the hard work on the slave, who made his job easier," most workers were shrewd enough to realize the inherent dangers in the formation of a skilled slave class.[25] The intangible "race" benefit working-class whites received from foisting filthy, heavy, or dangerous work onto slaves did not make up for the loss of wages or job security. White workingmen wanted more than the republican rhetoric about the unity of white citizenship. Those in Atlanta demanded some protection for their position as free laborers. In an effort to secure their own class position, two hundred white mechanics in Atlanta appealed to the city's pecuniary interests, penning a letter on February 19, 1858, to the mayor and the city council in which they argued that slave labor cheapened their wages. They also pointed out that slaveowners who resided outside of the city were making money through their chattel while avoiding payment of city taxes. In 1861, the council, bowing to the pressure of lost revenue and fears about class-based intraracial friction on the eve of the Civil War, imposed a one hundred–dollar tax on absentee slaveowners who hired out their slaves in Atlanta. [26]

City officials worked to maintain control over all aspects of the black community even more fervently than they struggled to support white solidarity. Free blacks in Atlanta shared the experiences of racial oppression with their enslaved black peers. The free people of color in the city, even less numerically significant than the slave population, were also pressed to the racial wall. Only nineteen free blacks—thirteen females and six males—lived in the city in 1850, and a decade later their number had risen to only twenty-five. Relative to the numbers of free blacks in other Old South cities such as Charleston or Savannah, such figures are minuscule. Charleston's free black population hovered around three thousand in the two decades prior to the war, roughly 8 percent of the total population. Similarly, the proportion of free blacks in Savannah had reached 8.3 percent by 1860, a figure unimaginable in Atlanta. [27]

Atlanta was very invested in limiting the number of free blacks residing within the city and passed restrictive legislation to control the population. Each free person of color admitted to the city was required, under threat of imprisonment and possible reenslavement, to pay a freedom bond of two hundred dollars to the city council within ten days of arrival. The same ordinance that restricted slaves from living out prevented free blacks from relocating in the city unless he/she had both a white guardian and express permission of the city council. Four such requests, three from free persons of color, and a fourth from a white man asking to bring his black daughter-in-law to the city, were denied in 1854. [28] Atlanta also imposed an annual tax of five dollars on each free person of color living within the city limits. [29]

Federal, state, and local laws worked in conjunction with race-based social custom to corral and control free people of color. Their legal status—"free" but without the advantage of whiteness—and social status—residents but without the rights of citizens—was only slightly above that of slaves. A series of city ordinances regulated everything from their style of dress to their mode of transportation. Free people of color were prohibited from wearing a cape or carrying a cane or firearm. Laws restricted their movements after dark and forbade them to lease a horse or carriage. Public gatherings were also restricted; approved gatherings required legal surveillance by a white marshal. Designed to "safeguard public order," laws prohibited free blacks from indulging in the use of spirits, dice, or other games of chance.[30] Legal authorities missed no opportunity to remind free blacks of their inferior status and lack of rights.

The tiny free black population that managed to maintain residence in pre-Sherman Atlanta was largely working class, unskilled, illiterate, and young. Free people of color hired out as day laborers and domestic service workers. Free African American "professionals," such as dentist Roderick Dhu Badger and barbers Robert Yancey and Dougherty Hutchins, were quite the exception. In 1850, plagued by poor wages and less than secure employment, free people of color lived in a variety of situations. There were some family units. Laundress Elizabeth (Betty) Edgar, age thirty, lived with her daughters Eliza Longstreet, seventeen, Laura Longstreet, fourteen (both of whom also took in wash), and baby Betsy, one. Joice Young, twenty-six, also worked as a laundress and shared her quarters with Catherine Young, sixteen, and William Young, age five. Rhonda Map, twenty-nine, lived with Barney Riley, a sixty-year-old railroad worker from Ireland, and her three children, an eight-year-old son and two daughters, Georgia, three, and one-year-old Eliza. Walker Ruff, a thirty-year-old blacksmith, lived with his wife, Melley Ruff, age twenty-five. They shared their home with twenty-year-old Mary. Both women worked as laundresses. The balance of the nineteen had an assortment of housing arrangements. Ruebin Nordman, a thirty-nine-year-old barber, and Felix Nevoyoles, twenty-three, shared quarters. Rebecca Sweat, seventeen, lived and worked as a domestic in a white household, as did laborer Richard Smith, age twenty-eight. Laura Combs, thirty, lived alone.[31]

There was no continuity in the free population from 1850 to 1860, no correlation between the names of individuals listed as people of color on free schedules for 1860 and those listed in 1850. The decade before the outbreak of the Civil War was a difficult one for free people of color all across the South. Political saber rattling at the national level often translated into greater restrictions for free blacks within southern states and municipalities. The 1851 legislation was the beginning of a process designed to tighten the restrictions on free blacks in Atlanta, to diminish their freedom, and to drive them either back toward slavery or out of the community. Undoubtedly, many opted, as did free blacks in other southern locales, to leave an enslaved family and loved ones and head north or west in search of breathing room.

Twenty-three of the twenty-five freed African Americans in the city in 1860 lived in the fifth ward, which was also home to the largest population of enslaved African Americans. Housing in the area was poorly built but rented cheaply. More important, however, it offered freed blacks the option of living near still-enslaved kin. The 1860 census did reveal three family groupings. Laborer John

Smith, nineteen, lived with his brother Riley, eleven, who was also listed as a laborer. Julia Gibbs, a twenty-eight-year-old washerwoman, lived with forty-year-old Neal (who also did laundry) and her two sons Willis and Issac, aged ten and eleven. William and Laura Gifford, ages forty-eight and thirty, lived with their six children: thirteen-year-old William, eleven-year-old Martha, eight-year-old James, six-year-old Eunice, two-year-old Marion, and Anna who was six months old.[32] The senior William Gifford worked as a railroad fireman while his wife Laura took in wash. They shared their home with Paton Drew, a twenty-eight-year-old railroad hand. Millie Locke, a thirty-year-old washerwoman, lived with her white employers. Elizabeth Anderson, seventy, Susan Johnson, twenty-five, Betsy Galfin, eleven, and a five-year-old identified only as Virginia lived in a rooming house with forty other residents. Johnson made her living as a washerwoman. Sarah Edwards, twenty-five, and Martha Nales, twenty, shared a residence, though no occupation was listed for either woman. Millie Locke and Julia Gibbs were the only free people of color listed as being able to both read and write (sadly, Gibbs, perhaps as a result of accident or disease, was also legally blind by 1860). Gibbs's son Willis could also write.[33]

Whites continually expressed hostility toward, and concern about economic competition from, free people of color in the city, despite their tiny number. Citizens of Atlanta and the city council attempted to control them by enforcing regulation upon black employment, business ventures, and lifestyle. Black masons and construction workers were denied the right to contract for the repair or construction of buildings by an 1845 act of the Georgia State Assembly.[34] Dentist Roderick Badger was harassed by whites on at least two occasions before the Civil War. White dentists in Atlanta sent a letter to the city council in July 1859, expressing their outrage "that your honorable body tolerates a negro Dentist Roderick Badger." Two years later the council received yet another letter from "many citizens calling the attention of the council to the professional pretensions of a colored man styleing [sic] himself R. D. Badger."[35] Jo Miller, a free black man who hoped to open an ice cream parlor in the city, hired white lawyer L. C. Simpson to petition the city on his behalf. Arguing that it would be "unwise, unjust and impolitic to grant" such a license to Miller, Councilmen L. J. Parr and A. R. Neanleiter stressed that it was "not our policy to train negroes whether bond or free, to become tradesmen merchants or speculators." Miller's request for a business license, like that of a Miss Edeleman, was denied on the basis of the 1853 Ordinance.[36]

Free blacks faced restrictions on their rights to assemble similar to those imposed upon slaves. When a group of free "colored citizens" sought approval to form a temperance society in 1852, permission was granted with the stipulation that the marshal or watchman or "some white persons approved by council attend this meeting."[37] A petition requesting approval to form a moral society was also granted in 1854, with similar restrictions, but apparently the presence of white persons did not constitute sufficient supervision; in 1856, the society was disbanded by the order of the city council.[38] Undaunted, slave barber Solomon Luckie, who lived independent of his master, petitioned the city council for permission to form a "Musical Band" a mere two weeks after the moral society was disbanded. Permission was granted, despite early efforts on the part of "sundry citizens praying the passage of an ordinance forbidding the assembly of colored persons after certain hours of the night, for the purpose of fiddling and dancing." But the capricious nature of the council asserted itself yet again: less than three weeks later, on October 3, 1856, the police committee revoked the license of the band "for good and sufficient cause."[39]

Free African Americans struggled to form community liaisons amongst themselves and with their enslaved peers despite legal restrictions imposed by white society. The religious groups that the small number of free African Americans and slaves in Atlanta were able to organize gave them an opportunity to share community. A group of black worshippers formed Atlanta's first black congregation within the white Union Methodist Church in 1847. (The group would evolve into Bethel African Methodist Episcopal Church after the Civil War.)[40] Both enslaved and free African Americans worshiped at this first church. African American Baptists also sought independence from their white brethren; in 1848 they moved to separate from the white First Baptist Church. A group of slaves belonging to members of the First Baptist Church asked permission to meet separately as the African Church. Slave minister Frank Quarles, who became an important social activist in post–Civil War Atlanta, joined the congregation in 1858. Both churches would prove essential to the political, economic, and social life of the African American community in Atlanta, though a lack of resources and privacy limited their antebellum activities. Pressed, regulated, and controlled in every aspect of their lives, free people of color in Atlanta nevertheless joined with their black enslaved peers to create spiritual homes for themselves and in the process laid the first foundations for the institutions that would sustain their lives in freedom.

There is little evidence to suggest that this repressed population was stratified on the basis of color. The white ancestry or light complexions that may have benefited free people of color in other parts of the South did not seem to have an effect on the level of literacy, employment, or wealth of free African Americans in antebellum Atlanta.[41] Robert Yancey (also known as Robert Webster) and Roderick Dhu Badger stand out as important exceptions to this rule. Neither one appeared as a slave, or as a person of color on the free population schedules for 1850 or 1860, though by all accounts, they lived as free men. Extraordinarily fair-skinned mulattos, they were both listed as white on later census and tax lists for the city. Both men, literate and propertied, were able to pass for white and may have done so to circumvent racial barriers.

Within the tiny population of free people of color in antebellum Atlanta, the life of Roderick Dhu Badger most reflects the privileged advantages of the southern mulatto elite. Born well before the Georgia state legislature passed a more restrictive antimiscegenation law (1852), Roderick Dhu and his older brother, Robert H., were the sons of DeKalb County dentist Josiah Bostwick Badger (1792–1859), who was white, propertied, middle class, and married. Josiah sired Robert in 1829 with Martha, a slave woman who worked as a cook in the Badger household. His son Roderick was born to Jemima, another household slave, in 1834. Josiah Badger trained both his mulatto sons in dentistry, perhaps even financing Roderick Dhu's office.

Each Badger boy, following the pattern of other southern mulattos who sought to pass their light skin on to their progeny, married fair, mixed-race women. Robert married Caroline Thomas, a quadroon with both Native American and white ancestry, who bore him at least six children. Roderick's wife, Mary A. Murphy, was both fair and well connected: she was the mulatto daughter of prominent DeKalb County resident Charles A. Murphy and half-sister to Eliza Murphy. Eliza, who inherited her father's wealth (and her illegitimate half-sister) when he died in 1861, married Milton A. Candler, statesman and older brother of Coca-Cola magnate Asa Candler. The connections established among the three white men—Badger, Murphy, and Candler—by the marriages between members of the white or black portions of their families undoubtedly contributed to Roderick Dhu's purported service as Milton A. Candler's aide-de-camp during the Civil War. Roderick's ties to two influential white patrons also contributed to his ability to survive public criticism from his white peers. Indeed, both the 1859 and 1861 letters to the city council condemning Badger's practice in dentistry came after the death of first his father, Josiah, and then his father-in-law, Charles A. Murphy. Despite those attacks on his status, Roderick continued to practice dentistry throughout the Civil War and returned to reopen his practice in Atlanta after a two-year (1864–66) retreat to Chicago. He was later joined in the Badger family practice of dentistry by his older brother Robert and his white half-brother Ralph. The black Badger brothers would go on to attain status and wealth in the African American community in the post–Civil War period.[42]

The Badger brothers' experience stands in stark contrast to that of their free African American peers in Atlanta.[43] Most free people of color in Atlanta did not share the combination of ancestry and class status that provided access to education and political protection for the Badgers. Of the nineteen free persons

Affluent and well-connected black dentist Roderick Dhu Badger. (DeKalb Historical Society Collection, DeKalb History Center.)

of color listed on the 1850 Free Schedule, ten were black and the remaining eight designated as mulatto. Betty Edgar, black, was the mother of mulatto Laura. Walker Ruff, black, was married to mulatto Melley Ruff. Rhonda Map and her children were listed as black and the Young family as mulatto. All mulattos listed were illiterate and without property. Two tradesmen, the barber and the blacksmith, were both blacks; of the two, only Ruff was literate.

A similar pattern held for the 1860 schedule that listed fourteen free blacks and nine mulattos, not including Badger and Yancey. William Gifford was mulatto, while his wife Laura was listed as black—as were all six of the Gifford children. The single females were listed as black and without occupation, with the exception of mulatto washerwomen Millie Locke and Susan Johnson. All males listed were employed. Three unattached males were mulattos; two worked as laborers, and the third was a train hand. Two mulatto women, Julia Gibbs and Millie Locke, were literate. No persons of color in the city owned taxable property.[44]

As this examination of antebellum records suggests, Atlanta's small, marginalized black population was not, prior to slavery's end, divided against itself along the lines of class and color. On the contrary, it was united in a fight for existence. The few free blacks in antebellum Atlanta were policed and taxed at every turn, their livelihood proscribed by city council action and their social life both monitored and censured. Free black Atlantans had little in common with Charleston's free people of color, who manipulated relationships with white patrons in an effort to circumvent South Carolina's racial codes and, in some cases, owned slaves and amassed fortunes.[45] Atlanta's tiny, harassed population had neither the resources nor the space to negotiate a "middle ground" between black and white, slave and free.

The enslaved population was, of course, even more repressed and controlled. There is no evidence of negotiated privilege rooted in either a post-Revolutionary progressive ideology or in maritime or industrial labor relations. Up-country farmers, merchants, railroad men, bureaucrats, and free laborers in Atlanta were not concerned with the long-cold embers of Revolutionary ideology. Their city developed well after the window of racial opportunity that marked the Revolutionary period had closed. More likely to remember Andrew Jackson's language of conquest and expansion than the waves of post-Revolution southern manumissions, whites—laborers, farmers, entrepreneurs, and city councilmen—were bent on establishing a sustainable economy and a functional city government. Despite conflict among themselves, they worked to secure a firm hold over their black workers, slave and free.

The efforts of the white community were largely successful. Whether free and harried or enslaved and controlled, blacks in antebellum Atlanta were propertyless, uneducated, and nearly powerless. However, a small number struggled to build a island community in the up-country. They tried, with limited success, to create social groups and develop activities for themselves in the face of white repression. They did succeed in forming two separate church groups, congregations that met some of their religious needs and helped create some distance from white society. Significantly for this examination of the black community in the postwar era, the marked social divisions found among blacks in Charleston, New Orleans, and Savannah were absent from Atlanta. This small black community experienced a rough equality of opportunity and status. Consequently, there was much less opportunity for a holdover of class or color barriers in the structure of the community as it developed after the war. The freed African Americans who flooded the city in the postwar period did not find highly stratified intraracial cliques; such color-coded structures were simply not there. Equally important, the new immigrants, the vast majority of whom were Georgian by birth, were far less likely to bring such an understanding of intraracial relations with them. Postwar Atlanta was a young city in a maturing South, complete with the promise of a new beginning for African Americans who hoped to build their future upon the ashes of slavery.

The 1864 Atlanta campaign and Sherman's march to the sea were part and parcel of the last great push of the Civil War. Within eight months of the burning of Atlanta, the peace treaty was signed at Appomattox Court House. In the wake of the war's destruction, both the city and the region faced the process of rebuilding. Beyond the issue of physical restoration was the question of how to reconstruct southern society without the institution of slavery. White southerners who had struggled to evade nascent class conflict by building a "republican equality" based on whiteness were soon to be confronted by both working-class whites who had lost their faith in such rhetoric and by former slaves made citizens by a more powerful federal government. The devastation and displacements of the war meant, too, that there was only a partial continuity in the black population in Atlanta. Black Atlantans would play a significant role in rebuilding the city from the ground up after the war, though they would also continue to face resistance to their freedom and to the idea of their citizenship from Atlanta's white population. The ensuing chapters will detail the history of a persistent and valiant struggle waged by the growing community of African Americans in Atlanta in an evolving context increasingly governed by the ideology of white supremacy and the strategies of Jim Crow. Throughout the South, African Americans, including those stranded on this island in the up-country, had their own understanding of how the pieces of southern society should be rearranged. As Stanley Engerman reminds us, "Freedom was obviously a dramatic step, but the nature of responses to it were greatly influenced by what had happened to the African Americans and how they had perceived it, in those preceding centuries of slavery."[46] The perception of freedom shared by many blacks in Atlanta was rooted in the experiences of slavery in the up-country and some slight experiences of being "freed but not free" in the city. Stories about the struggle both to maintain home and family and to build community as a population oppressed and excluded on the basis of race would be passed down for generations. Alienation and abuse at the hands of southern white society left a wound that served to reinforce a consciousness grounded in the idea of black racial solidarity and support. These newly freed people acted from such a consciousness as they went about pushing back the boundaries of the Old South and rebuilding their own lives in freedom.

Phoenix Rising

African Americans and the Economy in
Postwar Atlanta

The six men meeting in the basement room of Friendship Baptist Church in the fall of 1866 came together to organize an association that would provide African Americans in Atlanta with the means to bury their dead with respect and decorum. Five of the six were successful black businessmen, each of whom would contribute a portion of his resources to finance a joint stock company, the South View Cemetery Association. Grocers Albert Watts and Charles Morgan, drayman John Render, carpenter George Graham, and grocer-turned–rock contractor Jacob McKinley, along with minister Robert Grant, were the original charter members and represented a new breed of black entrepreneur and community builder in post-Reconstruction Atlanta. In time the South View Cemetery Association would expand to twenty-five members, numbering on its board of directors black morticians David T. Howard and Mitchell Cargile, shoemaker William Allen, and clerk Charles William Thomas. Howard and Alonzo Herndon, barber and later insurance mogul, would become substantial shareholders. South View Cemetery became a profitable concern by the turn of the century, paying investors small dividends from the appreciation and expansion of the original twenty-five-acre site. It also provided a much-needed social service to Atlanta's growing black community while enhancing the status and wealth of its organizers.[1]

In the three and a half decades following the Civil War, Black Atlantans established a small but solid economic base upon which they built a thriving community. Blacks, organizing cooperatively, created institutions and financed business development and growth. These early organizations provided models for development of, and avenues for advancement within, the black community. Freedmen were able to pursue new opportunities presented by the destruction of the institution of slavery and the city of Atlanta. Indeed, the burning of Atlanta accelerated the transformation from slavery to freedom, from Old to New

South. Blacks embraced their freedom and moved to acquire true independence through employment. They cultivated their human capital through education, business development, and property accumulation.[2]

Institutions such as South View Cemetery Association, Georgia Real Estate and Loan, and the Atlanta Loan and Trust are examples of fledgling black capitalism in the postwar period and evidence of black commitment to racial solidarity in the face of continuing white supremacy. Such efforts were not simply instances of either "race consciousness" or "the strong impulse of so many blacks to integrate themselves into American civilization," as argued by economic historian Loren Schweninger[3]; the collective economic efforts of black laborers and businessmen in Atlanta also represented a desire to have financial assets and to help their own. African Americans, free from slavery and thrust into the marketplace, learned to negotiate for wages, to budget and save, and to invest. Black entrepreneurs developed marketable skills, pursued business opportunities, and pooled their wealth in joint stock concerns to secure their freedom and build their economic future. The belief or the hope that such efforts would, as in the vision of Booker T. Washington, open the doors to an integrated society was regarded only as a possible, long-distant bonus. The stark reality was that, in the immediate postwar period, most blacks waged a difficult battle for survival and only after years of effort would some succeed in accumulating modest amounts of wealth.

Atlanta's white politicians, entrepreneurs, and common laborers also set about the business of crafting their future and rebuilding the city in the aftermath of the war. Contemporary observers noted that an unusual southern zeal made Atlanta rise from the ashes of Sherman's fires like a phoenix from the flames. The resurrection of the city required more than the rebuilding of physical structures. The social structure, which had been supported by the system of slavery, also needed rebuilding. Whites planned to return southern race relations to the prewar status quo. In their vision of the future white supremacy in things economic, political, and social figured large.[4]

Atlanta had been physically transformed well before the official end of the war. The once-open crossroads town had been fortified against attack. Streets filled previously with farmers and businessmen were clogged with marching soldiers and panicked refugees. Soldiers, first Confederate and then Union, were quartered in the city. Confederate forces made the city a military headquarters and took advantage of local industry, especially Atlanta Rolling Mills, which furnished precious iron rails to the South's traveling army.[5] Confederate troops and support personnel substantially increased the city's population within the first year of the war. Moreover, the presence of a military hospital meant that Confederate wounded inundated the city.[6] Refugees, too, poured in to escape the marching armies, both the retreating Confederate and the advancing Union troops. White families pushed south and west seeking refuge behind Confederate lines. Such migrations served to disrupt already fractured families, as some slaves were forced to travel with their masters while others were left behind. This new refugee population put a strain on local housing and limited food supplies. Confederate officers were forced to dole out rations to civilian personnel.[7]

Black men, both enslaved and free, also increased the city's population. Slaves impressed or on loan from their masters, free black men, and captured runaways conscripted by the Confederate army were all forced to work to support the war effort. Some blacks worked for hours each day digging trenches and sharpening wooden poles for Confederate fortifications on the edges of the city. Others made and loaded munitions wagons or ferried supplies from Atlanta to awaiting southern troops. Slaves also worked hospital duty for the Confederate wounded, tending to menial tasks that undoubtedly included removing and burying the dead.[8]

Still other blacks arrived in the city without their masters, having taken advantage of the disruption of war to leave the surrounding countryside and seek their freedom on the city streets. Hundreds of freed and escaped slaves arrived in Atlanta as camp followers on the heels of Sherman's army in 1864. Finding employment in war industries or working independently as day laborers and domestics, or perhaps securing their livelihood by indulging in the theft and resale of pilfered goods, black Georgians pushed the boundaries of their enslavement.[9] Soldiers, refugees, slaves, and those who had freed themselves increased the city's population by eight to ten thousand during the course of war. This trend was ultimately reversed by troop movement, bombardment, and forced evacuation, but not before the growing population had put a strain on social custom, especially traditional race relations.

African Americans seized the opportunity to challenge the limits of white control in the face of the dislocation and disorder caused by the war. Atlanta's city council—faced with blacks who moved freely through the streets, who contracted for and kept their own wages, and who clearly lived outside proper guardianship as established by local law—tried to address the chaos created by this increasing black population. Pass laws were strengthened in 1862. Slave balls, designed as fundraisers for the Confederate army, were outlawed the next year. The council even considered organizing a holding facility to help keep track of errant blacks.[10] Ultimately, the combination of the sheer number of unregulated blacks and war worries overwhelmed the efforts of the council. As historian Clarence Mohr notes, white authorities in Atlanta were forced to develop a high level of tolerance toward black misbehavior that they were unable to police effectively.[11]

The arrival of the Union army in the late summer of 1864 had the opposite effect upon the city's rebel population. Thousands of Atlantans fled as Union general William Tecumseh Sherman and the Army of Tennessee held the city of Atlanta under siege, subjecting the local population to bombardment by cannon for more than twenty days in August. The steady rain of shells rattled nerves and damaged hundreds of homes yet failed to make the city a used-up community, as envisioned by Sherman. Indeed, estimates suggest that shells fired during the siege killed less than fifty people. Many residents survived by hiding out in homemade dugouts that served as bomb shelters. A black barber, poorly named Solomon Luckie, was one of the few people killed by a shell.[12]

Confederate forces under General John Bell Hood, having failed to repulse Sherman's army, withdrew from the city on September 1, 1864. Hood's fleeing forces destroyed railroad cars, exploded thousands of pounds of ammunition, and engaged in widespread looting, this last being an activity in which they were joined by many of the local citizens. Mayor James M. Calhoun surrendered the city the next day. Sherman arrived a few days later and made Atlanta headquarters for himself, over twenty thousand Union troops, and several hundred camp followers. Writing first to General Hood and then to Mayor Calhoun, Sherman issued orders of evacuation designed to effect the removal of most of the remaining civilian population from the city. To Hood he noted "Atlanta is no place for families or noncombatants." He spoke more plainly to Mayor Calhoun: "The use of Atlanta for warlike purposes is inconsistent with its character as a home for families"; "inhabitants," he insisted, should leave before "want . . . compel[s] [them] to go." Finally, in a letter to Union Chief of Staff Henry Halleck, Sherman formally laid claim to the city. "Atlanta is a fortified town, was stubbornly defended and fairly captured. As captors, we have a right to it."[13]

White residents were shipped either north or south to the transportation station of their choice. They were allowed to take their "servants," white and black, with the proviso that no force was to be used toward blacks. Countless slaveowners ignored this proviso; George Mason was forced to return to the Ormond family after he "ran away" following the formal pronouncement of freedom. Black residents were not given the option of departure. Able-bodied black males were pressed to remain in the city where, as per Sherman's instructions, "they may be employed by our quartermaster."[14]

Black females, though not addressed directly in Sherman's missive, fell under the title of noncombatants and yet were given little choice save that of leaving the city with their former owners. Dozens of black women who had trailed Sherman to the city were employed in domestic service for the army. They remained, as did some other black women who struggled along with their male peers to find housing and eke out a living in the war-torn city.

The Union army occupied Atlanta for two months, resting and making plans for the march to the sea. Determined to leave the Confederate army nothing with which to continue the war effort, Sherman ordered the destruction by fire of the railroad depot, warehouses, and factories in the city, including Gate City Rolling Mill. The fires spread by the combustion of stored explosives in conjunction with the deliberate, but independent, firing of residential buildings by his troops. Sherman left Atlanta with far more fanfare than had accompanied his arrival. The November 16 departure was highlighted by his soldiers marching steadily and rapidly forward, "with a cheery look and swinging pace," boldly singing the chorus of the "Battle Hymn of the Republic" as they moved away from the blackened hull of the city.[15]

The march to Savannah was one of the last great pushes of the war that ended at Appomattox Court House, six months after the firing on Atlanta. In the wake of the war's destruction both the city and the region faced the prospect of rebuilding. Beyond the physical restoration was the equally pressing question of how to reconstruct southern society without the institution of slavery.

The population of Atlanta continued to grow after the war. Both blacks and whites returned to Atlanta, and the presence of the Freedmen's Bureau, the promise of employment, and a desire to escape their former masters lured additional freedmen to the city. Former slaves and free people of color traveled to Atlanta from Alabama, Mississippi, and South Carolina, but the majority came from the Georgia countryside—over 70 percent of the former slaves interviewed for the census of 1870 identified Georgia as their place of birth.[16] Many migrated to the city from surrounding areas including Henry, Walton, Gwinnett, Meriwether, and Jackson counties. Former slaves George Eason and Hattie Johnson traveled to Atlanta as young children under the "guardianship" of their previous owners. Camilla (Hoyle) Jackson, Henry Wright, Milton Hammond, David Goodman Gullins, and Lewis Favor migrated to the city as young adults, after working for former masters or hiring themselves out while searching the countryside for family members.[17]

The migrants pouring into the city of Atlanta were very similar in makeup to those arriving in other urban centers in the South. Men and women came from rural communities with resources limited to a few articles of clothing, their muscle power, and their desire to make a change in their lives. Such working-class migrants soon made up the vast majority of the African American population in Atlanta.[18]

Many new arrivals lacked the basic requirements for subsistence. Four years of war and two pillaging armies had left plantations and small farmers alike with empty larders. Shipments of grain were effectively ended by the Union capture of railroad lines that transported goods from the Midwest to the South.

Neither were local crops forthcoming. Rural populations remained in flux in 1865–66, which was disastrous during the planting season. Poor weather damaged harvests of both food crops and cotton between 1865 and 1867, further undermining agricultural recovery. Urban populations, both migrants who had fled the rural employment crisis and those who had remained in cities throughout the war, faced the triple threat of homelessness, hunger, and unemployment in the immediate postwar period. The Freedmen's Bureau, the American Missionary Association, the American Baptist Home Mission Society, and other organizations helped provide black refugees with food and clothing.[19]

The Freedmen's Bureau, the federal government's short-lived experiment in social welfare, set up operations in the city in June 1865. Its agents faced the hostility of southern whites and grappled with the extraordinary phenomenon of black freedom, and in so doing aided African Americans in the effort to reestablish their lives. The bureau's assistance in securing food, clothing, and shelter as well as medical care was indispensable: it provided much needed emergency rations to refugees, distributing some 95,000 pounds of food in the first month of its residence in Atlanta.[20]

Unfortunately, bureau policy was also inconsistent, offering aid in fits and starts. Fears of fostering black dependency upon federal assistance led the bureau at times to refuse or terminate aid, often leaving freedmen and -women in dire straits. Assistant Commissioner Davis Tilson, for example, instituted a policy prohibiting the distribution of rations to "able-bodied freedpeople" in 1866. Tilson apparently did not consider that the able-bodied were likely to be unemployed. His policy, followed by the bureau-wide decision to end the distribution of rations the next year, contributed to the hardships facing freedmen and -women.[21]

American Missionary Association missionaries helped fill the gap left by the bureau and were instrumental in offering assistance to refugees. AMA teachers were often shocked by the refugees' lack of basic garments. Jeannie Barnum reported sadly to agent Samuel Hunt in January 1866 that her students "have not been as regular in their attendance as one could but [they] have no clothing to make them comfortable and many came without shoes." The Friends Freedmen's Association of Philadelphia came to the aid of the city's ragged freedmen, providing, in the words of AMA matron Rebecca Craighead, "just the right sort of clothing" in a shipment that arrived two months later.[22] Yet, the Friends' clothing shipment and those of other philanthropic organizations were woefully inadequate to meet the level of need.

The Friends' clothing shipment did help Craighead and Superintendent E. M. Cravath provide clothing to thirty-eight orphaned children. Orphans and other displaced and homeless persons were in crisis in the postwar period. Family dislocation, a function of the chaos of the war, often resulted in the separation of children from parents and extended kin. The AMA opened the Washburn Orphanage and Asylum in May 1866 after both the city and the Freedmen's Bureau had denied assistance to black widows, orphans, and other indigent and disabled refugees. The problem of care for black orphans remained well beyond the end of Reconstruction. In 1890, black and white reformers opened the Leonard Street Orphans' Home, a facility for African American girls, on land adjacent to Spelman College. [23]

Shelter was a serious concern for all African Americans at the end of the war. The destruction of thousands of structures in the city, coupled with the massive influx of refugees, produced a severe housing shortage for all Atlantans. Black and white residents struggled to find adequate shelter with white residents pressing into housing they would have rejected prior to the war. Agent Frederick Ayers was alarmed at the scarcity, expense, and poor quality of housing available to AMA teachers and missionaries and equally dismayed by the housing situation facing the newly freed. Such scarcity led to a sharp increase in rental rates. Freedmen and -women in Atlanta were struggling to lease one-eighth- or one-quarter-acre lots with "a little house" for five dollars per month. Houses with a glass pane rented for four times as much. Ayers noted that it took nearly all of what African Americans could earn to pay rent and buy food. Exorbitant rents rather than de jure segregation established the pattern of black settlement in Atlanta. African Americans settled in those areas where they could pay the least rent. AMA workers noted freedmen and their families who had been living on the "outskirts of the city for 1, 2, or 3 years." [24]

The African American population remained interspersed throughout the city in the postwar period, developing enclaves in low-rent areas. The first and fourth wards, which had housed concentrations of African Americans before the war, became home to two significant black neighborhoods. Jenningstown in the first ward was the largest cluster, housing 2,490 African Americans. This settlement was in the hilly western portion of the city that was home to Atlanta University. Shermantown, located in the northeast, had the next largest black population, numbering 2,486. This neighborhood was built on land in the fourth ward that had been previously occupied by General Sherman and his troops. The third ward, in the southeast, was home to Summerhill, a smaller settlement with only 1,512 African Americans. The fifth ward, which had housed the greatest number of African Americans in the city prior to the war, retained a large number of freed people but dropped to third (2,436) in total black population. Mechanicsville, an additional enclave, developed in the second ward southwest of Whitehall Street in the late 1870s. [25]

These areas left much to be desired. Shermantown and Summerhill were

Post-Reconstruction-era sketch of residents and shanties in Atlanta's "Shermantown," originally published in *Harper's Weekly*. (Courtesy of the Atlanta History Center.)

low-lying areas in the city. Prone to flooding and to sewage overflow, they fostered a disease problem in the latter half of the nineteenth century. Only Jenningstown, located on the former battle site of Diamond Hill, was situated on high enough ground to avoid many of the problems of the "bottom lands." Further, the housing itself in all these areas was substandard. AMA missionaries were quick to point out that local whites were rapidly erecting poor, even primitive, housing to rent to African Americans, "expressly for securing a great profit."[26] Rebecca Craighead informed her superiors that many of the houses being rented to freedmen at inflated rates were little more than rickety shacks. She reported seeing "much, very much destitution wherever I go, some of the abodes of wretchedness, the doors of which are so small I have to stoop very low and when in, can scarcely stand without bumping my head against the apology for a roof."[27] Rather than struggling to pay such exorbitant rents for inadequate housing, some freed people squatted on small plots of land and erected their own huts from scrap wood and tin.

In such circumstances, Atlanta's struggling black population was not prepared to face the smallpox epidemic that hit in the winter of 1865. Illness descended on the barely recovering city in December and was widespread by New

Year's Day, 1866. City service providers were not equipped to handle such a health crisis. Hospital facilities were woefully inadequate, and doctors were few and far between. The disease had the greatest impact on the African American community. Freedmen and their families who lived in shotgun shanties that let in winter winds and rain were weakened from exposure; they sickened and died by the dozens.

City officials engaged in a deadly game of shifting accountabilities by pleading poverty and pressuring the Freedmen's Bureau to take responsibility for the care of the infected black population. AMA agent Ayers too exhorted the Freedmen's Bureau to provide for the sick and dying. Under pressure, the bureau established a makeshift smallpox hospital for African Americans outside the city limits. Merely a collection of tents, the hospital was poorly funded and understaffed. Freedmen and their families lay shivering and naked, often unattended and dying without the care of medical professionals. The impoverished African American community worked to fill the void left by the Freedman's Bureau and the AMA. Despite their poverty, local blacks combined their efforts, as recorded by the AMA, "to raise $200 per month to pay for the services of nurses in the hospital of Colored People."[28]

Illness continued to stalk the city as a second wave of smallpox hit in the fall of 1866 and lingered into the new year: 375 blacks died in 1866; another 252 died the following year. The mortality rate for African Americans was higher than that of whites in both years.[29] The epidemic had a lingering effect on the black population, especially the children. Of the 265 blacks who died in Atlanta in 1868, the greatest numbers were children under the age of ten.[30]

The search for work provided freedmen and -women with yet another challenge after that of securing food, clothing, shelter, and necessary medical care. The vast majority of migrants were unskilled laborers; of the black laborers in the city in the 1870s, 92 percent were unskilled. This percentage decreased slightly over the next two decades but did not drop below 86 percent.[31] Employment was neither stable nor lucrative. Common day laborers worked long hours for short pay performing such odd jobs as chopping and collecting wood, mucking out stables, running errands, sweeping streets, and whitewashing buildings. Former slave Milton Hammond recalled that he worked for anyone who would hire him in post–Civil War Atlanta, never earning more than twenty-five to thirty cents per day.[32]

Freedom, from the perspective of whites, was not to eliminate patterns of subservience established in slavery. Southern whites remained committed to the belief that blacks existed to provide service to some white master. African Americans were free but thrown into a racially stratified marketplace with no wealth and limited skills. Employed as bootblacks, cooks, drivers, hotel or railroad porters, and personal servants, freedmen and -women continued to take work providing intimate, often menial, service to whites. Racial segregation in hiring practices and discrimination in salary undermined black workers, skilled and unskilled. Unable to start their own business ventures, black men and women who did find steady work were paid significantly lower wages than their white counterparts. Skilled black workers might earn $1.50 to $3.00 per day. Most black migrants were employed at subsistence level and evidenced little upward mobility over time.[33]

The destruction of Atlanta, which created the housing shortage, also produced an employment boom in the immediate postwar period. Freedmen provided essential labor for the rebuilding of the city. Freedman's Bureau agent Frederick Ayers commented on the "business air" of Atlanta: "The great pecuniary losses by the war of the whites here affects of course the condition of the Freedmen. In addition to the loss of their slaves, they have, many of them had their houses and shops and other property, swept away by the deluge of fire that swept over their devoted city this furnishes employment to a larger number of colored people as masons, carpenters, teamsters and workmen."[34]

Ayers' observation was correct. Blacks were involved in every aspect of rebuilding the city. Black draymen who moved loads of wood, brick, and piping, as well as black carpenters, masons, plasterers, stonecutters, and common laborers, earned a living while contributing to the rapid transformation of the city. Railroads and manufacturing and service industries also provided job opportunities for African Americans. Hotels and restaurants expanded to provide assistance and relief to railroad passengers. The Western Atlantic and Georgia Railroads trisected Atlanta, creating the central business district triangle that became the heart of the city. The railroads gave local manufacturers direct access to markets in the hinterlands and along the coast.[35]

Railroad work offered wages that were amongst the highest in the city: skilled workers could earn as much as eighteen to thirty dollars per week. Unskilled laborers commanded considerably less, as low as eighty-six cents per day. Black laborers were for the most part denied more highly skilled jobs with Atlanta's railroads.[36] Neither the Western and Atlantic nor the Georgia Railroad employed blacks as conductors or engineers. Few black hands found employment as railroad workers. Black employment with the railroad increased from just under 100 in 1870 to 133 in 1880. Unskilled workers accounted for most of this increase.[37] Blacks were assigned dangerous, labor-intensive jobs, heavy cleaning and lifting work, or service work as hostlers and porters. Twenty-five-year-old Lucius Herd was employed in the dangerous position of brakeman. Herd, who by January 1870 had relocated to Atlanta from LaGrange, Georgia, would have been required to run alongside the moving train and risk life and limb to place the braking blocks under the still-moving wheels. As technological advances rendered such positions safe, black workers were replaced with white railroad hands.

Still, even unskilled railroad labor paid better than common day labor in the Reconstruction era and also offered some job security. For railroad hand George Grant, whose missing right eye may have been a result of a railroad accident, proportionally higher wages may not have been just compensation. His salary, however, in conjunction with job stability, undoubtedly helped him and his wife, Mollie, to feed, house, and clothe their six children.[38]

When the nation's economy slowed and then stalled in the 1870s, railroads first cut wages and then ultimately downsized their workforce. Employers, including the Western and Atlantic, demonstrated a preference for dismissing black workers first. White railroad labor unions offered some resistance on behalf of their own but black hands were unsuccessful in their efforts to stop wage erosion and the waves of job cuts. Even before the national railroad strike of 1877, black workers had challenged discrimination and staged work actions to protest unfair labor practices, both efforts resulting only in lower wages and dismissals.[39]

As a trade center rather than an industrial town, Atlanta had few large-scale industries. The Atlanta Rolling Mill, the focus of much attention during the war, employed fewer than 750 workers in the two decades following the conflict. Similarly, the city's half-dozen foundries, Jacob Elsas's Southern Bag Factory established in 1874 (replaced in 1889 by Elsas's Fulton Bag and Cotton Mills), and the Fulton Paper Mill combined had fewer than 1,000 workers.[40] Blacks accounted for a very small part of the total number of workers employed in Gate City industries. Virginia native John Carter, thirty-six, was employed in the Winship and Company Foundry in February 1870, one of the few African American males who secured some employment in Atlanta's industrial plants, mills, or factories.[41] Most African American males were restricted to low-level maintenance jobs in the Atlanta Rolling Mill, and white management used the few who did move into skilled positions to undercut the wages of white workers. Foreshadowing a pattern that would haunt northern industrial labor in the early twentieth century, black workers became strikebreakers in 1881 after white workers had failed to cultivate a pro–trade union stance in them. Exclusion and discrimination marked the experience of black male workers in all industrial and factory work in the city.[42]

Some freedmen parlayed their work as draymen into well-paying businesses. At least nineteen black men operated drays in the city in the early 1870s and three had accumulated over one thousand dollars in taxable property by 1880. Their success was a result of specialization and expansion. John Perdue, Wesley

Black and white railroad workers working side by side laying rail on rough hewn beams, 1895. (Courtesy of the Atlanta History Center.)

Darden, and Crawford Monroe enlarged their businesses as draymen by hiring their black peers. Bob Loftin, twenty-nine, was in the employ of fellow Meriweather County native John Perdue, twenty-eight, in January 1872. By 1880, Perdue was paying taxes on $2,175 worth of property. Darden expanded his business concern as early as January 1870, employing twenty-two-year-old Summerhill resident Linsey Easterling as a drayman. Crawford Monroe was the most successful of the three. He originally earned his living as carriage trimmer in the employ of J. H. Boon, but eight years after emancipation, the forty-three-year-old father of seven children owned and operated ten drays in Atlanta. His personal wealth increased from $2,550 in 1873 to $5,450 in 1885.[43]

Few other black-owned businesses flourished in the immediate postwar period. Most migrants lacked the necessary capital to launch a commercial enterprise. Nevertheless, African Americans with specific marketable skills were able to parlay those skills into independent businesses. Black laborers trained as cabinetmakers, carpenters, shoemakers, blacksmiths, tailors and/or seamstresses could earn somewhat higher wages and find steadier employment. Black shoe- and bootmakers and blacksmiths were quite numerous in 1870s and 1880s Atlanta; second only to groceries, shoemaking and blacksmithing operations represented the greatest number of successful small business enterprises among African Americans. Hardy Curry was a self-employed shoemaker at age twenty-eight in 1873. By 1885 he had secured more than one thousand dollars' worth of property, with which he financed a change in careers: by 1890 he had become a grocer and remained in that profession for more than a decade.

Festus Flipper was still more successful. Trained and hired out as shoemaker while owned by slave dealer Ephraim G. Ponder, Flipper returned to the city with his wife (whom he had purchased from her master, Rev. Reuben H. Lucky) and his three sons—Festus Jr., Henry, and Joseph—in 1865. "A Manufacturer of Custom Made Boots and Shoes," he was able to buy a half-page ad (an ad that ran without designation of his race) in the 1870 Hanleiter's Atlanta City Directory. Flipper employed thirty-six-year-old James Esek Johnson in his shop in January of that year. Johnson, his wife Caroline, and their four children may have been new arrivals in search of accommodations, for they shared quarters at the orphan asylum on the edge of the city. William Smith of Alabama, twenty-six, joined Flipper and Johnson in the shop in 1872. Flipper's income allowed him and his wife, Isabella, to educate two of their three sons. Henry and Joseph Flipper attended Storrs School in 1870, and Henry moved on to Atlanta University in 1873. A college freshman, Henry was selected that year to attend the U.S. Military Academy at West Point, becoming that institution's first black graduate in 1877. Joseph Flipper also continued his studies, graduating from Atlanta Baptist Seminary and ascending to the pulpit at Bethel AME Church, where he served as pastor from 1886 to 1889.[44]

African Americans with limited resources often entered the business arena as peddlers, selling produce, poultry products, and baked goods. Both slaves and free people of color had participated in this practice before the war. Predictably, several ordinances were passed in the antebellum period to control these fledgling merchants. The council required vendors to seek permission and purchase a license from the city before they could peddle their wares; failure to obtain a license resulted in arrest and a fine.[45] Occasionally the city made exceptions and granted requests for free licenses, but emancipation and Reconstruction resulted in the elimination of this practice in 1869. The city henceforth denied free licenses to all but disabled applicants and required the recommendation of three "respectable" taxpayers who had resided in the city for at least two years.[46] In freedom as in slavery, the practice of selling foodstuffs persisted irrespective of these new restrictions.

Peddlers gave way to grocers as African Americans accumulated small amounts of capital. James Tate opened his grocery store in 1866 with a capital investment of six dollars. Five other black-owned grocery stores were operating in the city by 1870. Grocers continued to multiply and prosper between the end of Reconstruction and the turn of the century. Supplying goods to a black clientele, more than twenty African American male grocers had acquired one thousand dollars or more in property by 1900.[47]

Barbershops, restaurants, and boardinghouses complete the list of black-owned businesses in the late 1860s and 1870s. The pre–Civil War pattern of barbering as a black profession persisted after the war: six of the seven tonsorial artists listed in the 1859 city directory were African American, as were the majority of barbers in postwar Atlanta. Black men continued to dominate the profession for the remainder of the nineteenth century. Robert Yancey, a barber in antebellum Atlanta, continued his trade after the war and had, by 1873, accumulated $2,400 in taxable property. Wesley Dougherty Hutchins, also a barber, improved his capital accumulation ($1,900 in taxable income by 1885) and expanded his place of business in 1870 by employing thirty-five-year-old Augusta native Alexander Dobson to cut hair in his shop.[48] The intimate nature of their work required black barbers to cater either to whites exclusively or to blacks exclusively well before the passage of segregation laws in Atlanta. Not surprisingly, those who chose the former had accumulated more wealth and owned more property by the turn of century. The efforts of these men foreshadowed the success of business entrepreneur Alonzo Herndon.

African American women found fewer job opportunities as a result of their gender and their race and also received lower wages than did black men. Heavy industry and factory jobs just barely open to African American men were emphatically closed to their wives, sisters, and daughters. The railroad did not employ many women, black or white, though freedwoman Carrie Steele held the position of stewardess in the depot. Manufacturing concerns that hired whites did not employ black women. Hannibal Kimball, owner of Kimball Hall and the Atlanta Cotton Factory, employed black women as maids in the hotel but refused to hire them in his cotton factory. Similarly, neither of the city's straw goods manufacturers in the city hired black women to operate sewing machines.[49] White workers reinforced the gender and color line in labor relations even when white business owners were open to the possibility of hiring black women. An 1897 effort by Jacob Elsas to hire black women at the bag mill resulted in white workers, first female then male, staging a strike that temporarily closed the plant. Consequently, the black female workers were dismissed.[50]

Most African American women were confined to jobs as washerwomen, domestics, and cooks. In the last three decades of the nineteenth century 40 to 44 percent of the black women who worked in the city of Atlanta were washerwomen, continuing the antebellum pattern of employment for free black women.[51] Washing, drying, and ironing clothing and linen was heavy, dirty work. Domestic service was equally time-consuming and exhausting labor. Both kinds of work paid poorly. A laundress might earn four to twenty dollars per month; domestics (when they were paid) earned somewhat less, from four to eight dollars per month. Black women's working lives were further complicated by negotiations with white female employers about the hours they were to work and the exact nature of the work to be done in white homes. Black women rejected white expectations that they be live-in help and struggled to find employment that did not require them to abandon their own families six days per week.[52]

Some black women in Atlanta rose above these limited job opportunities, saving their meager earnings to acquire taxable property and later joining their male counterparts as entrepreneurs. Women, however, were slower to accumulate wealth. On average it took women a decade longer than the men to gain one thousand dollars' worth of property. Still, from 1880 to 1900 more than 150 black women's names with assets of more than one thousand dollars appear on the city tax rolls. At least sixteen of these women were laundresses. Other black women turned their domestic skills to the operation of boardinghouses and restaurants, or worked as dressmakers. Seamstress Rosa Baldwin had $1,810 in property in 1880.

Most women who secured more than one thousand dollars in taxable property were part of dual-income households, with spouses or other family members who were also employed. Seamstress Emma Dukes lived with William Dukes, who worked for J. H. High and Company. Laundress Priscilla Bradford resided with James Bradford. Dressmaker Bette Beale lived with grocer Courtney Beale. Harriet Brown operated a boardinghouse at 50 Courtland Avenue where Felix Brown was a cook. Emma Steele owned and operated a lunchroom at 614 Marietta Street adjacent to the grocery store owned by her husband, Mack K. Steele.

The African American professional class, consisting mostly of ministers and educators, was minute. The eight black physicians in Atlanta in 1900 had not been there two decades earlier. Dr. J. B. Bass, listed in the 1881 city directory, was no longer practicing in Atlanta in 1900; neither was J. Powell nor James E. Ashley. Henry E. Baulden, the city's first black doctor, faced white harassment in the 1870s similar to the treatment received by dentist Badger. Harassment as well as the likelihood, given the poverty of the black population, of low income contributed to the transience of black professionals.[53]

There were several black ministers in the city in the decade after the war, but none had accumulated one thousand dollars in property by 1880. Historian Jerry Thornbery suggests that some of the forty-seven men listed as ministers in the 1880 census, which designates only twenty-two churches, may have been lay preachers or exhorters who spread the gospel outside a formal church setting. Yet, even men who operated inside church hierarchy, such as Rev. Joseph A. Wood of Bethel AME and later Wood's Chapel, and Bishop Wesley Gaines, also of Bethel AME, often failed to accumulate taxable property in the 1870s. None

Unidentified women learning the womanly art and practical skill of sewing, undated. (Neighborhood Union Collection, box 14, folder 27, Atlanta University Center, Robert W. Woodruff Library.)

of the seven ministers with deposits at the Freedman's Savings Bank in the early 1870s earned sufficient income to pay taxes in that decade.[54] Since most could not count on their congregations to provide a sufficient salary, some supplemented their income through extra-pulpit labor. The experiences of black tailor and part-time minister William Finch serve as a case in point. As a slave, Finch had learned to read and write and hired himself out on his own time as a tailor. Despite the privileged circumstance of his literacy, as well as his involvement in Atlanta city politics in the 1870s, Finch made his living and amassed two thousand dollars in taxable property not as a minister (he was ordained in the American Methodist Episcopal Church in 1868), but as a tailor.

Educators, also a part of the small professional class, faced the same problem of discrimination in wages as did common and skilled laborers. The first generation of black teachers in the city were committed to providing black children and adults with basic education but were themselves semiliterate and self-taught. They were also poorly paid. Robert and Roderick Dhu Badger, who were educated in slavery and helped benevolent association workers teach school in the First African Church, donated their time and efforts, as did self-taught grocer James Tate. Northern white educators and the black students they trained to be teachers barely made sufficient wages to keep body and soul together, let alone accumulate wealth. Mitchell Street School teachers Nellie Crawford with $1,500, Ruth Ford with $1,000, and Mattie A. Ford with $2,225 in taxable property in 1895 were certainly exceptional women in their ability to save on meager teacher salaries, yet even these three did not break the $1,000 mark before then.[55]

In the 1860s, the city of Atlanta and the state of Georgia established a pattern of paying black teachers less than their white counterparts. Indeed, City Councilman Powell ultimately argued in favor of hiring black teachers for black schools because it was more economical. On average, African American teachers were paid fifteen to twenty dollars less per month than white teachers from 1877 until the mid–twentieth century (see chapter 4).

Low wages and job instability limited the accumulation of wealth for most blacks in Atlanta. Gradations of wealth were very slight in the postwar era with many freedmen and -women living at subsistence levels into the last decade of the nineteenth century. Nearly ten thousand African Americans lived in the city in 1873, yet fewer than seven hundred owned any property, and fewer than fifty owned as much as one thousand dollars in property.[56] The number of black property holders increased over the next three decades as did the total percentage of black-owned property. The bulk of property owners were invested in smallholdings (i.e., their home and personal effects) rather than business. By 1900 the number of African Americans in Atlanta had more than tripled, to thirty-five thousand—nearly 40 percent of the city's total population—but the number with one thousand dollars in property approached only three hundred, still less than 1 percent of the total black population. The process of capital accumulation in the black community was painfully slow, and most of the population remained decidedly poor and working class at the turn of the century.

The wealthiest blacks in Atlanta in the last decade of the nineteenth century were successful businessmen such as drayman Frank Boykin, mortician David T. Howard, grocer James Tate, and dentist Roderick Dhu Badger. Badger died in 1891, by which time he had accumulated considerable wealth. His $9,600 in taxable income was nearly three times that of Alonzo Herndon, who would become the wealthiest black man in the city in the next decade. By way of comparison, the wealthiest whites in Atlanta owned fifty thousand dollars or more in property. Former governor Joseph E. Brown, then president of the Georgia Railroad, was worth $312,400 in 1890.

Despite the efforts of black entrepreneurs, white wealth continued to outdistance black wealth by leaps and bounds throughout the period.[57] In addition to low wages, limited access to credit within the black community hampered business ownership, development, and expansion. African American entrepreneurs in Atlanta, as in other major urban centers, encountered resistance in their search for capital in the Gilded Age. Both Loren Schweninger and Juliet E. K. Walker note that barriers to credit slowed black economic development. Southern banking concerns had a long history of denying blacks access to investment opportunities. Since antebellum laws had forbidden black ownership of bank stock in many parts of the lower South, free people of color who lived in urban areas in high concentrations developed raced networks of collective investment and credit opportunities inside the black community. This pattern of financial activity continued well into the postwar period as freedmen and -women searched for ways to finance their future.[58]

Old paternalistic patterns did allow some individual whites to offer financial assistance to some individual blacks. Successful grocer Floyd Crumbly financed his shop with three hundred dollars in credit he received from two local white merchants.[59] Similarly, undertaker David T. Howard's inheritance of $175 from a white benefactor allowed him to open his mortuary in 1882. Howard, assumed to be the mulatto son of white attorney Thomas Cook Howard and "half" brother of U.S. Congressman William Schley Howard, had, like Roderick Dhu Badger, important links to an individual with the means to offer financial assistance.[60] Howard would observe years later that "had it not been for the kindly considerations shown us in a business way by our white neighbors from time to time when our business needed financing, success would have been impossible."[61] John T. Schell, son of white lawyer and Confederate Colonel William Fletcher and a slave mother, may have received an inheritance or other forms of financial assistance from his father.[62] This form of credit, an extension of the privilege of being born to a white patriarch, was not available to most African Americans in Atlanta and had the drawback of reinforcing black dependence upon whites.[63]

Other forms of credit were also compromised in Black Atlanta. A branch of the National Freedman's Savings and Trust Company opened in the city in July 1870. The Freedman's Bank, as it was most commonly known, gave most blacks in Atlanta their first experiences with a financial institution.[64] The Atlanta branch of the bank was frequented by a broad variety of community residents. Savannah minister and Georgia State Congressman Ulysses L. Houston had an account, as did black schoolteacher Jesse Thornton and lathe worker Edward Dawson. Young Albert Watts, then a freighthouse laborer, opened an account in January 1870. The single greatest concentration of accounts were held by students (69)—elementary, normal-school, and university level—some as young as six. Among their number were the children of Robert and Roderick Badger, Festus Flipper, and Henry Finch. General laborers (29), waiters (21), draymen (19), carpenters (16), cooks (16), and washerwomen (12) made up the next largest groups of depositors.[65]

However, the phoenix city's branch was less successful than the older, more established, branches in Savannah, Charleston, and Baltimore. Poor employment opportunities and limited wages were reflected in the saving patterns of Black Atlantans: depositors in Atlanta had small accounts averaging between three and fifty dollars.[66] The Atlanta branch had a mere $28,404 on account six months before the final 1874 collapse of the Freedman's Bank. In contrast, the Savannah branch had $153,425, Charleston $255,345, and Baltimore $303,947.[67]

Still, the presence of the Freedman's Bank may have given Atlanta's black population some flexibility on the issue of credit. A few high-status African American males were associated with the bank: Roderick Dhu Badger was secretary; ministers Joseph Wood and Frank Quarles were members of the executive committee. Modifications in its original national charter allowed the bank to make small loans beginning in 1870, but policy required that they be granted only on property at least twice the value of the loan to prevent high-risk investments. This dictate was disregarded across the system, however. Loans were made to "a dangerous class of borrowers, who would have received scant consideration at the ordinary bank."[68] Perhaps some Black Atlantans benefited from this policy, but the close of the bank in the summer of 1874 left African Americans in the city with few options for pursuing financial investments.[69] They had to develop other financial strategies in the pursuit of capital for investment.

The pattern of investment of African Americans in Atlanta at the time reveals something about community and race solidarity among blacks in the city at the close of the nineteenth century. Black businessmen expanded their wealth by investing in real estate. First as individuals, then collectively, established business owners reinvested their surplus capital in land, thereby increasing their personal holdings and at the same time providing employment opportunities and service centers for the black community. Mitchell Cargile, David T. Howard, and Alonzo Herndon exemplify black entrepreneurship in late-nineteenth- and early-twentieth-century Atlanta. All three men entered the city after the Civil War. Their careers as successful laborers provided them with capital for investment and subsequent upward mobility. Cargile was a skilled laborer who made his living as a cabinetmaker on Ivy Street in the early 1870s. He was the father of six children and served as superintendent of the First AME Church. The least wealthy of the early entrepreneurs, his net worth fluctuated between fifteen hundred and two thousand dollars. He maintained roughly 70 percent of his holdings in real estate from 1878 through the 1890s. Other blacks in Atlanta duplicated this pattern of investment in the late nineteenth century. (See Tables 1 and 2 in the appendix.)

David T. Howard worked first as a laborer and then as a porter. Both Cargile and Howard amassed more than one thousand dollars in taxable property while working as laborers. This financial success allowed them to pursue training at Clark University (later Clark College) in mortuary science. Despite Howard's 1891 advertisement in the Atlanta city directory self-identifying himself as "the first colored undertaker who graduated from the Clark School of Embalming," Mitchell Cargile had opened a mortuary business in 1874. Howard, presumably short on capital, opened his shop three years later.[70]

Mortician and successful businessman David T. Howard. (Caroline Bond Day Collection, Robert S. Peabody Museum of Archaeology and Ethnology, Harvard University. All Rights Reserved. Used by Permission.)

David T. Howard with Ella B. (Banner) Howard, his wife and the mother of his six children. (Caroline Bond Day Collection, Robert S. Peabody Museum of Archaeology and Ethnology, Harvard University. All Rights Reserved. Used by Permission.)

Herndon arrived in Atlanta only in 1883, having worked as a farm laborer in Walton County, Georgia, immediately after the war and then as a barber in Covington. Although born of a slave woman and her white master, Herndon was afforded none of the privilege or financial support of the Badgers or Howard. He received little education and found employment in Atlanta with the aforementioned black barber Wesley Dougherty Hutchins, who later took him on as a full partner. Within three years Herndon acquired his own shop on Whitehall Street and soon solidified his position as Atlanta's preeminent barber by taking a job as house barber at Markham Hotel, a position he would hold for nearly a decade. By 1904, he owned three barbershops including the elegant and palatial facility at 66 Peachtree Street equipped with "sixteen-foot front doors of solid mahogany and beveled plate glass."[71] Herndon, like his former employer, hired black male barbers and served an exclusively white clientele.

Barber Herndon became the single most financially successful black entrepreneur in Atlanta in the early twentieth century. In 1885, however, his total worth was a paltry $615, 82 percent of which was invested in real estate. Herndon's wealth grew considerably in the last decade of the nineteenth century; indeed, he amassed a small fortune, far outstripping the wealth of his black peers. By 1900 his net worth was $12,750, $5,000 ahead of grocers Peter Eskridge, Willis Murphy, and I. P. Moyer. A decade later, Herndon had a total worth of $10,300, 97 percent of it invested in real estate within the city of Atlanta.[72]

Cargile, Howard, and Herndon, as well as older businessmen James Tate and Roderick Badger, all invested heavily in real estate. Tate and Badger had been the two wealthiest African Americans in Atlanta in the 1870s and 1880.[73] Tate, who owned $3,507 in taxable property in 1880, had 77 percent of his wealth invested in real estate. Badger was wealthier still, paying taxes on a total worth of $5,850 in 1880, 77 percent of which was in land. Five years later, Badger's net worth had risen to $8,000, with 88 percent invested in real estate (see Tables 1 and 2 in the appendix).

Such individual investment in city and county real estate was supplemented by joint real estate endeavors in Black Atlanta, duplicating prewar patterns of investment found among African Americans in other southern cities. South View Cemetery Association, the earliest and perhaps most successful, was joined by Georgia Real Estate Loan and Trust and Atlanta Loan and Trust before the turn of the century. Joint real estate investment firms offered individual black investors the opportunity to increase their private wealth while at the same time providing the community with much-needed financial institutions, which in turn offered would-be entrepreneurs within the black community access to start-up loans. Fledging businessmen and -women, who might otherwise have been denied financial support to open a grocery store, boardinghouse, or kitchenette, could turn to members of their own community to secure funds.

Barber turned insurance mogul
Alonzo Herndon. (The Amistad
Research Center at Tulane University,
New Orleans, Louisiana.)

Georgia Real Estate Loan and Trust Company, a joint investment firm, was established in 1890. Floyd H. Crumbly was the chief organizer of the concern. Born in Rome, Georgia, Crumbly had moved to Atlanta with his family while still in his teens during the decade after the war. He was a successful grocer by 1890 with $2,275 in taxable property, 65 percent of which was invested in real estate. (His wife, Lulu, was worth an additional $2,500 in her own right.) Crumbly pooled resources with shoemaker turned dry goods vendor John T. Schell, contractor Alexander Hamilton, and customs house official and politician Henry Rucker to establish the trust company. William Allen and Charles William Thomas, members of the board of directors of South View Cemetery, were also investors in the Georgia Real Estate Loan and Trust.

All six men were experienced in the real estate market. Crumbly and Schell both owned the buildings that housed their businesses. Crumbly purchased the lot adjacent to his original store and built a two-story structure that housed his family in apartments upstairs.[74] Schell also owned his own home. Rucker operated a barbershop on Decatur Street distinguished for serving a black clientele. He was less affluent than the others in 1890, but he too invested the bulk of his wealth in real estate. Building contractor Hamilton owned $4,150 in taxable property in 1890, $3,000 of which was invested in city and county property.[75]

Georgia Real Estate Loan and Trust invested in land and rental properties in the city. No records of the organization survive, but there is evidence that it had some success. The Atlanta University conference on black efforts toward self-improvement listed the concern as a cooperative business with twenty-five members. The firm's total worth, including real estate, mortgages, and cash, was

$3,500.[76] The company first appeared on the Fulton County tax digest in 1900 with $1,650 in property.[77]

A third group of real estate investors established a firm a year after Georgia Real Estate was opened. The Atlanta Loan and Trust Company, housed at the corner of Bell and Auburn Avenues, had fifteen stockholders. Wesley Redding was the chief organizer, and the company invested in city rental properties. Four years after its establishment the firm opened the European Hotel to serve visitors to Atlanta during the 1895 Cotton Exposition. The company's total worth was listed as seven thousand dollars three years later.[78] The collective purchase and rental of residential properties generated income with less of an investment per capita than would have been required of a single investor.[79] These profits were then reinvested in the purchase of commercial real estate. The Schell Opera House and Hall, the Rucker office building, and the Odd Fellows Hall (jointly owned by the Odd Fellows, David T. Howard, and G. Young) were all important social and cultural institutions for the black community. These buildings were privately owned and publicly utilized after the development of joint real estate concerns. In addition, firms such as Hamilton and Son hired black workers as they constructed residential and commercial buildings. The money turned over within the community once again.

Black entrepreneurs invested in properties other than commercial ones. The Carrie Steele Logan Orphanage may have been a beneficiary of collective real estate investment. The orphanage opened was chartered by the state of Georgia in 1888. Carrie Steele and her teenaged son, Robert, were part of the freed population that migrated into the city after the war. She first earned her livelihood by selling candies and baked goods and then secured a job as the stewardess in Atlanta's train depot, saving sufficient funds to buy a modest $1,600 home by 1885. Robert Steele worked as a porter for several years before joining the ranks of the city's black barbers. His Marietta Street barbershop did not produce Herndon's wealth but Steele did achieve some status in Atlanta: he served as an elder of Bethel AME Church and also purchased a home in the late 1880s.

The number of orphaned and homeless black children in the city distressed Carrie Steele. Her own experiences as a seventeen-year-old slave mother undoubtedly influenced her understanding of the difficulties of negotiating life with limited resources. (Steele later married Josiah Logan, who joined her in the work of caring for orphans.) Steele began to take in small children, "placing them in a boxcar during her workday" and bringing them to her home at night. Recognizing her approach to the problem could only provide temporary relief, Steele sought a more permanent solution. According to E. R. Carter, she petitioned the city council for a sales permit and sold printed material to raise funds to establish a black orphans' home. Then she prevailed upon the city to let her use a portion of the municipal pesthouse to shelter the children temporarily. She also solicited funds from community members. Reportedly having raised five thousand dollars through the sale of her autobiography, direct solicitation, and the sale of her home, she purchased a small lot and financed the construction of the orphanage.

The Carrie Steele Logan Orphanage opened in 1889 (though Carter notes an official celebration of the opening in 1892). The chief organizer of the Georgia Real Estate Loan and Trust Company, Floyd Crumbly, served as secretary of the board of trustees of the orphanage.[80] It is likely that he and other investors aided Steele in her efforts at fund-raising and may have even helped facilitate the sale of her home. The Carrie Steele Logan Orphanage represented an important effort on the part of the black community to tend to parentless children. In this case, the process of investing in real estate, individually and collectively, did more than generate wealth. It built community, physically and socially. The individual investors profited, and the total wealth of these men expanded significantly over time.

Real estate investment gave African Americans in Atlanta spaces for cultural and social events. In the early 1870s, once freedom had brought an end to the process of seeking white permission to gather to sing or to pray or to dance, black churches, fraternal organizations, women's clubs, and dramatic and literary societies began to form. These institutions were the social threads with which African Americans wove a community in post–Civil War Atlanta. The possession of privately owned spaces meant the black public—political activists, benevolent societies, and cultural groups—had meeting and gathering places of their own.[81] Real estate investment moved the community one step further from the dependence of slavery. African Americans invested in their future and the future of the phoenix city.

A perhaps apocryphal story reports that when General Oliver Otis Howard visited black schools in Atlanta and asked what should be said about the condition of freedmen in the South, a young student remarked, "Tell them we are rising!"[82] The restoration and development of Black Atlanta is a story of a slow rising. African Americans were given "nothing but freedom" at the war's end. Those stranded in up-country Georgia and other rural areas flocked to the crossroads, to the city, in search of opportunities that would shape their future. As men and women who had endured the ordeal of slavery, these migrants intended to do more than just survive in the new market economy, though for a while even survival was tenuous. They set to work, building shacks in any available space, scrounging for clothing, hunting for work. Those with skills quickly formed their own small businesses, while those less skilled marketed themselves to potential employers for pennies a day. Racism, job discrimination, and segregation limited economic development; most African Americans in Atlanta remained part of the working poor throughout the nineteenth century. While slow, the accumulation of capital in the hands of a few hundred black men and women resulted in individual and collective investment in real estate. This process secured and multiplied investors' wealth and created autonomous social spaces, owned and controlled by African Americans. Black laborers, businessmen, and entrepreneurs created the material base on which layers of community came to rest.

CHAPTER THREE

The Black Church in Atlanta

Brush Arbors in Freedom

A free, independent black church was central to the postwar transformation of the African American community in Atlanta. Freedmen and -women expressed and acted upon their desire to tend to the needs of the spirit just as they had worked to tend to the needs of the body. The informal and often hidden "brush arbors" concealed from the sight of their oppressors, in which enslaved African Americans had transformed the white man's Christianity into something more truly their own, gave way to organized and highly visible religious congregations in freedom. Both spiritual haven and community center, the black church addressed the moral, economic, and social needs of freed African Americans. Spirituality as practiced in black churches was at the center of their way of being, part of a racial consciousness that linked African Americans to the culture of their slave past and gave them the necessary hope and energy to build their future.

The spiritual life of slaves, like much else in their world, was a contested space. White Christian slaveowners vacillated between their hope that religion would make their chattels obedient and docile and their fear that the central tenet of Protestantism—equality before God—would encourage enslaved blacks to rise up against their oppressors. Religious teachings that linked the spiritual salvation of black souls with the liberation of black bodies deterred slaveowners from tending to the conversion of their slaves early in the history of the institution. This issue was largely resolved before the end of the Revolutionary period. Some masters continued to complain that conversion and lessons in faith occasionally led their slaves to overstep their bounds. Others voiced stronger concerns that Christianity fostered (in the view of whites) a misguided belief in social justice that might foment revolutionary insurrections by slaves on the order of the uprising in Saint Domingue or, closer to home, the rebellion of Gabriel Prosser. Most, however, placed greater store in the lessons of obedience, including the oft-repeated dictum "servant obey thy master," as preached by white ministers to black congregants in mandatory religious services. These moral lessons, in conjunction with white southerners' steadfast belief in their ability to regulate and, under the constant threat of violence, control the behavior of their chattels, led most owners to Christianize their slaves.[1]

Black slaves in the antebellum South did not passively accept Christianity as it was force-fed to them by their masters but significantly reshaped it in the way they received, interpreted, and performed it. Enslaved Africans and their American-born descendants had their own cosmologies, their own understanding of the spirit world, and their own styles of worship. African-based belief systems and forms of religious expression marked by song and dance, offerings, and verbal appeals to their ancestors and their God were married to a base of Christianity. Forms of Christianity that allowed for a rich and highly demonstrative religiosity, especially as espoused by Methodists and Baptists during the Second Great Awakening, found many converts among black slaves. Emotional camp meetings filled with the cries of men and women caught in the spiritual crises of conversion, or voices lifted in songs of praise, won many blacks to the faith of John Wesley and George Whitfield.[2]

Slaves required to attend religious services under the watchful eye of masters or appointed white guardians sat quietly and formally as they listened to biblical tales of Cain and Ham designed to encourage complicity in their oppression. Former slave George Womble reported that all slaves were required to attend Sunday services at the master's church where the white minister "would walk back to where the slaves sat and tell them not to steal their master's chickens, eggs or his hogs." Ex-slave William Ward recalled being ministered to by a black rather than white man but noted that the black preacher, under the watchful eye of the overseer, also preached obedience. Indeed, the black preacher's sermon was "always built according to the master's instructions" and focused on reminding slaves "that they belonged to the masters and were intended to lead a life of loyal servitude."[3] Significantly, Ward also noted that "none of the slaves believed [in the black preacher's message of obedience] although they pretended to believe because of the presence of the white overseer . . . if he preached exactly what he thought and felt, he was given a sound whipping."

In addition to noting that slaves were required to attend Sunday services, Womble also offered evidence that slaves celebrated their faith in a manner inconsistent with the wishes of their owners. His description of a nighttime "brush arbor" service where slaves secretly "knelt and turned their faces toward the ground and then . . . began . . . moaning and praying" so that "the sound would not travel very far" reveals the ways blacks struggled to embrace Christianity outside of the control of their masters. Former slave Emmaline Heard also described a "brush arbor" church on the Harper Plantation in Henry County, Georgia. "The trees and underbrush were cleared away to provide a sufficient space to accommodate the slaves and the trees evened off at a good height and the brush and limbs piled on top to form a roof." Adelia Dixon too recalled a "brush arbor" church community in rural Georgia.

> At the beginning, several trees were felled, and the brush and forked branches separated. Four heavy branches with forks formed the framework. Straight poles were laid across to form a crude imitation of beams and other framework of a building. The top and sides were formed of the brush which was thickly placed so that it formed a solid wall. A hole left in one side formed a doorway from which beaten paths extended in all directions. Seats made from slabs obtained at local sawmills completed the furnishings. In inclement weather, it was not possible to conduct services here.[4]

African Americans often used the expression "hush harbor" to describe such a forested place of shelter in which they practiced their faith. Whites, slave masters, and later scholars, however, understood the expression as merely a garbled pronunciation of "brush arbor," not considering the way blacks might communicate meaning by naming. Womble's recollection of services in such a site, where African Americans gathered to offer praises but bent low to muffle the sounds of their songs and prayers for deliverance, offers a glimpse of the distinct spiritual style of the enslaved. Indeed, many former slaves related tales of secret gatherings in secluded spots where worshippers gathered around iron pots to "catch the sounds" of celebration that might alert whites to services taking place without "proper" supervision. Hence, the expression "hush harbor" conveys quite literally the need slaves had for a safe space—a separate haven in which they might worship. Historian Robert L. Hall suggests that the presence of the iron pot at black spiritual gatherings was less about helping to prevent being found out by whites and more a consequence of surviving Congo-Angolan religious beliefs. Both the artifact and the practice highlight a form of Christianity that was reminiscent of African traditions.[5]

Owing both to their West African origins and the circumstance of their bondage, then, the religion practiced by the enslaved was of necessity different in form and in style from that of their masters; more importantly enslaved Christians held beliefs different from those of their masters. As was true of the material trappings of their lives—food, clothing, domiciles—African Americans took the religion that was offered them and refashioned it to meet their own aesthetic and spiritual sensibilities and needs. The Christianity of enslaved blacks offered the abused a faith steeped in love; the oppressed a concept of divine justice and retribution; and the sorrowful a hope for a life redeemed from the control of their masters. The enslaved embraced Christianity because it gave them joy and the psychological power to negotiate in a world in which they had very little control.[6]

The paucity of black churches in antebellum Atlanta was not the result of spiritual lack. Rather, it was the direct consequence of the high level of repression in up-country Georgia. Policed, regulated, and controlled, African Americans in Atlanta simply were not able to develop a broad range of social institutions or churches before the Civil War. Atlanta had no counterpart to Charleston's African Methodist Episcopal Church, famous for sheltering Denmark Vesey's plot for insurrection. Neither did Atlanta possess the equivalent of the independent Baptist church in New Orleans, with a slave congregation five hundred strong.[7] The two African American congregations that existed in the city prior to 1865 were closely monitored and dependent on white largess for their very existence.[8] These first congregations and the half-dozen churches they helped create in postwar Atlanta struggled to possess their freedom more fully. Black congregants bridled at southern white leadership, ownership, and restraint, and hoped to build autonomous churches in which they could worship as they chose.

Their efforts yielded mixed results. On one hand, African Americans produced large, "institutional" churches that fostered educational organizations and groups for social reform and uplift, both of which contributed to community building in Black Atlanta. On the other hand, these institutions often struggled with staggering debt, which kept them (and their black ministers and parishioners) in patron-client relationships with northern white philanthropic and religious organizations. Smaller, less well-connected, and infinitely poorer black churches could offer their congregants a spiritual place but little of the social clout or services of larger churches. Freedom and the search for a religious autonomy were compromised by the need for capital and the limits of white racism.

The African American population in Atlanta multiplied rapidly, growing from roughly two thousand in 1860 to ten thousand a decade later.[9] By the turn of the century the black population was thirty-five thousand, and, correspondingly, more than twenty new churches serving African Americans had opened in the city. Baptist churches dominated the field, followed by African Methodist Episcopal and Methodist Episcopal.[10] The history of these churches and their development is tightly correlated to the development of Atlanta's black community as a whole.

As noted, black Christians had first moved to distance themselves from white congregations while still slaves in the 1840s. The city's first black congregation developed within the white United Methodist Episcopal Church in 1847. A year later, black Baptists were organized within the First Baptist Church of Atlanta.[11] These groups provided for the spiritual needs of enslaved Black Atlantans.

First Congregational joined these two antebellum congregations in 1867.

Wheat Street Baptist and Ebenezer Baptist, both of which played a crucial role in the modern Civil Rights movement, came into being along with dozens of other congregations in the 1870s and 1880s as the city's black population grew and diversified. Their efforts to secure and finance houses of worship, the form of their religious practice, and the social outreach programs African Americans developed in their churches will be examined here by focusing on Black Atlanta's big three: Bethel AME, Friendship Baptist, and First Congregational churches. These churches dominated the scene because of their size, social activism, and influential ministers.[12]

In the antebellum period African Americans who were in bondage to white members of the Union Methodist Episcopal Church sought permission to attend afternoon and evening worship services independent of their owners. They held services inside the church, supervised by an appointed white custodian, for roughly three years.[13] Seeking still more independence, black congregants secured a separate place of worship from Colonel Lemuel P. Grant, where they held services led by black lay minister Joseph Wood from 1855 until the war.[14] Under the auspices of Bishop Daniel Payne in 1865, Rev. Wood brought this independent congregation into the national African Methodist Episcopal Church through the South Carolina Conference.

The congregation at Bethel AME grew from a handful in the antebellum period to over sixteen hundred by the turn of the century.[15] Bethel's congregation would have reached this number in the 1880s if not for the establishment of Wood's Chapel AME in 1867 and Shiloh AME in 1872. These churches, offshoots of Bethel, reflected population growth and community expansion rather than congregational disputes.[16] Bethel AME was an important and successful church even before the turn of the century. It hosted the North Georgia Annual AME conference in 1881, which figured prominently in the national organization's decision to establish an "institution for the higher education of the negro," Morris Brown College, in Atlanta. Ministers Joseph Wood, Randall Hall, and Wesley J. Gaines, who made up three-fifths of Morris Brown's board of trustees, had each served a term as pastor of Bethel in previous years. The church gained national attention in 1895 when President Grover Cleveland attended services there and addressed the congregation during the Atlanta Exposition.

Friendship Baptist, the second oldest black congregation in the city, grew out of Atlanta's First Baptist Church. First Baptist Church was the religious home of men of wealth and influence in the city, including Drs. Jones and Fagan as well as Judge J. O. Whittaker. Thirteen slaves, including some owned by the aforementioned patriarchs, were the first to ask, on June 13, 1848, for a letter of dismission to be allowed to worship independently as "an African Church." Approval having been granted, the newly formed congregation met in First Baptist on Tuesday evenings, supervised by at least one white member of the church.[17]

After enslaved lay minister Frank Ponder (who later changed his surname to Quarles) joined the black congregation in 1858, black members rapidly fled First Baptist to join the African Baptist Church. Seven members joined Quarles in July, followed by another eight in August. By September, beleaguered by requests for letters of dismission to the African Church, elders at First Baptist granted "as many are disposed too [sic] transfer to this Church." First Baptist also terminated Tuesday evening services and direct supervision of black worship, granting members of the African Church "the privilege of this house every Sabbath at 3 o'clock when it does not conflict with more important assignments" and ordering that "the gallery be opened for their use at all times." First Baptist maintained stewardship of the black congregation, however, appointing five white members to serve as trustees and treasurer in 1862.[18]

The African Baptist Church continued to grow between 1859 and 1864 as a steadily increasing number of slaves requested dismission.[19] Quarles was formally ordained in 1862 and continued to minister to the city's enslaved Baptists.[20] Quarles relocated, temporarily, to Macon, Georgia, where he founded St. James Baptist Church, but returned home to his church in Atlanta in the winter of 1863. There, in a February 1864 ceremony presided over by a presbytery of white Baptist ministers, Quarles was, "by imposition of hands," made pastor of the African Church. First Baptist was still not yet ready to relinquish full control of the African Church, however, reappointing in March 1864 a committee of five white deacons to continue to oversee the Quarles' congregation.[21]

Established in May 1867, First Congregational, the third black church in Atlanta, was founded by white teachers and staff from the American Missionary Association and in 1877 moved into a new building situated in Shermantown at North Calhoun and Houston streets.[22] The congregation was, at first, interracial: white AMA agent Frederick Ayers and his wife, and teacher Edmund Asa Ware, were joined by black grocer Charles H. Morgan and his wife, Anna, and eight other African Americans who entered First Congregational by a profession of faith. In March 1868, after Ayers' death in September 1867, Cyrus West Francis was the first of many white "Yankee" ministers from New England to take over as pastor. However, fifteen years later, First Congregational Church was a "black" church with the exception of white minister Evarts Kent and a few faculty members from Atlanta University.[23]

First Congregational became a black church as a result of white flight rather than willful black separation. As blacks continued to join in increasing numbers in the 1860s and 1870s, the darkening of First Congregational was aided by several white members, mostly teachers and administrators, who chose to meet in a separate chapel at Atlanta University rather than trek to Shermantown for services. Although that chapel remained interracial, open to black students who attended the college, it was distinguished by a critical mass of white members. Edmund Asa Ware would later challenge the notion of segregated Congregationalism, but in December 1873 he joined Cyprus West Francis (who was invited back to First Congregational as pastor in June 1874), and George Walker and his wife, Emily (a teacher at Storrs School), in leaving the church to attend the chapel, by then called the Church of Christ, at Atlanta University. The Walkers' son, Lewis G. Walker, also defected. White cashier Philip Cory, convicted of embezzlement at the Freedman's Savings Bank, went further still, leaving Congregationalism to join the white Methodist Episcopal Church in June 1873.[24]

The movement to form a whites-only Congregationalist church culminated in the formation of Piedmont Congregational Church in 1882. The Congregationalist community was divided on the issue of segregated churches. Atlanta University's president, Edmund Asa Ware, confronted American Home Missionary Society Superintendent James Harwood and others on the issue. As part of an effort to stave off the growing segregation of his denomination, Ware condemned "segregated Congregationalism in the South, on both ethical and practical grounds." Despite Ware's efforts, white Congregationalists continued to pursue a system of segregation in Atlanta and other parts of the state. As a result of this policy of racial exclusion, Georgia Congregationalists were not admitted to the Congregational Council of Churches until 1892.[25]

Black Congregationalists, officially segregated from their white peers, continued to worship under the control of white missionary ministers appointed by the American Home Missionary Society until 1894, when Henry Hugh Proctor was chosen as pastor.[26] Proctor was the first man of color to serve as minister of First Congregational. Pastor to a flock of African Americans who had watched their white brothers and sisters in Christ reject integrated fellowship at the church, Proctor nonetheless maintained an "open door" policy. Committed to interracial cooperation, he invited all Atlantans, black and white, to worship at First Congregational until his resignation in 1919.

Black Christians continued their efforts to develop independent churches and to practice their faith separate and apart from whites during the remainder of the nineteenth century. Southern white churches and missionary groups made some attempts to retain black parishioners, even establishing separate black churches. Clark Chapel was organized in the Summerhill section of Atlanta in 1866 under the auspices of the white Southern Methodist Episcopal Church. White Presbyterians and Episcopalians also worked to keep black members within the fold by continuing the practice of either segregated pews or segregated services within white-controlled churches. Issues of space and finances did force some black congregations to remain semidependent on white religious institutions in the first decades after freedom. Yet African Americans, recognizing the paternalism involved in white efforts to maintain biracial congregations that drew the color line, for the most part rejected religious race mixing in which they were to remain subservient to southern whites. They chose instead to establish and maintain their own churches.

In their bid for independence, however, black worshipers struggled to find homes for their congregations. Lack of buildings, lack of resources, and white hostility infringed upon their efforts. Wartime destruction dislocated both black and white parishioners in the immediate postwar period. Immaculate Conception Catholic Church, Trinity Methodist Episcopal Church, and Central Presbyterian Church had survived the bombardment of the city; First Baptist, Christian, and First Methodist Churches were all damaged. Members of the African Church continued to hold worship services in First Baptist, despite the condition of the building. In November 1865, the "colored congregation" was given notice that their continued presence compromised white religious services: "so better order may be observed during the Sabbath Service of the church both morning and night . . . the Gallery will be kept for the use of the white congregation."[27] Pressed for space and undoubtedly tired of white overseers, Quarles moved to form a physically as well as spiritually separate church. His March 1866 request for a full separation of the two congregations was followed by a May proposal that the black congregation "make some other arrangements for a place of worship during the summer."[28] Quarles's congregation relocated in the summer of 1866 after being formally dismissed from First Baptist. The African Church, renamed Friendship Baptist, held services in a freight boxcar provided by the 9th Street Baptist Church in Cincinnati, Ohio, and located on property owned by First Baptist Church.[29]

Free from First Baptist, Friendship Baptist had only the resources of its poor, recently freed, congregation to finance church life. Its members may have had the will but certainly not the wealth "to make monthly tithes . . . to support the building of a pastor's home and provide his salary" or to hire a black sexton to "take care of the church," as did the congregation of First Baptist.[30] Quarles acted quickly to address the concerns of his now independent congregation. He negotiated with American Missionary Association official Frederick Ayers to establish a school for black children, and by offering Ayers the church site to house said school, Quarles guaranteed access to free education for his parishioners at the same time that he secured financial resources for the church. Ayers had a chapel dismantled, transported from Chattanooga, and reconstructed in Atlanta to serve as a school for black students—the school later became Atlanta

University. The link between Friendship Baptist and educational institutions and missionary associations would continue throughout the nineteenth century.[31]

White Atlantans were not appreciative of Quarles's progressive thinking. The congregation was forced to relocate less than two months after separating from First Baptist when white residents nearby complained about the location of the AMA school for black children. On June 20, 1866, the First Baptist Church authorized Quarles, as trustee of the Baptist-owned property on which the boxcar and school stood, to "make the best settlement [he] could with the city council for their church lot to reinvest the funds in another lot." The black congregation purchased and moved to a site at the corner of Haynes and Markham on the west side of the city, away from First Baptist and its neighbors.[32]

Relocation did not, however, solve the financial problems facing the church. Once again, Quarles and church deacons turned to northern whites to solve their financial crisis. Friendship Baptist secured a fifteen hundred–dollar loan from the American Baptist Home Mission Society to cover part of the cost of construction of a permanent church building. The ABHMS earned an extra return on this loan in 1879 when the organization relocated Augusta Institute to the city. Renamed Atlanta Baptist Seminary, the school started out in the basement of the ABHMS-financed Friendship Baptist Church building. Two years later, ABHMS organized a school for women—ultimately, Spelman College—in Friendship's basement rooms.

As he negotiated with philanthropists to help build community institutions, Quarles's Friendship Baptist Church grew tremendously: the congregation of less than thirty in 1859 had increased by 1881 to more than fifteen hundred. Quarles certainly recognized the advantages of developing a relationship with both the AMA and ABHMS. The institutions developed by these organizations provided black men and women with vital educational opportunities that produced generations of "teachers and preachers," social reformers, and politicians. The link between African American churches and white-sponsored institutions for black education did not relieve churches of debt, however. Quarles's negotiations created opportunities for black uplift and raised the profile of the church, but it also left the congregation of Friendship Baptist indebted to its white benefactors.

Reverend Edward Randolph (E. R.) Carter, graduate of Atlanta Baptist Seminary and Quarles's successor, discovered that Friendship was three thousand dollars in debt when he assumed the helm in 1881. This debt, largely a result of Quarles's program to provide yet another new home for his burgeoning congregation by building a freestanding church a few blocks away at Haynes and Mitchell, took years to repay. Carter, following the established pattern, began

E. R. Carter, future minister of Friendship Baptist Church, as a young man. (Archives Division, Auburn Avenue Research Library on African American Culture and History, Atlanta-Fulton Public Library System.)

Friendship Baptist Church. (Courtesy of the Atlanta History Center.)

his career at Friendship with a full-scale fund raising campaign. He took to the stump, traveling nationally and internationally, lecturing to church and philanthropic organizations in order to raise funds, as well as constantly urged church members to share their limited resources with the church.[33]

Bethel AME also struggled with issues of finance, though less so than the independent Friendship Baptist. As part of a large, hierarchical denomination, the congregation of Bethel did not control the appointment of its ministers. Eight different men served Bethel in the same years that Quarles led Friendship Baptist. But there were benefits to this lack of congregational authority; Bethel could rely upon some funds from the North Georgia Conference of the African Methodist Episcopal Church. The congregation built its first small church on Jenkins Street during the three years after the war. When growth forced the expansion of the church, Wesley J. Gaines, who succeeded Woods, serving from 1866 to 1869 (and again from 1881 to 1884), oversaw the relocation from Jenkins Street to Wheat Street (renamed Auburn Avenue in 1893) some time in 1869.[34] The demands of an ever-growing population led to expansion at the new location as well, and the church undertook a thirty-year building campaign beginning in 1891. Nine ministers and some twenty-five thousand dollars later, "Big Bethel" had erected the largest black-owned church in Atlanta and had avoided the debt that plagued many black churches by raising subscriptions to pay for the new building as it was being constructed.

White ministers associated with the American Missionary Association, from Frederick Ayers to Samuel H. Robinson, led First Congregational Church from its founding until the last decade of the nineteenth century. This link between a northern missionary society and a growing black congregation worked to the fiscal advantage of First Church. All congregants were asked to raise $30 to give to the AMA in order "to make a special effort to secure a church lot"; in addition, each was expected to pledge "a contribution according to his ability" on the first and second Sabbath of the month. These local fund-raising efforts were in addition to whatever money came from the AMA. First Congregational Church continued to be housed in Storrs Chapel, which doubled as a school, until 1877. This situation was remedied when students from the AMA-affiliated Atlanta University were recruited to erect a five thousand–dollar brick church and a sixteen hundred–dollar parsonage on ground deeded to First Congregational by the AMA. In the early years of operation, then, the church was spared the frantic scramble for housing or funding as a result of its relationship with the AMA.[35]

Henry H. Proctor arrived in Atlanta in 1894, committed to transforming First Congregational into an "institutional" church. He set out to expand the church's social services to the black community by supporting several "neighborhood missions." The violent attacks on blacks and their property during the riot of 1906 inspired Proctor to expand the boundaries of his ministry further. He also began work on a new, more modern church building in 1908. Designed to lure African Americans from "the wide open, illuminated, and attractive dive," Proctor's new church was intended to become a community center as well as a house of worship, providing a gym for the colored YMCA and meeting rooms for the YWCA. AMA funds had dwindled as a result of the separation of congregations and Proctor was forced to find other means to finance his dreams of expansion. Initially embraced by Booker T. Washington as an example of "new colored leadership," Proctor worked "the circuit," giving speeches and raising funds from white Congregationalists and philanthropic organizations both north and south of the Mason-Dixon line. The search for funds for his black church pressed Proctor into a patron-client relationship with several elite whites in the city. Each new church project sent him, hat in hand, to moneyed whites in search of financial support.

Black churches continued to develop and expand in Atlanta despite financial struggles. The black population continued to grow, reaching nearly thirty-five thousand by the turn of the century, and the number of churches grew to meet the demand. Baptists had the greatest number of churches. Black residents, who lived in small enclaves and neighborhoods around the city, wanted churches within walking distance of their work and homes, and Friendship Baptist aided in this process, helping to organize some seven of the thirteen Baptist churches formed in Atlanta before 1900.

Wheat Street Baptist was one of the most significant of these new congregations. Organized in 1870 to serve the black community east of Jenkins Street, the congregation later moved to a building on Wheat Street where, along with Bethel AME, it helped provide social and religious guidance to black residents. Wheat Street Baptist grew slowly, changing ministers twice before settling on William Henry Tillman, who oversaw both the church relocation and the expansion of its rolls between 1875 and 1897. Morehouse graduate Peter James Bryant took the helm of Wheat Street the next year and guided the church until his death. Destroyed by the great fire of 1917, the building remained in a state of partial reconstruction for nearly two decades while the congregation worked to retire a debt of more than one hundred thousand dollars.[36]

AME churches were the second most numerous in the city between 1875 and the turn of the century. First African Church, later Bethel AME, was joined by Wood's Chapel and St. Paul's African Church in the 1870s. There were four AME churches in the city in 1880 and a dozen by 1900. Although they did not share the Baptists' intense relationship with slave-based religious traditions, these traditions remained part of their worship style. When a "hush arbor" was established

Henry Hugh Proctor, Yale-educated minister of First Congregational Church. (The Amistad Research Center at Tulane University, New Orleans, Louisiana.)

Activist minister Henry Hugh Proctor with civic leaders. Proctor was determined to communicate his understanding that Atlanta's First Congregational Church was significant for its "institutional" efforts to uplift the race as expressed by the banner, "First Institutional Church welcomes President William Howard Taft." (The Amistad Research Center at Tulane University, New Orleans, Louisiana.)

in the Summerhill area in Atlanta in 1866, Rev. Joseph Wood of Bethel AME reached out to minister to the group. The arbor gathering was formalized as Wood's Chapel and was brought into the AME diocese.

In late-nineteenth-century Atlanta, dozens of other black congregations established small churches that struggled to survive. Meeting in different locations over a number of years, these churches scrambled for funds to secure a permanent location and pastor. These small groups of working-class men and women, who stretched extremely limited resources in an attempt to support their churches, represent the effort of African Americans to create a place that would provide spiritual and social connections and re-create a familiar sense of community in an alien urban landscape. Such churches were often short lived, opening and closing within a year or two, as parishioners joined larger congregations where many more small contributions helped sustain the church.

Atlanta's churches differed among themselves in their organizational structure and their worship styles. Big Bethel and First Congregational were part of larger state and national conferences that selected and assigned ministers to specific posts.[37] Friendship and Wheat Street Baptist were independent churches whose ministers were selected by and answered to the congregation. Perhaps more important than these structural differences were the churches' varied worship styles. The end of slavery meant the end of the specific social framework in which slave religion had been cultivated. As freedom brought the hidden religion of slaves into the light, the movement from hidden "hush arbors" to independent churches led to changes in the nature of religion. Literacy, too, brought changes: preachers who had relied solely on memorization and oral tradition in slavery learned in freedom to read the word of God. The form and style of slave religion was further altered by stimuli from "outsiders." The gaze and critique of northern and southern whites as well as elite blacks all worked to transform slave religion in the decades after the Civil War. This transformation was slow and piecemeal. In religion, as in all other cultural spaces, freed people did not reject slave traditions in a wholesale fashion. Some denominations retained more of their slave-based religious traditions than did others. The retention of these traditions was tied to the larger phenomena of race consciousness and assimilation and was linked at some level to status and aspirations.[38]

Ministers were influential in the maintenance or rejection of black religious traditions. Doctrinal policy emanated from the top down in both the AME and the Congregational Church, and their ministers were called upon to see that denominational instructions concerning worship practices were followed in individual churches. Churches with less hierarchical structures, in contrast, gave ministers more freedom to design worship services that best fit the needs and desires of their congregation. Black Baptist, Independent Baptist, Free Baptist,

Pentecostal, and Sanctified churches were less hierarchical and less connected to mainstream churches than were Presbyterian, Colored Methodist Episcopal, or Lutheran churches. The religious traditions of the former developed from the "ground up" and so they retained more slave-based practices than the latter.[39]

Slave-based religious traditions of African Americans were manifest in spirit-filled, often physically demonstrative, worship services in the postwar era. Emphasis was on "getting the spirit," physically and emotionally feeling the presence of the Holy Spirit and Jesus Christ. Spiritual passion encouraged members of the congregation to punctuate the minister's sermons with shouting, wails of joy, and tears. The often-discussed pattern of call and response rooted in slave religion continued in these services, and music and song were essential. Music helped to free the soul from the limits of the body, and song elevated the soul to the Lord. The songs of choice were old-style hymns and favorite slave spirituals.[40]

African American religious traditions expressed cultural and ethical values different from those of whites. Spiritual practices and religious beliefs supported the larger cultural ethos of enslaved African Americans, at the center of which was communality. African Americans valued communality as part of their African cultural heritage and because it made practical sense in the American slave system. As historian John Blassingame has noted, slaves "united to preserve their self esteem . . . Group identification [assured] that slaves were not solely dependent on the white man's cultural frames of reference for their ideals and values." Communality resulted in neither homogenization nor a melting away of individual identity. The creation and maintenance of their own values and culture allowed those who were enslaved to cultivate a sense of autonomy. Blassingame concludes that "the slave's culture bolstered his self-esteem, courage and confidence and served as his defense against personal degradation."[41] Whittington B. Johnson, too, stresses the black churches' role in creating and sustaining black community in slavery. "The black church," he explains, "brought African Americans together, slaves and free persons of color, blacks and mulattoes—in a positive meaningful way; there could have been no viable black community without it."[42] Communality encouraged mutual cooperation and a sense of interdependence that aided slaves in facing the harsh realities of their existence.

Even though Christian conversion was an individual experience, the practice of worship in slavery was a communal activity. Shouting, call and response, and the singing of spirituals all worked as part of a group dynamic.[43] More important, the spiritual activity of slaves provided African Americans with a safe space in which to build a life for themselves, outside of the religious services required and controlled by their masters. This space was crucial both to slave survival and resistance. Historian Donald Mathews has addressed the powerful role of the black church in creating spaces of resistance: "Any organization which exists independently of the ruling elites, selects their own leadership, and is able to attract loyalty from dependent groups, even in the guise of religious worship, provides an important basis for social solidarity and personal security."[44]

The survival of slave-based religious traditions and cultural values in black churches was linked to the social, economic, and political circumstances of African Americans in the post–Civil War period. African Americans faced dire economic circumstances as well as white southerners—who, as the period progressed, embraced a renewed commitment to racial supremacy. Freed blacks were thrown, in large measure, on their own resources, including the resources of cultural traditions and values carried over from slavery, in order to survive.

Many whites, however, misunderstood and disapproved of the continuation of blacks' religious traditions. Northern missionaries and teachers who entered the South during Reconstruction expressed dismay upon observing the spirit-filled religious services of the freedmen and -women. Well meaning but paternalistic, the missionaries identified such behavior as heathen and barbaric, evidence of the evil consequences of slavery and the degradation of the Negro. Northern missionaries who planned to redeem the souls of freedmen focused their efforts on proselytizing southern blacks to transform their "childlike" faith and "animalistic" worship practices into something that more closely resembled their own religious beliefs and customs.[45] Southern whites appealed to the fact that freed blacks retained these traditions to rationalize racial segregation of various denominations in the postwar era.

More important in the context of this discussion, some African Americans, too, objected to these traditions. Northern blacks were also involved in the effort to provide aid to their southern brethren recently freed from slavery. Black educators, ministers, doctors, and would-be politicians were part of the population of northern carpetbaggers descending on the South in the postwar period. These men and women were products of mainstream educational and religious institutions in the North. Such institutions of higher learning as Oberlin and Berea College had been the source of knowledge for northern free blacks and fugitive slaves, as well as the source of mechanisms for their acculturation. Consequently, many black carpetbaggers shared ethical and cultural values with their white middle-class peers.[46] They, too, criticized slave-based religious traditions as superstitious and overly emotional.

Educated northern blacks, including those who had escaped from slavery, spoke of the degradation of the race under the slave system and of the need for "racial uplift." For northern black ministers, uplift meant erasing much of the religious tradition that had been carried over from slavery. For them, proper Christian practices involved an appropriate celebration of the Eucharist, stately hymns sung in calm moderate tones, and, perhaps most important, a silent, attentive congregation obediently absorbing the sacred word delivered in quiet, measured, and standard English by a literate minister. Freed people, they thought, would acquire these new behaviors through education. Literacy would allow for a deliberate and serious study of scripture and the evolution of proper church traditions. In theory, the education of emancipated men and women would serve to transform them on other cultural levels as it had these elite African American missionaries from the North.

Consequently northern black missionaries "pledged themselves to root out every religious practice that could not be found in Scripture." This effort brought northern black ministers into direct confrontation with "old-time" southern black pastors. Black missionaries from the North, positioning themselves as the new religious leaders of the race, condemned southern preachers for their lack of education and knowledge of scripture, labeling them ignorant, superstitious, and sometimes criminal.

This attitude on the part of northern black as well as white ministers and missionaries provoked conflicts with southern preachers. Savannah's First African Baptist Church pastor William J. Campbell was infamous for challenging "Yankee nigger" ministers who entered his domain.[47] Peter James Bryant, the Atlanta Baptist Seminary-educated pastor of Wheat Street Baptist Church, also rejected mainstream religiosity. Speaking before the Negro Young People's Christian and Educational Congress held in Atlanta in August 1902, he cautioned his fellow college-educated peers against confusing "churchanity" with "Christianity." Bryant began by praising the "marvelous progress" toward civilization made by individual blacks and by the race as a whole. But he balked at the idea that civilized black men and women ought to worship in the style of "white folks," and launched into the tale of a recent church revival. During the evening meetings, he said, black worshipers had reached "a fever heat, great was the preachers [sic] lung power, and many were the amens." One white man, who had been disturbed by the "long and loud" screams of joy, confronted Mary, a female attendee; "You people ought to quit," he said. "It is not intelligent. Have you not read how Solomon built the temple without the sound of hammer or driving of nail?" Mary replied, "We ain't near ready to build dat temple yet. We are simply blasting the rocks and ain't near done yet." Clearly, Bryant believed that the style and form were as important as the theology of faith.[48]

White missionaries in Georgia complained of "intemperate and illiterate" black southern ministers who "hate the school and the teachers, and oppose them in all secret and underhanded ways."[49] Lay preachers who objected to and resisted the biblical and theological interpretations of new professional, college-educated ministers were the source of many of the interdenominational conflicts of the post–Civil War era, especially within the Baptist and Methodist Episcopal faiths.[50]

Daniel Payne, an AME bishop and the founder of Wilberforce College in Ohio, was appalled by the survival of the "ring shout" and other "heathen" traditions in the AME churches in the South and North. Payne stressed the need for worshipers to leave behind any touches of slavery and Africa. He described slave-based religious traditions as "heathenish . . . disgraceful to themselves, the race, and the Christian name."[51] Not all AME parishioners endorsed Payne's perspective; he was physically attacked in one church after attempting to interrupt spirituals. Payne continued to lament the failure of the race to set aside slave-based religious traditions in the 1870s.[52] Like other educated black ministers and missionaries in the South, Payne believed that the only solution to the problem of such uncivilized religious traditions was an educated ministry.

Northern workers from benevolent societies failed to recognize the freedmen and -women's loyalty to their southern preachers and slave-based religious traditions. Black Atlantans overwhelmingly expressed their support of "old-fashioned" religion. The vast majority of blacks in Atlanta belonged to the continually expanding Baptist churches; First Congregational saw several members defect to AME and Baptist churches in the 1870s. The city had eight black Baptist congregations by 1875; ten years later their number had grown to thirteen, and by 1900 the number of black Baptist churches had doubled to a total of twenty-six. The old-time religion of the Baptist church attracted most working-class Black Atlantans, who filled their pews.

Unique among Atlanta's big three, First Congregational Church was distinctly *not* rooted in slave-based religious traditions.[53] The leadership was very much a part of the white mainstream; its ministers were white, upper middle class, and college (specifically Yale) educated. White Congregationalist doctrine marked the religious traditions of First Congregational. Black college students, and later faculty, joined First Church as a result of its association with Atlanta University. Acculturated, educated, and sometimes, though not exclusively, wealthier blacks were increasingly drawn to First Church. Robert Badger left Bethel AME to join First Congregational in May 1876 and Alex D. Hamilton, son of contractor Alexander Hamilton, joined in 1881. The appointment as pastor of Henry Hugh Proctor, a graduate of Fisk and Yale Divinity School, and part of a new group of educated, elite black male leadership in Atlanta, intensified this trend and made the congregation less inclined to incorporate a traditional African American worship style.[54]

Congregants at First Congregational left no report of their attitudes toward religious practices; however, Proctor boasted of more than one hundred college graduates in his congregation. He also recorded his opinions on slave religion in a book of autobiographical sketches, *Between Black and White*. He began his essay "A New Ethnic Contribution to Christianity" by arguing that "every race that has embraced Christianity has brought to the system its own peculiar contribution." He went to detail the contributions of Jews, Greeks, and Romans before he reached the last, and most important, that of Africans, who, he explained, had added "humility, fidelity, patience, large-heartedness, love" to Christianity. Proof for his claim, he noted, could be found in the example of Harriet Beecher Stowe's Uncle Tom, who was "more than a character of fiction. He was a real representative of the Christian slave."[55]

Proctor proceeded to analyze the slave's concept of God, Jesus Christ, heaven and hell, and the Christian life as manifested in slave spirituals. Africans, observed Proctor, learned Christian doctrine from their white masters. Like sponges, they soaked this belief system up, taking it to their hearts and maintaining it in pure form. Slaves "worked over in their minds" the themes of this new faith by adding "burning rhythmic utterances" in songs of faith, but they had not, argued Proctor, tampered with the theology of Christianity: "Their conceptions are orthodox. Doubtless they heard unorthodox preaching, but that none of it is manifest in their songs shows that it requires truth to inspire the genuinely religious heart." More significant than the "absence of certain heretical . . . elements" was the lack of hostile or vengeful thoughts: "Although these songs comprised, as I have said, the whole public utterance of a people for two and half centuries, yet there cannot be found in them a single trace of ill will!"[56]

Proctor's romantic vision of the theology of slave religion was part of an effort to find a place for Africans within the "family of man." Africans, according to Proctor, had borne their status as "servants to All . . . and drawn the water of others with a fidelity that is wonderful and a patience that is marvelous." Despite their oppression they had returned only love and loyalty to their masters. This not only belied judgments about African inferiority; it was evidence, suggested Proctor, of a moral superiority, making Africans worthy of respect. "When public prejudice shall have passed away and the future historian shall write unbiased by race feeling he will dip his pen in the clear sunlight of justice and catalogue this among the virtues of the American slave. Coming generations will read with admiring wonder of this oppressed people who so forcibly remind one of Him who was oppressed, yet humbled himself and opened not his mouth." Without a trace of self-conscious irony, with no criticism of Stowe's racist and paternalistic images, Proctor argued that, in exchange for this future acceptance and admiration, African Americans must embrace the depiction of "Uncle Tom" as a reflection of their true, best selves.[57]

Proctor saw slave religion as the simple and pure faith of the "unlettered." As evidence of the "original qualities of mind and heart of the Negro people," it had been of some value. Yet it did not follow, according to Proctor, that it ought to be the religion of free people striving to rise in American society. Because he so misunderstood the nature of slave religion, Proctor had no desire to maintain its traditions in freedom.[58]

Black churches served as centers of moral leadership as well as houses of worship, for religious leaders believed that the church was the proper instrument for reforming the race. Made "ignorant and vicious brutes" by the oppression of slavery, African Americans could redeem their humanity only through moral transformation. Ministers, deacons, and elders established and held congregants to a high moral code. Church members were expected to be monogamous and sober, examples of virtuous Christian souls redeemed by God's grace. Members who constantly strayed from church teachings were first warned, then suspended, and ultimately excommunicated if they failed to mend their ways.

First Congregational Church, which kept detailed records of church enrollment, "excluded" or excommunicated one or two members per year, for a total of twenty between 1867 and 1881, as a result of moral infractions. Amanda Powell was suspended for adultery and having a child out of wedlock. Ann Brown was suspended for "walking disorderly" and finally excommunicated after the failure of "prayer for divine intervention"; she had apparently continued her association with unnamed "persons of bad reputation [and] attended public dancing parties and other places of bad repute." Styles Lincoln Dougherty, Atlanta's first black lawyer and son of barber Wesley Dougherty, was excommunicated in September 1869 as a result of "drunkenness, profanity and fighting." Porter Wimby, who with his father Lucius had joined First Congregational in spring of 1868, was suspended after being charged with theft. Convicted of robbery and sentenced to the penitentiary, Wimby was excommunicated April 26, 1871.[59]

Ministers from all denominations were committed to the project of moral uplift during the last quarter of the nineteenth century. Baptist and AME churches also lectured members and excluded from the church those congregants who refused to adopt a chaste lifestyle. E. R. Carter, Peter James Bryant, and Wesley J. Gaines were well known for sermons and public lectures advocating temperance and the virtuous life. AME Bishop Henry McNeal Turner, editor of the *Southern Recorder*, used the newspaper as a bully pulpit from which he instructed members of the race to live in accordance with the dictates of the Bible. Reformed sinners, ministers argued, would benefit from the change to an upright life. Money that might otherwise be spent on liquor in lowlife "jooks" could be saved to secure ownership of a carriage or home. Time spent in pursuit of the "gaming life" was better spent in socializing with family and friends at home or at church. Church buildings therefore doubled as social centers, hosting teas, socials, and even the occasional dance. Pastors also opened their churches to scholars, reformers, and visiting ministers for public lectures on temperance, marital fidelity, and progressive child rearing. The church, even more than the schoolhouse, was considered a necessary alternative to the "dive" and central to the moral reformation of the race.

Black ministers were expected to organize and take the lead in overseeing black community efforts to secure public services, from education to political access. In the early years of emancipation, minister Frank Quarles had been at the forefront of the battle for education. At the turn of the century outspoken *Atlanta Independent* editor Ben Davis still looked to "the colored preachers [to] start the ball rolling for more room and better school facilities" for black children. Black ministers were also in the vanguard of the city's 1880s prohibition battles. Former politician and AME Bishop Henry McNeal Turner struggled in the winter of 1903/1904 to organize a protest against Atlanta's newly segregated streetcars.[60] Armed with moral suasion rather than political clout or wealth, men of the cloth reached beyond their pulpits to advocate social change for African Americans in Atlanta.

Churches, at the heart of community building in Black Atlanta, pooled their resources to meet the social needs of their congregations. The informal church had provided enslaved African Americans with the necessary space to affirm their existence. In freedom, black churches offered social support and material assistance as African Americans extended their limited assets to share the burden of caring for the living and the dead. Bethel AME, Friendship Baptist, and First Congregational Churches provided a large part of Black Atlanta with support services. Each one had ties to either a mutual aid society or a fraternal order that offered funeral and other services to members and the community at large.

African Americans had organized burial societies in slavery, some linked to African traditions and beliefs surrounding proper preparation of the dead.[61] Slaves acted to maintain the spiritual traditions they believed would assure their dead friends and family members safe passage to their next home, whether that be Africa or Heaven. The survival of African traditions associated with burials is well documented. Customs such as the dancing funeral processional, the shuffling ring, and the Kongo practice of leaving broken crocks or urns at the gravesite all survived the Middle Passage to become part of slave cosmology.[62] Slave burial societies reinforced African customs and beliefs every time a member of the community died. Even if the knowledge of the meaning of the rituals faded from one generation to the next, burial societies routinized the customs, guaranteeing their survival and, consequently, a distinctive African American culture.

Before emancipation, free people of color too had relied upon burial societies to pay the expenses of a proper funeral. Individuals who did not have membership in such a society were buried at the public's expense, and relatives lived in fear of their dead being placed in graves in poorly tended areas of the public cemetery. Worse yet, they could suffer the additional indignity of their dead being disinterred as a result of some municipal transaction. For example, in March 1852 the Atlanta City Council graveyard committee designated the easternmost portion of the local cemetery to be used "for the purpose of burying the black population."[63] Twenty-five years later the city exhumed the bodies so that it could rearrange plot size to allow for the burial of additional African Americans. Those whose families could not pay for individual reinterment were unceremoniously buried in unmarked mass graves.

As they left plantations or small farms and entered the cities, freedmen and -women entered a market economy, a cash nexus where relations were determined by financial resources. All arrangements for life, and death, required capital or access to credit. Fraternal societies that flourished in conjunction with churches in Atlanta allowed Black Atlantans to bury their dead with dignity. Several different societies offered burial services to their members.

Bethel AME entered the field of social service work early in its post–Civil War career. Rev. Francis J. Peck established two of Atlanta's early mutual aid associations. The first, founded in 1870, was the Daughters of Bethel. It was designed to provide sick relief and burial services for its members, who paid a fee of twenty-five cents per week in exchange for sick benefits of two dollars per week and death benefits of thirty-five dollars. In addition, members assisted one another with nursing care and provided floral arrangements for the memorial services.[64]

In 1871, Peck also helped to organize both a lodge of the Independent Order of Odd Fellows (Star of the South No. 1456) and a Masonic Lodge (Saint James Lodge No. 4, Free and Accepted Masons). African Americans had a relationship with the Odd Fellows, "the poor man's Masonry," dating back to 1843.[65] Peck had been affiliated with a lodge in Boston prior to his assignment to Atlanta. The Odd Fellows, like the Daughters of Bethel, provided sick relief and burial benefits for members, who paid dues of roughly a dollar per year. The lodge increased from the twenty-five members necessary to gain a charter in 1871 to sixty-five in 1898.[66] The Odd Fellows lodge and the Daughters of Bethel also provided members with the opportunity to socialize; both organizations held fairs and socials to raise funds and allow young adults to interact with members of the opposite sex under proper supervision.[67] The Masons of the Saint James

Lodge No. 4 were less successful than the Odd Fellows—of sixty-two original members, only thirty-seven remained active in 1898, and the lodge functioned with fewer total resources.

Friendship Baptist Church also provided social services for its members. By 1900, this second largest church in the city had a congregation that exceeded fifteen hundred. Like the other benevolent groups, the Daughters of Friendship Union No. 1, established at Friendship Baptist under Frank Quarles in 1869, provided sick pay and burial services for its members. E. R. Carter, Quarles' successor as pastor of Friendship, embarked on his own expansion campaign designed to increase the social work of the church. In 1884, Carter first acquired the mortgage of properties near the church. Eight years later, he secured twelve hundred dollars in loans from Atlas Savings and Loan Association and Citizens Bank and Trust Company to buy additional land slightly south of Friendship and directly north of his own home on Tatnell Avenue. Carter sold a building on this second property in 1893 but retained the land, charging three hundred dollars in rent annually. His purchase of three additional properties on Dover Street in 1895 gave him control over much land south and southwest of Friendship Baptist. This was the initial step in his turn-of-the-century campaign to finance and build first a Baptist home for the aged and then a "reformatory to care for the orphaned and wayward of the race," the Baptist Center for Wayward Youths.

The Carter Home for the Aged was funded by Friendship and cost some three thousand dollars to complete. The costs of expansion were beyond the congregation's means, so Carter appealed yet again to white elites—those in the city, across the South, and in Europe—for funds. In 1905 he secured a letter of endorsement from Georgia's Governor Joseph Terrell, validating the worthiness of his person and his cause. Carter's attendance at the Baptist World Congress that year was part of his fund-raising campaign. Five years later, now armed with letters of introduction from Henry Rucker and Booker T. Washington, he was still appealing for funds.[68]

Friendship Baptist Church also sponsored a chapter of the Women's Christian Temperance Union, organized by Mrs. Carter in March 1887. The wctu promoted temperance and clean living among the city's black poor. Its members lectured young women on the virtue of temperance and sexual abstinence. wctu members also delivered lectures on personal hygiene, motherhood, and "character building" to female students at Atlanta University and families on the western side of the city. In addition, the group raised funds to aid poor families, visited the sick, and distributed literature to prisoners on the city's infamous chain gang. wctu members held a celebration in the spring of 1894 at the inauguration of the one-room library they founded on the city's west side.[69]

First Congregational Church provided "institutional charity" for its members and the black community in Atlanta. Its link with Atlanta University gave the church special prominence in the university's published research on the condition of the Negro. *Some Efforts of American Negroes for Their Own Social Betterment*, third in the sociological series edited by W. E. B. Du Bois, offers some unique insights on Rev. Henry Proctor and the social politics of First Congregational Church. The population of the congregation had reached four hundred by 1898 and the church had a real estate value of ten thousand dollars with an indebtedness of only one hundred dollars.[70] The First Church was given the first slot in the listing of Atlanta churches in the Du Bois study, and although all three of the churches had suppers, socials, and fairs to help raise money and recruit new members, the Atlanta University publication listed only those of First Congregational (ten suppers and socials and twelve fairs). Similarly, although all three churches gave money to charity, only First Church was recognized for providing charity in a systematic way "along institutional lines."[71]

Two benevolent societies were attached to First Church. Helping Hand, organized between 1870 and 1872, followed the pattern of most black church-based mutual aid societies. Helping Hand collected an annual income of $140, expended $255 over five years for benefits to its members, and by the turn of the century had purchased a city lot. No more than fifty members were involved with Helping Hand in 1898, a mere fraction of the congregation, perhaps because of Proctor's disapproval of traditional benevolent and mutual aid societies. First Church's pastor looked to create a different type of charitable organization within the black church. He acknowledged that charity toward the poor was limited among African Americans as a result of their own continued poverty, "low wages," and "lack of organization for this specific purpose." Proctor also acknowledged that benevolent or insurance societies were "strongly entrenched" and "doing much good." Yet, he argued, such organizations ultimately sapped the financial energy of the black church. Specifically, "the small insurance business is greatly overdone and hinders thrift and benevolence."[72]

A second organization backed by First Church, the Florence Crittenton Home, established in Atlanta in 1898 to "rescue fallen women," was more in line with Proctor's vision of church-based social services. Unlike Carter's locally based home for the aged, the Crittenton Home was part of a New York City–based reform organization that established homes of refuge for unwed mothers and women who wished to escape a life of prostitution. Originally the Sleeker Street Mission, later renamed in honor of Charles N. Crittenton's daughter Florence, the home was relocated to Simpson Street. Crittenton helped finance the building but raised the remainder of the funds from philanthropic organizations in Atlanta, including five hundred from First Congregational Church.[73]

First Congregational's affiliation with the Crittenton Home grew directly out of Proctor's concern with the "moral decay" of the poor women of the Gate City—specifically his concern over the rising number of unwed mothers in the black community—and his hopes for developing institutional charity. Proctor argued that the mission of the black churches should be "rescue and reform among the lower classes of Negroes" in Atlanta. Linking institutional charity and moral reform to his disregard for traditional African American worship styles, Proctor questioned, "Is it not high time we stop our shouting, be sober and do something to save the little black girls that are tripping headlong down to hell?" He encouraged "all churches to unite to support the New Florence Crittenden [sic] Home" as the first step in transforming the style and form of social services in the black churches in Atlanta.[74]

Proctor's perspective on social outreach was influenced by his academic training and his increasing distance from working-class African Americans. In the case of the Florence Crittenton Home, it was also tied to the physical location of his church and the larger social circumstances affecting his congregation. First Congregational was located on Courtland Street, formerly known as Collins Street. The name of the street had been changed at the insistence of residents in 1886 because "Collins" was linked to the numerous brothels and houses of prostitution that lined the thoroughfare. The white purveyors of flesh relocated to the Mechanic Street area in 1910, but not before a crude limerick— "Peters Street for wagon yards, Whitehall Street for stores, Peachtree Street for dressy feet, and Collins Street for whores"—had made the rounds in the city and beyond. The women arrested and formally charged with soliciting along Collins/Courtland Street in the 1880s were white rather than African American. This, however, does not rule out the possibility that black women too were also involved in the sex trade on Collins Street. Proctor, ever mindful of the negative racial stereotypes associated with black women's sexuality, was quite anxious about the presence of prostitutes of any color on the same street as his church. His commitment to the Crittenton Home grew out of his desire to clean up the city of Atlanta, beginning with his neighborhood. However, Proctor's moral reform efforts, which predated those of the Men and Religion Forward Movement, could not supersede patterns of racial segregation in the city.[75] Black and white women might "walk the stroll" together but they could not be saved together: the failure of the Crittenton Home to take in black female clients forced Proctor to build his own home for working girls. Once again, in search of resources for this ambitious project, Proctor appealed to wealthy whites for funds. In 1912 his "institutional church" borrowed three thousand dollars from Coca-Cola founder Asa G. Candler in order to finance the new home for working girls.[76]

In criticizing the lack of "proper" charity coming from Atlanta's black churches, Proctor failed to understand the historical legacy and the immediate need that reinforced the continued existence of mutual aid societies. Nor did he fully appreciate the desperate straits of most of the working poor in the city's black population. For men who worked as day laborers and women as laundresses, the contribution of twenty-five cents a week to guarantee proper burial or to provide some relief from financial pressure for themselves, their peers, and their families *was* a proper act of benevolence. Mutual aid societies helped stretch the limited resources of an impoverished community. Charity was given openly and directly, face-to-face between neighbors: in times of need, observers noted, "immediately in a whirl of sympathy or enthusiasm a collection is taken up and the money given, although no official record remains of the deed."[77] This behavior was neither an inappropriate nor necessarily ineffective means of providing aid. The methods of helping the less fortunate within most African American churches distinctively reflected the traditional sharing of resources common in slave-based culture rather than a mainstream, progressive understanding of charity as the upper class doling out surplus resources to the lower class.

Small black churches, whose ministers were not high-status members of the community, were unlikely to receive gifts or loans of funds from Atlanta's white elite, nor could they engage in the kinds of "institutional" expansion envisioned by Proctor, Quarles, and Carter. Proctor and other high-profile ministers failed to recognize that their model of progress for the race was not the only viable one. Other African Americans too had visions of advancement. Some of the "lower classes of Negroes" did in fact belong to other black churches in the city. The working class who shouted and seemed less sober also gave to and joined organizations as part of their own understanding of uplift and race improvement.

Historian Roger Lane, speaking of the black church life in post–Civil War–era Philadelphia, notes that "to join a church was to join a community." Indeed, in the city of brotherly love, despite differences in class and denomination, black clergy struggled and sometimes successfully affirmed "a racial kinship that transcended the differences that usually divided them."[78] Similarly, black churches in Atlanta served as the spiritual and social heart of the multilayered African American community. Between 1865 and 1900, church growth kept pace with the expanding black population. Differing cultural orientations promoted diversity in religious practices in Atlanta. Baptist churches with overwhelmingly working-class congregations were the most numerous. The city's black elite, distinguished by education and social status, was dispersed among higher profile churches, joining First Congregational, Bethel AME, Friendship Baptist, or

Wheat Street Baptist Church. Yet, most importantly, church activities united Black Atlantans of diverse backgrounds by giving them social options in a city segregated first by custom, then by law. Black churches grew to be an integral part of efforts to provide for the sick and bury the dead, and to "uplift the race." Ultimately, the black churches of Atlanta reflect the transition from slavery to freedom; they simultaneously linked Black Atlantans to their past and were instrumental in the task of crafting the future.

CHAPTER FOUR

Community Action and Resistance

Black Atlanta and the Fight for Education

The creation of a system of free public education, perhaps the most enduring achievement of the Reconstruction era, resulted, in part, from the desire and efforts of African Americans to gain access to education for themselves and their children. The collective action of the black community in Atlanta between 1870 and 1900 supports W. E. B. Du Bois's contention that autonomous action by African Americans was instrumental in the success of post–Civil War educational reform.[1] The continued efforts of the community to secure basic rights for its members prevented the complete exclusion of blacks from Atlanta's economic, educational and political arenas during and after Reconstruction.

African Americans in their social and political activities, which were rooted in community organizations and institutions, shared a commitment to racial solidarity and progress. The planning and implementation of progressive action was communal in nature. Meetings held in black churches were announced in black newspapers. Black ministers as well as members of fraternal organizations and militia groups acted as community organizers and leaders. Despite the diversity of status, complexion, and religion, members of the black community in Atlanta, especially in the first three decades of freedom, were united in their desire for and their efforts to achieve economic, political, and social success for the race. They all worked toward racial progress as a common goal.

Few historians would challenge the premise that African Americans came out of slavery with a burning desire for education. While still enslaved, blacks had understood the power of the written word. Many risked dire punishment and sacrificed much needed rest to steal away and struggle to teach themselves or have others teach them to read and write. Freedom only heightened this determination. Indeed, Du Bois noted, "the very feeling of inferiority which slavery forced upon them fathered an intense desire to rise out of their condition by means of education."[2]

Freedom brought new opportunities to use the transforming power of literacy. Many freedmen and -women were committed to learning the true words of the Gospel away from the watchful eye of the overseer or master. More important, freedom brought the labor contract and other written documents on which livelihood and, therefore, true freedom rested. Illiteracy, in contrast, endangered freedom. Former slaves understood the connection between the ability to read and their future success as free people. Education would secure freedom and independence as surely as would land ownership and voting rights. Freedmen and -women wanted education for both themselves and their children. Eric Foner notes that the "most striking illustration of the freedmen's quest for self improvement was their seemingly unquenchable thirst for education."[3]

Northern benevolent societies and the Freedmen's Bureau were instrumental in providing education. Jacqueline Jones's *Soldiers of Light and Love* tells the story of the efforts of northern teachers to bring knowledge and moral regeneration to the freed people in Georgia. But less emphasis has been placed on what blacks in the state did to secure education for themselves. African Americans in Georgia had, by the end of the Civil War, a long history of educational activism. Blacks in Augusta and Savannah defied an 1829 state law that forbade the education of free blacks and slaves, establishing both Sunday Schools and private academies for their children. Whittington B. Johnson notes the existence of a black school that thrived in the city of Savannah from 1833 until the close of the Civil War. The desire to secure education for black children did not fade after the war; African Americans in Augusta continued to organize and eventually oversaw the establishment of the state's first public high school for blacks.[4] Blacks in Atlanta, whose educational activism lagged behind that of their peers in other urban centers, worked in a systematic, organized fashion to help establish and then augment educational opportunities for their children in the post–Civil War period. The black community pushed even harder than did the American Missionary Association or the Freedmen's Bureau, using all the tools at its disposal to improve the chances that African American children in Atlanta would have access to education.

When the American Missionary Association arrived in Atlanta in 1865, two ex-slaves, James Tate and Granithan Daniel, were already teaching in a school on Ivy Street. The two men taught the basic elements of reading and writing to a few dozen African American children and adults although the school was small and poorly furnished.[5] The American Missionary Association with the help of the Freedmen's Bureau and the Ohio congregation of Rev. Storrs established the Storrs School two years later. At the same time, the Freedmen's Aid Society created the Summer Hill School.[6] Blacks contributed to both these schools by raising funds to pay the salaries of the white teachers.[7] Moreover, before the organizations established these two permanent locations, they had depended on the African American community, specifically churches, to house their schools. The first school staffed by the AMA was housed in Rev. Joseph Wood's African Methodist Episcopal Church on Jenkins Street and subsequently became known as the Jenkins Street School. The Walton Springs or Car Box School, as noted in chapter 3, shared facilities with the congregation of what would become Friendship Baptist Church, headed by Rev. Frank Quarles.[8]

The African American community welcomed the Storrs and Summer Hill Schools with much fanfare and great appreciation. White teachers complained about the lack of discipline and the poor facilities but also marveled at the lust for knowledge on the part of the freed people. The two facilities fell far short of providing enough classroom space for all the black children and adults who wished to attend school in Atlanta. Not only was there heavy enrollment in the day school, but night schools designed to accommodate working adults soon filled to capacity as well. Black students explained to the teaching staff that they took their texts to work, studying while pursuing their livelihoods.[9] The two schools housed roughly 900 of the city's 3,129 black school-age children in 1870.[10] True to Du Bois's observation that "the first great mass movement for public education at the expense of the state, in the South, came from Negroes," black citizens went to work by pressuring the city of Atlanta to develop a public school system.[11]

The community's battle for educational access for African American children must be placed against the backdrop of action at the state level. As early as 1866, Georgia blacks had organized the Georgia Educational Association, "whose object was to induce the freedmen to establish and support schools in their own counties and neighborhoods."[12] The GEA was instrumental in organizing schools around the state and in educating the new black voting public about their rights as citizens. In 1870, James Porter, a black member of the Georgia state legislature, introduced a bill to authorize a public school system.[13] The law empowered local governments to develop such programs, but it was not immediately acted on in all parts of the state. The city of Atlanta, for example, stalled for two years.

During those two years, African Americans in Atlanta worked to encourage the city to establish a public school system. Black tailor William Finch was deeply involved in the effort. Finch was affiliated with the Georgia Educational Association in Augusta and understood the value of education. He became Republican Party chairman in the fourth ward shortly after his arrival in Atlanta. Finch was elected to city council from the predominantly black fourth ward in December 1870.[14] Fellow black Republican, George Graham, was elected to the council from the third ward. Both men worked within the city council to pressure the city to act on public school legislation. The city council created the twelve-member board of education in 1869. Voters (especially those from the predominantly black third and fourth wards) approved a measure to allow the sale of one hundred thousand dollars in city bonds to finance the public school system the next year.

Still, city council officials were reluctant. White council members had qualms about establishing at taxpayer expense a public school system that would also benefit "other people's children," that is, African Americans.[15] They argued that black children clearly could not be educated in the same facilities as white children; providing facilities for black students would require additional resources. Council members were of the opinion that if African Americans must have equal access to educational facilities, then there would be no facilities. The board of education took a slightly different tack, arguing that, indeed, black children already had an advantage over their white peers.

> At present, through the aid of the Freedmen's Bureau, and voluntary contributions from various sources, the facilities for the gratuitous education of the colored children are more extensive than those for the gratuitous education of the white children. The wants of the white children are more immediate and more pressing. This committee, therefore, do [sic] not propose . . . to complicate this subject by making specific recommendations in regard to the charge of education of colored children. It can safely be left for future action.[16]

Finch urged African American taxpayers to demand their rights from a publicly funded system of instruction. Despite his encouragement, the city council refused to inaugurate a school system. Undaunted, Finch submitted a proposal in May 1871 that gave white city officials a viable alternative: the board of education would assume "control" of the two private schools created by the benevolent associations for the education of black children. The city would rent the properties from the American Missionary Association and the Methodist Freedmen's Aid Society and pay the salaries of the teachers. In this way, Atlanta could have a public school system that was segregated and that did not require the creation of new, separate facilities for "colored" students. The proposal anticipated the decision of the Georgia state legislature to amend the 1870 law by requiring segregation in public schools. Atlanta finally established its school system in 1872, providing seven schools for white children and two—Storrs and Summer Hill—for blacks. William Finch lost his bid for reelection to the city council in the fall of 1871. Blacks in Atlanta would not succeed in electing a black to the council or to the school board until the mid–twentieth century. Although now outside the political machinery of the city, Finch remained a combatant in the fight for black children's access to public education in Atlanta.

The next battle in the conflict involved plans to add high-school instruction to the menu of educational services provided to black students. There were, by the fall of 1872, five grade schools and two high schools for white children. Yet, the two public schools for black youth stopped at grade eight. Finch and twenty-five other black citizens petitioned the city in September 1872 asking that arrangements be made to pay Atlanta University a per-student fee such that qualified African American students might receive high-school-level instruction free of charge like their white peers in city-funded high schools. Atlanta University President Edmund A. Ware endorsed Finch's proposal, informing the board of education that the university would be willing to teach the students for three dollars per month, per pupil. The board was not swayed; the proposal was tabled and no action was taken.[17]

Although unsuccessful in their bid for a high school, African Americans continued to press for access to the school system. William Finch, working in conjunction with Rev. Frank Quarles and the congregation of Friendship Baptist Church, quickly developed a new plan to expand facilities for black students. Quarles's petition to the board of education offered to sell the Baptist Church on Magnum Street to the city for use as a public school for African American children. One week later, Finch and thirty black community members petitioned the board, asking that the city build schoolhouses for black children.[18] The board declined the offer to buy Friendship Baptist Church but was sufficiently convinced of the need for another schoolhouse for black children (and of the commitment of the African American community to keeping the issue before the board) to rent the facility. In 1873, the Haynes Street School, housed in the Friendship Baptist Church building and using church benches as desks, opened to accommodate 250 students.[19]

The addition of Haynes Street School brought the total enrollment of African American students to 1,153. An additional two thousand, however, were still without classroom space. The Finch-Quarles team continued to press the city council and the board of education about this discrepancy. On August 15, 1873, Quarles again offered to sell the church and lot to the city. Within thirty days Finch and another twenty community members again petitioned the city for more public schools for black children. Although these petitions were tabled with no action, Finch, Quarles, and other black community members continued to keep issues affecting public education of African American children before the board.

The community's efforts to expand educational opportunities for black children must be placed within the context of other challenges faced by the school board. The pending passage of a federal civil rights act created havoc in the administration of the Atlanta public school system in 1874–75. Whites feared that the act would require integration of the state's schools, and local newspapers were full of outraged concern about the possibility; the board of education rec-ommended the abolition of high schools and other drastic changes in the sys-tem rather than submission to integration.[20] Sadly, the Civil Rights Act of 1875 failed to include education when specifying integration policy: integration was mandated only for public accommodations and transportation. The exclusion of education from federal legislation prohibiting discrimination set the tone of the discussion about access to education for African Americans all over the nation.

The school board was faced with a new provocation immediately on the heels of the civil rights "scare." Catholic citizens petitioned for the creation of separate schools for their children. The Catholics argued that "Negroes" were granted separate schools on the basis of difference; consequently, their disparate reli-gious perspectives and "conscientious scruples against sending their children to schools where their religion is not taught" should be considered difference enough to allow for the creation of separate Catholic schools. The board re-jected the petition from Catholics on the grounds that "there is no analogy in the cases. The general system of the State [following the 1872 amendment] re-quires them [i.e., blacks] to be taught separately. Considering their social status we could have no public schools without such separation."[21] Catholics might indeed be different from most Atlantans, who tended to be members of main-stream Protestant denominations, but more important, they were white. In this era of white supremacy, the unifying factor of race was far more significant than the minor inconvenience of religion.

More significant than the challenge of Catholic citizens for the Atlanta school board was the constant threat of insufficient funds. Indeed, the board was in a state of financial crisis from its inception in 1869. The Georgia Real Estate tax, $\frac{1}{10}$ of 1 percent on property in the county—or one dollar on each one thou-sand dollars' worth of property—would have been insufficient had the city been operating a unified, integrated schools system. It was doubly so in the face of dual system developed under Jim Crow. An 1873 resolution authorized borrow-ing money "from time to time as their absolute wants require to meet . . . cur-rent school expenses at the lowest rate of interest . . . until the taxes due . . . are collected."[22] Despite this deficit-spending policy, the school board remained chronically short of funds. In October 1875 the board considered a petition to suspend schools in order to avoid the tax increase that would have been required to meet the system's financial needs. During this period both the board of ed-ucation and the city council were continually lobbied by Atlantans opposed to an increase in taxes for education. The next year the board was compelled to go to the council to ask for an increase in the appropriation for public schools. By the spring of 1877, again unable to meet its monthly bills, the board requested funds from the city council to stay afloat for the remainder of the school year. By December of the next year, the board had slashed teachers' salaries by 50 percent in order to balance the budget.[23]

In the midst of this turmoil, black citizens continued their efforts to keep the issue of education for black children before the board. Quarles petitioned the board in the fall of 1875 to buy a house on Mitchell Street for the purpose of opening another public school for black children. Other African Americans focused their energies on developing private educational facilities. Mrs. E. A. Chapman, wife of black mattress-maker Edward Chapman, petitioned the board in June 1876 asking if she could rent a building in the city's fairgrounds "to keep school." During the next two decades, black women developed several small schools for black children. Sparingly furnished and often short on supplies, these independent schools were funded by small tuition payments, fifty cents to a dollar per month per child. These schools could not adequately serve the minority children in the city, but their development does speak to the desire of the black community to educate its children.

While the issue of the development of facilities to house African American schoolchildren remained central to the community's agenda of equal access, there were other educational issues as well. The question of who would teach African American children had come to the fore by mid-decade. Rev. Frank Quarles petitioned the board in August 1874 for the appointment of African American teachers for Haynes Street School. The timing of this action was, undoubtedly, connected to the 1873 graduation of Atlanta University's first class of young teachers. A product of the character-building curriculum of Atlanta University, these graduates were also well prepared to teach literature, science, grammar, and mathematics to the city's hundreds of black children.[24] Although the black community persisted, the board failed to endorse the petition that year.

Quarles's 1874 petition had specified black appointments at the Haynes Street School, which, at the time, was the only black public school completely under the control of the city. Both Storrs and Summer Hill Schools remained tied to the American Missionary Association and Methodist Freedmen's Aid Society respectively.[25] The black community found itself at odds with the AMA regarding the race of teachers of black children: opposed to depriving loyal white teachers of employment, the Association rejected African American requests for black teachers. Northern white teachers whose philanthropy "saved the Negro Public School" had endured poor working conditions, even poorer living conditions, and social ostracism from southern whites in order to work for the education and moral regeneration of black children.[26] AMA agents perceived the demand for black teachers as evidence of a lack of proper gratitude for all that had been done on their behalf.

African Americans, though initially concerned about the availability of qualified black teachers, were convinced that Atlanta, Clark, and other educational institutions were graduating sufficiently accomplished black candidates to fill posts in the city's public school system. High-status blacks who were invested in the idea of racial uplift had been indoctrinated with a belief in the transformative powers of education. In the process of receiving their own education, they had also been socialized to understand that their duty was to return to their communities as teachers and future leaders of the race rather than capitalize upon their advantages for themselves alone.[27] Educated blacks then were quick to demonstrate their willingness to help the race progress by becoming teachers. Black educator, political activist, and novelist Frances Ellen Watkins Harper articulated the value of personal sacrifice for the higher purpose of teaching and uplifting the race. In her 1892 novel *Iola Leroy, or Shadows Uplifted,* Harper places selfless and inspired words in the mouth of her female protagonist, Iola, as she explains her commitment to uplift her race and her role in that struggle: "To be . . . the leader of a race to higher planes of thought and action, to teach men clearer views of life and duty, to inspire their souls with loftier aims, is a far greater privilege than it is to open the gates of material prosperity and fill every home with sensuous enjoyment."[28]

Both John Hope, Atlanta Baptist College professor, and W. E. B. Du Bois, Atlanta University sociology professor, educator, and activist, who made Atlanta their home after the initial battle for black teachers had been waged, endorsed Harper's view. And of course, the Atlanta University–educated black men and women who became the teachers of the city's black youth also endorsed this worldview. There can be no doubt that high-status blacks in Atlanta shared Du Bois' belief in the need for liberal arts education for African Americans, especially for the "talented tenth" whose task it was to lead the race forward on a civilizing mission.[29]

It was in this spirit that Lugenia Burns Hope, social reformer and wife of John Hope, joined forces with other blacks in the city to organize the Gate City Free Kindergarten Association. The Gate City Free Kindergarten Association predated by two years the founding of the Neighborhood Union, the social-work organization for which Lugenia Hope is best known. Lugenia Hope joined Du Bois and others affiliated with Atlanta University to try to address the lack of educational facilities for the hundreds of black children in the city who were without supervision when their mothers were at work. Designated as the chair of the fund-raising committee of the association, Hope appealed to

more affluent members of the black community to finance the proposed kindergartens. Adrienne Herndon, Atlanta University instructor and wife of successful
barber Alonzo Herndon, was on the board of the association as was mortician
David T. Howard. Herndon devoted a portion of his substantial resources to
the association, as, no doubt, did Howard. Within two years, the association
was operating four kindergartens for the city's "under-privileged children."[30]
The association was status marked, which is to say that high-status blacks, educators, and businessmen committed to the ideology of racial solidarity and uplift developed the association and low-status blacks, working mothers without
childcare, benefited. Yet the Gate City Free Kindergarten Association highlights
once again the collective efforts of Black Atlantans to pool their resources to
provide for the educational needs of all members of the community.

In addition to being motivated by uplift ideology to request black teachers,
Black Atlantans also agitated for black teachers because of the racism of white
teachers toward black students. This especially became the case when school
boards began to replace northern missionary teachers with their white southern
sisters who revised the curriculum to reflect southern racial sensibilities. For
example, black students were made to line the streets of the city in the spring
of 1886 to cheer as former Confederate President Jefferson Davis passed.[31] They
were forced to repeat this performance three years later when Davis's body was
paraded through the Southland to allow Georgians to pay their respects to a
fallen icon. Black parents who had no reason to celebrate the life of Jefferson
Davis were not pleased with this use of valuable school time.

Not all African Americans endorsed the idea of black teachers for black
schoolchildren, however. Black physician Henry E. Baulden, acting in conjunction with "several hundred colored citizens," presented a petition in August
1877 "asking that the [white] teachers of last year be retained in Storrs School."
Baulden's petition argued that the "intellectual and moral education of our
children is rapidly advancing" and that change in the school's staff would "work
disorganization and damage" in the progress of the race. Black men and women
who signed their names to this petition may have in fact been concerned that
the more militant stance of such activists as Finch and Quarles would give the
school board an excuse simply to terminate black schools altogether. Given the
history of the Atlanta school board, such a fear was not completely unfounded.
Dr. Baulden may have also been acting upon his bias as an elite northern black;
he was something of a carpetbagger, having being trained and licensed as a
physician in Illinois. Baulden may have simply assumed southern blacks had
had insufficient time and distance from slavery to have mastered the level of
education and acculturation necessary to educate the next generation of free
black people. Regardless of his motivations, or his argument that "nineteen

twentieths of the colored people would oppose the change to colored teachers," Baulden was unsuccessful in his efforts to sway the board.[32]

The issue of black teachers was central to the relationship between the American Missionary Association and the Atlanta school board. The city's original contract with the association required the city to pay six hundred dollars in rent for the use of the Storrs Street building. In addition, the board was to appoint teachers from a pool of nominees selected by the AMA. Crying poverty, the board renegotiated the contract with the AMA in anticipation of the 1877–78 school year, slashing two hundred dollars off the rent of the building. Four years after Quarles's initial petition, school board members expressed interest in appointing black teachers in accordance with the "request of black citizens," though for much more mercenary reasons: black teachers could be paid less than white teachers. The school board proposed appointing a female principal for the same reason—female principals were paid less than males. In the end, the school board mandated the appointment of a female principal and five black teachers to staff the Storrs School, "provided that they are found competent upon examination." Arrangements were made to advertise an open examination for candidates to be held the second Wednesday in August 1877.[33]

AMA officers were not pleased with the reduction in rent but were much more concerned about the possibility of a core of five African American teachers displacing five white missionary teachers. The association refused the board's offer of contract renewal for the school with a black teaching staff, proposing instead the appointment of two "colored" teachers and noting that they "hope[d] that colored teachers . . . [might] gradually [be] put into these positions to the satisfaction of all concerned." The city accepted the counterproposal, and on October 9, 1877, "Fannie Norris and Julia Turner, both colored, were elected to the Storrs school seventh and eighth grades." Their salary was "fixed at $35" per month—the lowest wages in the school district—as of October 23, 1877.[34]

The black community continued to pressure the city for more African American teachers. A "convention of leading [black] citizens" elected a council in June 1878 to petition the school board for "the appointment of colored teachers in all the colored public schools of the city." Quarles was listed as president of the council. A mixture of concerned businessmen and ministers including William Finch, James Tate, Joseph Wood, Squire Turner, Jonas Solomon, Hilliard Darden, and Emmanual King joined him. The men observed that "the colored people almost universally desired to have their children taught by colored teachers." Quarles urged the school board "on the score of expediency and of justice to the colored people" to act quickly to hire black teachers as soon as competent ones could be obtained.[35]

At the close of the 1877–78 school year the conflict between the school board and the AMA over the issue of black teachers (and rental costs) erupted again, resulting in the city terminating the contract with the school as of July 15, 1878. Thus the Atlanta school board was left with the responsibility for finding another facility for some three hundred black children who were without access to education in the city. The black community, represented by the Bethel AME Church on Wheat Street, stepped in on August 3, 1877, to provide a solution to the problem of facilities. Church trustees Mitchell Cargile, W. Ware, Porter Freeman, William Carter, David Howard, Francis Grant, Stewart Wigley, W. H. Harrison, and John Johnson agreed to rent the church basement to the city for ninety dollars per month. The Wheat Street School opened in September 1878, serving the three hundred former Storrs students and an additional fifty new students. An added bonus was the employment by the school of five African American teachers.[36]

That same month, at the urging of board member John A. Beatie, the board purchased property on the corner of Houston and Butler Streets to provide another school for black children.[37] The Houston Street School was completed in 1881, and the children attending Wheat Street School were relocated to the new facility. After more than eleven years of struggle with the school board, the Houston Street School was the first new schoolhouse the city provided for black children. Replacing older, cramped, poorly lit buildings, Houston Street was "well lighted, well ventilated and contained 8 rooms."[38]

Houston Street was also the city's first black public school staffed entirely with black personnel from the first grade teacher to the principal. The president of the school board noted in the tenth annual report that "the colored people insisted on having persons of their own race teach their children." The superintendent added, "the building is the pride of our colored people. It is officered entirely by colored teachers . . . They understand their own race and can discipline and teach to the satisfaction of their patrons."[39]

In the next eleven years, Atlanta opened three more public schools for black children. The Haynes Street building was sold, and the Mitchell Street School opened in 1882, also staffed by African American teachers. Gray Street School opened in 1888 with an all-black staff. The last of the schools to open in this period, Roach Street, opened in 1892. Of the three, Gray Street was the jewel in the crown of Atlanta's black schools. The superintendent of schools rhapsodized in the eighteenth Annual Report of the Board of Education: "The Gray Street School, for colored children[,] . . . is, in my opinion, the best schoolhouse in Atlanta. It was built on the most modern plan, wisely arranged in regard to the admission of light, furnished with Smead's system of heating and ventilating, furnished with Andrews' best desks, supplied with maps, charts and other aids in teaching."[40] Unfortunately, the standards set at Gray Street were not matched

Houston Street School, second grade, circa 1900. Miss L. M. Coleman, teacher, third row, far right. W. B. Matthews, principal, first row, far right. (Courtesy of the Atlanta History Center.)

by most of the rest of the city's black public schools. The praise for Gray Street would be repeated, ad nauseam, in the annual reports of the Board of Education, while the city made no attempt to address the educational crises facing black children in the other city schools. Even Gray Street School fell into disrepair as a result of inadequate funding and poor maintenance.

Acting to achieve a shared goal, the black community did realize a measure of success in the eighteen-year battle for public education for its children. The community succeeded in acquiring five public schools for black children and in staffing all of them with black teachers. Yet success was tempered in Atlanta by the limits of community action in the face of white efforts to prevent black access. Black children had five public schools in 1900, but there were fifteen for white children. This disparity meant that the 3,731 school-age black children in Atlanta attended public schools in incredibly overcrowded classrooms. A petition drafted by a community meeting at Bethel AME church in the fall of 1886 requested additional teachers "in ordrr [sic] that more of the children out of school could obtain admittance."[41] Wheat Street Baptist Church minister Tilman, Jackson McHenry, and Major Easley presented the signed petition to the board of education. In response, beginning in 1886, the board required teachers to hold double sessions in the three black schools that existed at the time.

Double sessions proved to be a less than ideal solution. Two hundred fifty to five hundred children at a time attended classes for three-and-a-half hours; then after a half-hour break, the next wave of students attended class for another three-and-a-half-hours. Black students had to absorb what they could of a full day of lessons in less than half the time. The children were shortchanged in the content and the quality of their lessons. Black teachers, working an eight-hour shift, taught up to 120 students per day, twice as many as their white counterparts.[42]

The frustration of the double workload was compounded by the discrepancy in wages: black teachers earned two hundred dollars less per year than did white teachers. Black principals also earned less than did their white peers. The black community struggled to rectify this situation. Blacks petitioned the school board to increase if not to equalize the salaries of black teachers. Their petitions and concerns fell on deaf ears: African American teachers earned less than white teachers well beyond the turn of the century.[43]

Black schools were poorly maintained and faced a chronic shortage of supplies in addition to overcrowding and an overworked, underpaid staff. Three of the school buildings were old, drafty, and poorly lit. Summer Hill School, the oldest of the buildings, was continually being expanded to service more students despite the fact that it was in very poor shape.[44] Community members tried, unsuccessfully, to persuade school officials both to increase the number and to improve the condition of the facilities for black children.

The black clergy remained a strong advocate in the fight for equal access to education for African American children. The Evangelical Ministers' Union—an organization of black ministers in Atlanta that included E. P. Johnson, H. H. Proctor, C. C. Carrel, and J. E. Spring—resolved to improve school conditions for black children in the city. The union developed a committee of eighteen members, three to visit each of the six schools, to investigate and report on their condition. The findings of the investigative committee, published in the *Atlanta Independent,* praised the extraordinary efforts of black schoolteachers to provide a quality education for their students. But the report also addressed the negative effect of double sessions: "Of course, when she [the teacher] comes to work on the afternoon, her energies are so far spent that nothing but unsatisfactory results could be expected. Both teacher and pupil are put at a great disadvantage."[45] Investigators also made mention of the poor facilities in some schools, including the fact that only a thin partition separated the boys' and girls' toilets in the Houston Street School, which put the modesty of young black girls in jeopardy. Unfortunately, the Evangelical Ministers' Union had no more success in swaying the Atlanta school board than other community members; the board made no changes in the school situation of black children in response to the union's report.

African Americans tried to use their clout as voters to improve the situation for black children in the city. Black voters were important in the passage of a four hundred thousand–dollar city bond issue in 1903, but board members failed to live up to their commitments. The *Atlanta Independent* reminded the city fathers and the voting public of the debt owed black citizens. "The Negro was promised that if he would vote for the bonds, we would be given additional schoolhouses and teachers. The Negro always took the white man at his word, and did on this occasion, which meant so much to the development of Atlanta . . . [The Negro] used his vote to promote the best interest of the community."[46] *Independent* editor Benjamin Davis continued to encourage the local black clergy to petition the school board for better schools. Still, the community failed in its attempts to acquire a black public high school in Atlanta before 1924.[47]

Education for blacks in Atlanta did extend beyond elementary-school training despite the lack of a public high school. The American Missionary Association opened Atlanta University in 1865. The Freedmen's Aid Society provided a second university for blacks, Clark University (later Clark College), in 1869. The Augusta Institute relocated to Atlanta under the name of Atlanta Baptist Seminary ten years later.[48] Under the auspices of W. J. Gaines and the Georgia AME church in 1881, Morris Brown College became the first black-owned institution of higher education in the city. Spelman College, the first all-female black educational institution in the city, was also established that year. Gammon Theological Seminary, sponsored by the Methodist Episcopal Church and the Freedmen's Aid Society, opened its doors two years later.

The black community greeted these institutions of higher education with the same enthusiasm with which it welcomed the elementary schools. When Atlanta University began its second full term in the fall of 1870, students overflowed the dormitory. The relatively low cost of higher education provided by these institutions, a fact that was regularly advertised by the black press, made them accessible to a wide range of African Americans in the 1870s. Students could enroll in Clark University without paying tuition fees; room and board for the year cost only seventy-seven dollars if paid in advance. Young women could pursue an education at Spelman for sixty-five cents per month tuition as day students or seven dollars per month as residential scholars. But even though the costs remained relatively modest, the increase in tuition rates in the 1890s,

First graduating class to complete the English high school course, Spelman 1887: Ella N. Barksdale, Clara A. Howard, Lucinda Mitchell, Adeline J. Smith, Sallie B. Waugh, and Ella L. William. (Courtesy of Spelman College Archives.)

and beyond, limited access for working-class blacks and their children. Administrators attempted to bridge the gap by providing poorer day students with scholarships and a rudimentary work-study program.[49]

The words "university" and "college" in the titles of these institutions often spoke more to their aspirations for the future than to their contemporary capacity. AMA agent Frederick Ayers noted that there were not as many "reading colored people in Atlanta as in many other Southern cities." Atlanta University, Clark, Atlanta Baptist, Morris Brown, and Spelman functioned in their first few decades as high schools as much as colleges and universities. Clark University offered an eighth grade, a normal school, and a collegiate degree into the twentieth century. Of course, most of the first generation of freedmen and -women had little or no educational background and were ill-prepared for college-level courses in the 1870s; they often began their education as adults in evening courses at the missionary schools.[50] Black children in Atlanta who were denied a public high-school education took courses at AU and received high-school certificates. These students were then ready to continue in genuine college-level programs.

Graduating class of Clark College, 1890. Roderick Badger's daughter, Mary Jane Caroline Badger, identified as Janie C. Badger, is one of the graduates in this photo. (Clark College Collection, Atlanta University Center, Robert W. Woodruff Library.)

The schools offered a classic liberal arts program, courses in algebra, geometry, Latin, Greek, and music. Atlanta University and Atlanta Baptist stood fast in the commitment to a "classical" education for African Americans as the South increasingly turned against the idea. Conservative white politicians and social activists across the South, from Senator James K. Vardaman of Mississippi to Georgia's own Allen Candler, began in the last decade of the nineteenth century to condemn the effort to offer black men and women more than an industrial education. Such education, argued conservatives, only served to confuse blacks, encouraging them to be ambitious, specifically to strive toward a life above the station white southerners deemed appropriate for them, in other words, life above the level of servant.

Yet black educators in Atlanta, for the most part, rejected the vision of white conservatives as well as that of Booker T. Washington, whose accommodationist stance included an attack on liberal arts education. Du Bois weighed in on the role of liberal arts education and specifically of the black college, the job of which was "to create men," in his classic text *The Souls of Black Folk.* John Hope joined Du Bois, arguing that the future of the race depended upon higher education. Historian Leroy Davis notes that Hope believed higher education was necessary for the race to achieve "progress, dignity and respectability." What is

Poised to take their place among the Talented Tenth, graduates of Clark College, class of 1896. (Clark College Collection, Atlanta University Center, Robert W. Woodruff Library.)

more, Hope shared Du Bois's belief that the leadership of the race must come from the educated classes.[51]

Commitment to the liberal arts did not mean that either Atlanta or Clark University (or, for that matter, most black educational institutions in the South) did away with technical education. Atlanta, Clark, and the other universities and colleges also provided black adults with the chance to improve their economic circumstances through the acquisition of a trade. Students also studied mechanical courses including industrial drawing, blacksmithing, harness and wagon making, carriage trimming, painting, plumbing, carpentry, embalming, and masonry. The first generation of African American students who attended institutions of higher education often participated in work-study programs: they performed the carpentry, masonry, plumbing, smithing, and iron work necessary to maintain campuses. The young men at Atlanta University were pressed into service in the expansion of the parsonage of First Congregational Church.[52]

Similarly, the young women of Spelman pursued "ladies' courses" in literature, art, and music and were taught basic domestic skills as well, such as ironing, dressmaking, cooking, housekeeping, and laundry. Female students, especially those on scholarship, provided housekeeping services to the college faculty. Limited resources and the belief in the importance of industrial education made this model the rule well into the twentieth century.

From elementary school through college, moral training played a part in the curriculum in all of these institutions. The 1871 State Board of Visitors was pleased to observe "abundant evidences [sic] of the very judicious moral training" among the students at Atlanta University, commending "their polite behavior, general modesty of demeanor, and evident economy and neatness of dress."[53] Spelman women, both boarding students and day students, were required to follow a basic dress code. It mandated, among other things, "a simple white dress of cotton, linen or wool (preferably cotton) . . . [for] those who take part in public exercises." Regulations noted that clothes should be "inexpensive" and "appropriate," shoes low heeled and "not fancy," and that students should also acquire "work aprons, rubbers [rain boots][,] umbrella and coat."[54] The attire of Spelman girls was designed to be practical. It was also intended to distinguish Spelman girls, some of whom traveled from the east side of the city, from any low-status woman who "advertised herself" by the "loudness of her dress" and "the far from lady-like walk."[55]

An educational norm for the nineteenth century, moral education was perceived as especially significant for blacks. White missionaries and teachers saw newly freed African Americans as individuals in need of cultural transformation and moral regeneration. American Missionary Association records and those of the American Home Baptist Association are replete with criticisms of the supposed lack of morals and undeveloped Christian character of the freedmen and -women. Moral education was therefore thought to be a method of reversing the damage to character, values, and intellect inflicted upon blacks in slavery.

As noted, high-status blacks, especially ministers and educators, shared the perspective of white middle-class reformers and educators. Although their political perspectives may have differed on the issue of access to civil rights, both Booker T. Washington and W. E. B. Du Bois agreed that the progress of the race depended on moral education. Henry H. Proctor and John Hope as well as their reform-minded wives, Adeline Davis Proctor and Lugenia Burns Hope, also shared a commitment to this ideal. These high-status men and women played important roles in the city's black community on the eve of the new century and spread the gospel of moral education while they worked to secure and expand educational services for blacks. It does not follow, however, that low-status working people, who were also very interested in education to improve their lot in life, shared the idea that the progress of the race depended on moral education.

Teachers and missionaries observed that African Americans were "sensitive" and often resented what they considered meddling or interference in their spiritual lives beyond the classroom. They seemed to desire the education these self-appointed "raisers" had to offer but otherwise wanted to be left alone. Baptist missionary Rev. J. H. Conley noted that "when I first go into their homes [to share religious teachings] they look distant; but when they are asked how many children they have and how many are in school, then they are interested."[56] The pursuit of education by blacks in the South, including those in Atlanta, did not instantly translate to an acceptance of the cultural or social norms of their educators.

The African American community in Atlanta was a diverse population of laborers, ministers, tailors, carpenters, and shopkeepers, and of Methodists, Baptists, and Congregationalists, in the last three decades of the nineteenth century. Among the authors of proposals and signers of petitions, Rev. E. R. Carter, James Tate, and Jackson McHenry were working-class dark-skinned men. Ordained African Methodist Episcopal minister William Finch was high status and fair. Frank Quarles was a Baptist reverend. Carter was educated at Atlanta Baptist Seminary whereas McHenry, Tate, and Quarles received no formal education. Cargile and Darden were fledgling businessmen who owned at least one thousand dollars or more in property by 1885; Squire Turner and Handy Curry were laborers who would not reach that financial watermark for another decade. Despite their differences, however, all these individuals worked as part of a team. The pattern of their petitions was neither random nor coincidental. Finch and Quarles and others worked in tandem to keep the desires of the black community before the board of education: the common goal of access to public education for all black children.

The first generation of black men and women out of slavery, then, approached the world through the lens of racial solidarity and with a belief in the efficacy of community action. This worldview or ideology was carried over in large measure from the collective experience of slavery and stood them in good stead in the last decades of the nineteenth century. In the face of efforts by white politicians and civic leaders to exclude them completely from the political, economic, and educational arenas, they worked together to try to maintain basic rights and access for their community. Racial segregation and limited political recourse hampered their efforts to achieve full citizenship rights, and, as the long struggle for educational facilities indicates, community action was not always successful in the pitched battle with white supremacy. Still blacks persevered in their efforts to build their lives in freedom. They organized themselves into church communities, fraternal orders, and social clubs. From the base of such social institutions they continued to work toward the goal of race uplift and community progress.

CHAPTER FIVE

Fraternity, Community, and Status

Fraternal Organizations in Black Atlanta

African Americans' economic, social, and political needs determined the style and form of their community in Atlanta between 1875 and 1906. Their responses to these needs were connected to available resources and to the traditions and values that had governed their lives in the past. For, as the period advanced, it became increasingly clear that earlier hopes for freedom and full citizenship were systematically being denied by a combination of legal and social strategies put in motion by Atlanta's white majority. Black social institutions that developed in this period of white racial antipathy reflect a commitment to racial solidarity and the desire to craft a better future.

"Fraternity," argued historian Wilson Carey McWilliams, "grows from the recognition of kinship, likeness more important than unlikeness. All the fraternal relationships of man, in his progression from birth to death, teach the same lesson. A man is kin to his blood-brothers, like them more than he is unlike, because dependence and society are more important than physical isolation."[1] This sentiment is more than apt when used in reference to the black men and women thrown upon their own limited resources at slavery's end. Across the southern states, emancipation saw the rise of fraternal orders and lodges and brotherhoods (and their female auxiliaries referred to as "daughters"), organizations providing associative ties that moved beyond the foundation laid by black churches. These secret societies, among the most significant forms of social organization in postbellum Black Atlanta, were established to provide basic social services to African Americans, services provided only marginally, or not at all, by the larger white society. These fraternal orders and secret societies supplemented income for working-class African Americans during illness, provided funeral and death benefits, and offered opportunities for self-improvement and social interaction. They were thus crucial in the formation of community among African Americans.

Membership in fraternal orders or "upright" social clubs also improved one's social status within the larger black community. Status was equally important in the black community's relationship with white society. High-status blacks, who self-identified as part of "the better sort," "of the "better class," or as "best men and best women," struggled to present an image of a moral, conscientious, and virtuous black community to critical members of the white race. Long before Alain Locke would appropriate the term "New Negro" to define the forward-looking black men and women of the Harlem Renaissance, high-status blacks in Atlanta were working to show southern whites a new black community distinguished by mastery of mainstream middle-class values. Atlanta's New Negroes embraced these values, understanding that education, temperance, and stable families would help improve the material conditions of black life. They also hoped these behaviors would undercut arguments that advocated the exclusion of members of their race from American civic society on the basis of the "inferior" essence (manifested in "inappropriate" behavior) of black people. Arguments appealing to the "natural rights of man" to fight the racism and inequality instituted by white society seemed increasingly less viable for African Americans. Instead, the black community pointed to an internally constructed social stratification that facilitated arguments rooted in "the politics of respectability"—a new weapon in the battle against white supremacy.[2]

In late-nineteenth-century Atlanta, different social status levels within the greater economic category of "working class" among African Americans began to evolve. Status is rooted more in life situation and social behaviors than in economics, though status levels may be tied to economic class position. An individual may enjoy elevated social status within a particular group without occupying a correspondingly high economic class. As sociologist Max Weber has argued, status is linked to economics through specialization and individual groups achieve elite status in part through exclusive monopoly of a specific part of a larger economic market. For black fraternal orders, mutual aid associations, and benevolent societies, providing insurance (sickness and death benefits denied to blacks by the greater market) was the embodiment of such specialization.

African Americans determined status in Black Atlanta on the basis of character (manners and morals), education, occupation, and sometimes religious affiliation. They associated traits such as respectability, reliability, and temperance with high status within the black community and determined the basis for their criteria in accordance with the resources available within the community. Thus, for example, the kind of occupation, rather than the amount of salary it earned the jobholder, often determined status. Black schoolteachers and ministers were afforded the respect of high status despite their often extraordinarily low wages. This designation was linked, in part, to the level of education required for these professions. Although many black ministers in the immediate postwar period had a limited formal education, the required familiarity with and understanding of scripture often fulfilled the educational criterion.

Status was not a static category. Individuals could improve their status by acquiring education, undergoing religious conversion and joining a church, marrying an individual of higher status, or becoming the owner of a business. Similarly, associating with lower-status persons or frequenting their places of entertainment, such as pubs, brothels, and gaming houses, could diminish status. Individuals could lose status by being chastised for misconduct in the public eye (e.g., facing charges of adultery or drunkenness from a church council). Arrest on vice charges would also lower status. Divorce also signaled a decline in status for women. The solution to these problems was found in education, temperance, and obedience to the rule of law.

Sexual purity, especially in black women, was an important mark of high status. The Fifth Conference for the Study of the Negro Problems, held at Atlanta University, noted that "without doubt the greatest social problem of the American Negro at present is sexual purity." Du Bois argued in his essay on the family that slavery had provided "regularity" to the sexual practices of blacks, resulting in "as near the monogamic ideal as the slave trade and concubinage would allow." Emancipation and the "independent Negro home" run by Negro women of "poor training" and "field-hands" who "never had the responsibility of family life" had resulted in crises in the sexual purity of black women and the black family in that day.[3]

The pursuit of purity, the desire to cleanse and sanitize the soiled image of black femininity, was shared by both black men and black women. Sexual and social purity connoted chastity, temperance, modesty, all understood to be byproducts of Christian conversion and redemption. High-status black women, educators, wives of ministers, and social workers, shared Du Bois's vision. They lectured their lower-status female peers on the importance of "social purity" at every opportunity, both because they believed that sexual and social purity held the key to race uplift and because they recognized that they were judged by the lowest of their number. Members of the National Association of Colored Women Clubs, female reformers, educators, and activists struggled with middle-class notions of appropriate social behavior as they attempted to "lift" the race from the degradation of slavery. Historian Deborah Gray White notes that according to high-status black women, "chastity would liberate black women from 'their blighted past,'" and therefore became "the litmus test for middle-class respectability."[4] High-status women understood that black womanhood had been degraded as a result of black women's "brutal treatment," specifically "being valued according to their physical strength and ability to enrich their masters' wealth by adding other living slaves to their possessions, in any way, suited to their master's will, however illegitimate."[5] They also accepted the gendered division of labor that made women responsible for the cultivation of proper morals and the behavior of their children and husbands. Advocates of sexual and social purity did not necessarily argue that women who worked outside the home violated the rules of purity, but many did link working-class life, including low-status labor, with a poorly maintained home life and lack of quality childcare. Consequently, high-status "uplifters" devoted considerable time and energy to teaching lesser blacks about social purity. Colleges, social clubs, church sermons, and conferences provided forums for the process of inculcating the race with the message of sexual and social purification. Although high- and low-status blacks might share an interest in improving the image of black womanhood, solutions most often put forward by high-status women failed to recognize the behavioral restrictions imposed by limited wealth and access to opportunity.

Mrs. Adeline Davis Proctor, social reformer and wife of Hugh Henry Proctor, addressed social purity concerns in her pamphlet "Negro Womanhood— Its Present." She began by naming status divisions within the black community: "There are, roughly speaking, three classes of Negro women, lower, middle and upper. By the lower class I mean those lower in development. This is the class of women Southern newspapers hold up as typical . . . It is from this class that the inmates of the prison and evil resorts come. With their upliftment the redemption of the race is involved."[6] She went on to highlight the causes of "low development" in black women, namely, past oppression, poverty, and lack of proper training—circumstances that could be changed by education, temperance, and adherence to the rule of law.

Anna Bell Rhodes Penn, Shaw University graduate, poet, wife of black journalist and social activist Irvine Garland Penn (and mother of their seven children), added her words of guidance to the general discussion of social purity at the 1902 Negro Young People's Christian and Educational Congress. Encouraging black women to set a proper example for their children by being "truthful, honest and pure," Mrs. Penn also admonished the woman who was "so much absorbed by fashion and the things of the world that she had no time to gather the little ones about her and warn them against sin and punishment." Mrs. Penn recognized that "fathers, so full of ambition, so much in love with the things of the world . . . have no time nor heart for their religious instruction of their children," but she was quick to identify such behavior in women as "strange, unnatural, yes . . . shameful."[7]

Spelman graduate, and wife of Wheat Street Baptist Church minister Peter James Bryant, Sylvia Jenkins Bryant also weighed in on the proper role for women at the 1902 convention. She reminded her audience that social purity was "divine and heavenly in its origin" and advocated "society free from all vice and sin." The path toward this otherworldly perfection was paved by parents who were "models for their children by living pure and upright lives." Mrs. Bryant warned against "teaching girls how to paint and powder, and preparing them for dime parties, wine suppers and card parties." Instead, children, especially girls, were to be dressed in modest attire and kept close to "pleasant and attractive" homes ruled by "the sweet and modest action of a tender, loving mother."[8]

Teacher, activist, clubwoman turned World War I nurse, and wife of YMCA Secretary of the Colored Division William Alphaeus Hunton, Addie Waites Hunton, also presented a paper at the Negro Young People's Christian and Educational Congress. Hunton, who was instrumental in organizing the National Association of Women's Clubs (1906–10), stressed the importance of sexual purity and feminine virtue.[9] Her presentation, entitled "A Pure Motherhood—The Basis of Racial Integrity," reminded her audience that "upon the Negro woman rests a burden of responsibility peculiar in its demands." Charging women with "the salvation of the human race," Hunton noted that historically "inferior" races of white women might breed with "superior" races of white men to achieve the goal of improving their race. This option was not, however, open to "the Negro woman" who "must tear herself away from the sensual desires of the men of another race who seek only to debase her," and struggle to lift the members of her race, in "intelligent christian homes" through "womanly virtue and integrity."[10] While Hunton's belief that "Briton, Saxon and Normans" had "mixed their blood to give us the proud Anglo-Saxon" through "honorable wedlock" is historically naïve, her point that black women were more likely to be the sexual playmates than marriage partners of white men was not lost on her audience. Addie Hunton's concern with the sexual purity of black women, especially low-status black women, is tied to her larger concern, as noted in "Negro Womanhood Defended," that black women would be held accountable for the failings of the race.[11]

Young women attending Spelman College were groomed to accept the female role in maintaining standards of social purity. Branches of the YWCA (Colored), the WCTU (Colored), and the Christian Endeavor Society schooled Spelman girls in behavior deemed appropriately moral and proper for young "rising" black women. Sexual purity and social decorum were the key to "raising the high Christian standard of living which we endeavor to have among our girls." Toward that end, a Social Purity Club was formed at Spelman in the 1890s with the specific goals of "strengthen[ing] . . . and teach[ing] the girls along lines of purity of both soul and body." Girls over the age of twelve who joined the group were asked to sign a pledge and to strive to "resist the manifold temptations that shall present themselves."[12] Educated in the liberal arts, socialized toward racial purity, Spelman girls were well prepared to do the social service work necessary to morally transform the larger black community.

It is not coincidental that the Social Purity Club at Spelman was later renamed the White Shield Society. The emphasis on middle-class notions of femininity—proper deportment, matronly domesticity, and sexual purity—was part of a vision of gendered behavior designed to raise black women to the status of their white female peers, to whiten their image if not their skin. African Americans, especially those of high status, did internalize some racialist notions of white superiority and black inferiority; their efforts at cultural assimilation reflect, on one hand, the power and influence of such beliefs. On the other hand, the first generation of black men and women who exited slavery was well aware of the sexual exploitation of black women. African Americans developed a rigid code of behavior in part to build a protective shield of manners and morals around a vulnerable black womanhood.[13]

Fraternal orders, too, not only provided social services to black community members but helped African Americans in late-nineteenth-century Atlanta to build status and create a positive sense of self. In the 1860s–70s, freed black men in the South began to engage the discourse that sought to equate true liberty in America with the concept of a robust Christian masculinity. Indeed, historian Maurice Wallace argues that "probably no other cultural movement before the civil rights campaigns of the twentieth century has been more emblematic of the social and psychic drama of black masculinity in the American cultural context."[14] In the safe haven of the lodge, black men experimented with their identity as freedmen and cultivated challenges to white racism. The daily experience of nineteenth-century bigotry—from the social etiquette that named all black men "nigger" and "boy," to the job discrimination that eroded economic advance—threatened black self-worth and often thwarted black celebrations of manhood. Through ritual, secret greetings, and private renaming, lodge members created enclosed spaces, sanctuaries free from the intrusion of racism in which they could craft a masculine identity. Brotherhoods (and sisterhoods) provided African Americans with space for experimenting with political leadership at a time when other opportunities for engaging in political activity were wanting. Activities sponsored by lodges—picnics, bazaars, Sunday dinners, and fairs—were protected sites for social interaction among young men and women that did not bear the stigma of the dance or billiards hall. Thus, by pooling their resources, social and economic, lodge members provided cohesion within the African American population and focused energy on building and transforming community. They also provided forums for moral regeneration and tem-

White Shield Pledge

"Blessed are the pure in heart"

I _____

PROMISE BY THE HELP OF GOD

1. To uphold the law of purity as equally binding upon men and women.

2 To be modest in language, behavior and dress.

3. To avoid conversation, art and amusements which may put impure thoughts into the mind.

4. To guard the purity of others, especially of my companions and friends.

5. To strive after the special blessing promised to the pure in heart.

The White Shield Pledge. This form, complete with the angel logo denoting purity, was signed by each of the club members. (Courtesy of Spelman College Archives.)

perance and, as noted by historian Nick Salvatore, places for African American males to "explore the meaning of that elusive term, 'manhood.'"[15]

"The lodges," noted McWilliams, "provided, as they did for whites, an escape from daily life into a world where different ideals could be affirmed and emotions expressed."[16] Indeed, African Americans have a long history of affiliation with fraternal orders and benevolent societies. Black chapters of white orders such as the Masons and Odd Fellows were established between the American Revolution and the Civil War.[17] In addition, blacks formed independent societies designed to provide social services in struggling free communities in the North. Such fraternal orders and other benevolent societies spread into the South following the Civil War. They continued to act as social service agencies, providing aid and insurance to members of the black community. The Masons, Odd Fellows, and Knights of Pythias were the most prominent fraternal orders in Atlanta between 1875 and 1906. Big Bethel's Rev. Francis J. Peck, as noted in chapter 3, organized the city's first Masonic and first Odd Fellows Lodges in 1871.[18] Two decades later, four additional Masonic lodges and three new lodges of Odd Fellows had been established in the city. A third fraternal order, the Knights of Pythias, had six lodges by the turn of the century and two lodges of Good Samaritans had been established before 1898. In addition, women's auxiliaries of the Knights of Pythias, the Odd Fellows, and the Good Samaritans were active in Atlanta. Female auxiliary members were responsible for fund-raising and caretaking, and they provided the food for events, visited the sick, and comforted the grieving.

All fraternal orders were distinguished by the use of ritual and costume. Participation in an initiation ritual, mastery of a series of secret handshakes and code words for identification, and special attire marked by a unique design or combination of colors were required of all members. In addition to assigning members a new name, to be used only by other members of the brotherhood, the orders also conferred degrees upon their members. Titles of military rank or of pseudoroyalty reveal the hierarchical character of the organizations. Similarly, titles such as "Noble Father" and "Exalted Patriarch" for men and "Daughters of Love" and "Daughters of Faith" for women suggest the patriarchal nature of the orders. Parade divisions of these orders practiced standard military drills. Members prided themselves on public displays of this military pomp at lodge fairs or bazaars. Uniforms adorned with sashes and accompanied by ceremonial swords and medals reinforced a sense of masculinity and authority. Fraternal orders also encouraged proper moral behavior, especially temperance and the practice of Christianity. Members were to live a moral and "upright" life, keeping themselves and their fraternal brothers on the straight and narrow. Both the Masons and the Odd Fellows strongly encouraged thrift and homeownership as exercises in self-discipline and independence.

Lodges on average held business meetings twice per month. The corresponding male and female groups held their meetings on different days. In 1904, for example, Atlanta Lodge #103 of the Knights of Pythias (one of six such lodges in the city) met on the second and fourth Friday night of each month. The Ladies of the Household of Ruth No. 457, the female branch attached to the Knights, met the second and fourth Mondays of the month. The Saint James Lodge No. 4 met at the Mason Hall at 12½ Piedmont Avenue on the first and third Tuesdays, and the corresponding ladies group, the Saint James House of Ruth, met every Monday evening.[19]

Formed at the local level, chapters or lodges of these orders were connected to regional and national organizations. After a core group of would-be members gathered and appointed the necessary officers, the regional or national lodge then chartered the local group, usually by sending a representative whom the membership requesting accreditation hosted. This connection with lodges beyond the confines of the city linked members to a network of like-minded African Americans across the state and the country. Such affiliation also gave members access to additional financial resources.

Local lodges contributed to cooperative efforts to purchase real estate for the use of all members.[20] In the 1870s and 1880s monthly dues of fifty cents per member (rising to between one dollar and three dollars per member in the

1890s) allowed the orders to provide sickness and death benefits for their constituents. The Knights of Pythias, with a membership of 5,094 in Georgia in December 1903, provided a sickness or injury benefit of three dollars per week that year. At year's end, the Georgia chapter had a cash balance of $12,099.25, having paid $5,400 in benefits to members in the fourth quarter.

Funds were often used to purchase the necessary meeting halls. The lack of a privately held space forced lodges to seek access to public buildings. The Odd Fellows successfully petitioned for use of the Atlanta City Hall for a function in November 1871, but a similar request from the Star of the South Odd Fellows Lodge was denied in April 1874.[21] The unpredictable response to such requests on the part of the city council undoubtedly helped to drive the Odd Fellows to acquire their own space. By 1895 the Saint James Lodge had purchased a lot and erected a building worth some ten thousand dollars at 12 Piedmont Avenue.[22] (It would be another nine years before the Odd Fellows built their famed hall on Auburn Avenue.) The hundred names on its rolls included both working-class members of the black community and prominent black businessmen David T. Howard, J. D. Render, and Wesley Redding.[23]

The Crystal Fount Lodge of the Good Samaritans illustrates the connections between fraternal orders and economic uplift in Black Atlanta. When the order, "composed of the very best people in Atlanta," began in 1875, few of its members were particularly affluent. The list of twenty officers and twenty-five members (one quarter of the total) provided in E. R. Carter's *The Black Side* revealed only one person who owned taxable property of one thousand dollars in 1876—undertaker Mitchell Cargile Sr.[24] Yet the Crystal Fount Lodge collectively purchased several shares in South View Cemetery, allowing it to offer reduced rate plots to members as part of their death benefits package.[25] Individually, members of the Good Samaritans may not have been affluent enough to purchase burial sites.[26] By pooling their resources, however, they were able to free themselves from the fear of a pauper's grave.[27] The order thus provided a needed social service for its members. Simultaneously, the expenditure of capital supported the entrepreneurial efforts of all the shareholders of the South View Cemetery.

This connection between Crystal Fount and private enterprise benefited all parties concerned. The profits from the cemetery helped to make Crystal Fount Lodge one of the earliest black fraternal societies to own real estate in Atlanta: the order had erected a meeting hall on Ivy Street by 1895, which increased their taxable property by six thousand dollars for that year.[28] The black-owned contractor's firm of Hamilton and Son constructed the building, and it is likely that the rock-contracting firm of South View Association member Jacob McKinley provided the stone. Both businesses would have profited from the transaction, as would have the black laborers both firms employed. Thus, support services supplied to the association provided further opportunities for commerce and growth within the black community.

Members of the female equivalents of these societies engaged in the important "women's work" of home visitations and nursing the sick and dying.[29] The gender bias of the era was such that women were thought to be "naturally kind and friendly" and therefore the logical persons to provide caretaking in the community.[30] Mrs. Minnie Wright Price, an 1888 graduate of Atlanta University speaking at the second Atlanta University conference on the Negro, praised the Negro woman. "If cold, wet, hungry or sick, woman never stops to consider naught but the stranger's needs and will sacrifice her last stick or crumb to relieve him." She called upon her sisters not to let "the opportunity slip by . . . [to] visit some of our poor neighbors." "Our cheering words will give them hope, courage and strength to toil on," she went on, "[and] each and all of us by making friendly visits among our neighbors . . . can teach lessons of purity, cleanliness and economy."[31] Price admonished her audience not to let status barriers disrupt the important work of "friendly visitation." "Our neighborhoods are filled with families which need the sympathy and cheer that a friendly visit from you would give, but you withhold yourself because they are a little lower in the social scale than you are, or if they are higher, you fear that they will think you are seeking their recognition. How much better off we would be if we would cease to draw these lines of caste and each of us as we climb the ladder reach down and assist a struggling sister!"[32]

Price reminded her audience that it was a woman, a poor widow, who sacrificed to feed the prophet Elijah. This portrait of the selfless, Christian-minded female presented a positive image for African American women. The construction of a model of a moral, even saintly, black woman working for her race stood in opposition to the negative stereotypes perpetrated by white society of black women as lazy, dirty, dishonest, and morally "loose" (sexually inappropriate). Price's words also indicate her willingness to engage in the task of helping the community with all black women, regardless of their class. Lower-status women were to be embraced if they were open to social reform for the betterment of the race as a whole. Price also assumes that, through exemplary behavior, black citizens of Atlanta could refute the racist conceptions of the white community.

Rev. Henry Hugh Proctor of First Congregational Church presented a paper at the same conference with a similar theme. He stressed the need for friendly visitation as a means of putting "jackscrews under the mudsills of society." He also addressed the concerns of status mixing. To the question "Will not the upper class be dragged down by contact with the lower?" Proctor answered, "There is not the least danger of the plainest people mistaking our kindly interest for an invitation to our private social functions . . . it is not contact with the lower element that injures the higher; it is the kind of contact . . . Virtue is its possessor's shield. The immaculate swan comes unspotted from the vilest sewer."[33] Proctor's response indicated his commitment to "racial uplift." Yet the choice of metaphors also indicated his elitist leanings. In opposition to Price, he did not encourage his listeners to erase lines of caste but reassured them that by wrapping themselves in Christian virtue they could visit the "sewer" of lower-class life and return unsullied. High-status blacks in the North had long encouraged black women to try to conform to standards of white womanhood, and their southern counterparts joined in renovating the image of black womanhood. Virtuousness, deference, and fragility were held out to black women as ideal values. All African American women were reminded that their reputations and their behavior contributed to or detracted from the image of the entire race. The economic reality of most black women in Atlanta, however, required them to leave the "domestic sphere" and work outside the home—often leaving their own households and children unattended—as part of an effort to support their families. The poor wages of black men and women of low-status offered formidable obstacles in the pursuit of the Victorian-style womanhood for the vast majority of African American women.

Though, predictably, church leaders were among the most ardent advocates of moral uplift, other organizations began to develop programs that addressed community needs perhaps more pressing for Atlanta's black working class. The mutual aid societies, which provided insurance benefits to members, were not always rooted in church groups; rather it was more typical that individual working men and women joined to form mutual aid societies to provide the protection of industrial insurance. The True Reformers of Virginia and the Afro American Benevolent Association of Alabama began life as mutual aid societies and grew into the earliest black insurance concerns in the 1890s.[34] The Coachman's Benefit Society, established in Atlanta in 1896, was apparently another such insurance association.[35]

N. J. Jones, grocer, ordained minister and elder at Friendship Baptist Church, who had a long history of community activism, organized the Colored Men's Protective Association in 1886 with an eye toward providing support for African Americans in Atlanta. The state of Georgia chartered the group to provide sickness and death benefits for its members. An estimated fifty-four hundred dollars in sick benefits was paid to Atlanta members between 1886 and 1894. The association also provided poor relief for less fortunate blacks in the city. The group expanded beyond Atlanta and had chapters in Columbus and other cities in the state.[36]

The Atlanta Benevolent Protective Association was established in 1904. Although Reverend Bryant, pastor at Wheat Street Baptist Church, was the organizer, this association was not based on church membership in the same sense as Bethel AME's the Daughters of Bethel. Bryant organized the group in the face of rising unemployment and poverty in the city. Members paid five to twenty-five cents per week into a general fund that provided them benefits during times of illness and covered funeral costs.[37] An administrative team comprised of three physicians, two ministers, and a female member of the Wheat Street congregation ran the group.

The story of the Atlanta Benevolent Protective Association is similar to that of the Georgia Real Estate Loan and Trust Company. Changes in Georgia state law concerning the regulation of insurance companies required that all such groups deposit five thousand dollars with the state treasurer by January 1, 1906, as "guarantee that claims could be paid in case of a company's failure."[38] Since the association operated as a mutual aid society rather than a profit-generating business, neither Bryant nor the individual members had the necessary funds to meet the state's new requirements. But Alonzo Herndon, wealthy barber and, since 1885, real estate entrepreneur, did have the capital to invest. Herndon purchased the mutual aid society for $140 and transformed it, along with two similar groups, into the Atlanta Mutual Insurance Association. Thus a mutual aid society, one that had developed out of the commitment of the black working class to providing social security for its members, served as the economic base for entrepreneurial efforts in the black community. One of the administrators of the association noted that "there were bids by white institutions, [but we were] fully decided to let this institution remain as it began, a race institution."[39] Herndon and his investors were able to build a million-dollar insurance business in Atlanta in the early 1900s because the mutual aid, benevolent, and secret societies had already cultivated potential insurance buyers .

Fraternal orders and benevolent societies, in addition to providing aid and spurring economic development, supplied entertainment services for the black community. The social and educational programs of these organizations fostered a sense of community and shared political purpose for many Black Atlantans. Luncheons, fairs, and bazaars helped raise funds for the organizations while allowing community members to socialize in status-appropriate settings. Lectures and debates kept African Americans abreast of the political issues likely to affect their community. Black newspapers also provided a recap of events for those who had been unable to attend lodge meetings and other social gatherings.[40]

A local chapter of the Young Men's Christian Association (Colored) was organized in Atlanta in 1894 and was nurtured by the steady support of high-status black men such as William A. Hunton, Henry Proctor, and John Hope. Canadian-born Hunton took office as the first black international secretary of the YMCA eleven years before his arrival in Atlanta in September 1899. The Huntons would make their home in Atlanta for roughly eight years, building friendships with members of the city's black elite. The writings of Addie Waites Hunton, who remained in the city with the family as William Hunton traveled on YMCA duties, became something of a fixture in the pages of the *Atlanta Independent*. Dedicated to Christian-based interracialism, Hunton devoted his life to the mission of the YMCA. He died of tuberculosis in November 1916 at the age of fifty-three, but not before he oversaw the development of YMCAS across the southern United States and overseas.[41]

Henry Hugh Proctor was equally devoted to the local chapter of the black YMCA. He dedicated his considerable fund-raising abilities to ensuring the success of the Butler Street YMCA, aiding in the purchase of property on Auburn Avenue. Proctor argued that the YMCA, dubbed "the center of life activity for the Negro of Atlanta" long before the 1918–20 construction of a new building on Butler Street, should be debt free. (Black builder and rock contractor Alexander D. Hamilton won the contract to erect the later structure.) Along with dentist James R. Porter, Professor John Hope, insurance agent William D. Driskell, and others, Proctor urged members of the black community to support the YMCA by raising funds to pay off the mortgage. The building did provide space for various social activities. The Evangelical Ministers' Union, as well as the Board of Trustees of the Carrie Steele Logan Orphanage, held meetings in the YMCA building.

John Hope was involved in the Atlanta Baptist College chapter of the YMCA (Colored) of his own accord, but was also happy to be supporting the work of his friend William A. Hunton at the same time. Leroy Davis notes that Hope served as faculty advisor for the campus chapter as early as 1900. Ever concerned that young black men have vice-free activities to occupy their time, Hope lauded the "wholesome recreational activities" offered by the YMCA.[42] The YMCA (Colored) focused, as did the white chapters, on helping young men, especially those from poorer backgrounds, "develop their manly powers and strengthen their moral purpose and Christian resolution." Toward that end the YMCA sponsored religious lecturers, literary readings, concerts, and classes in citizenship. There were also classes designed to promote "muscular Christianity" by providing instruction in swimming and team sports. Other classes sought to teach basic hygiene (and those who took these classes were allowed access to bath facilities) and proper etiquette. The programs at the YMCA were endorsed as progressive methods for ensuring black uplift and "the development of Christian manhood."[43] The YMCA also held an annual debate designed to engage the minds of right-living young men in the social and political arguments of the day. The subject of the 1904 YMCA debate was the question of the federal government's obligation toward the education of the "descendants of the Freedmen."[44]

The Frederick Douglass Literary Society was founded February 14, 1904. The Society provided a forum for Black Atlantans, including ministers, businessmen, and educators, to speak on the social and political issues of the day. Beginning February 22 with the celebration of the first annual memorial exercise, activities included the reading of a formal address about Douglass, a vocal solo, and a musical duet. The gathering was held at Wheat Street Baptist church, and three Baptist ministers—J. S. Flipper, Peter James Bryant, and A. D. Williams—were on the program.[45]

These clubs and organizations brought members of the black community together to socialize and enjoy themselves while they simultaneously worked toward the uplift of the race. Community leaders observed that the YMCA and other such groups helped prevent young men from straying toward "coarseness and vice" by providing them with opportunities to fraternize in "decent" environments. At the same time, the presence of such groups provided white Atlantans with evidence of the social progress of the race.

Not all Black Atlantans, as historian Tera Hunter has observed, were interested in high-toned amusements or cared about providing whites with evidence of racial progress. While Henry Proctor and Odd Fellow member Ben Davis debated the relative merits of dances at the Odd Fellows Hall on Auburn Avenue, low-status men and women were engaging in more colorful activities. Hunter argues that those who walked on the rough side of life also sought amusement choosing "jooks" and "blind tigers" on Decatur Street in which to dance, drink and "carouse the night away."[46] High-status blacks interpreted such behavior as evidence of the lingering impact of slavery on the race and of the need for moral uplift and reform.

Scholars have addressed both the origins and meaning of white fraternal orders and secret societies in eighteenth- and nineteenth-century American political and social life, but less has been written about the importance of the fraternal orders in African American history and culture.[47] W. E. B. Du Bois recognized the importance of black fraternal orders and benevolent societies, identifying them as "business enterprises" that required and fostered specific manhood skills. "A higher average of intelligence and thrift in its membership, and a more quiet, business like persistence along selected lines of effort . . . these lodges . . . [are] not without a certain social value. It attracts members, and then, too, it allows the establishment of a hierarchy of authority . . . thus the more competent get a chance to guide and rule. They represent the saving, banking spirit among the Negroes and are the germ of commercial enterprise of a purer type."[48]

Yet Du Bois, ever the social analyst, was also quite critical of secret societies. He recognized an African connection in their origin but in a less than flattering light. "When the mystery and rites of African fetishism faded . . . the secret society rose especially among the Free Negro as a substitute for the primitive love of mystery." He argued that secret societies encouraged "extravagance and waste" in pursuit of "regalia and tinsel." Du Bois, like Proctor of First Congregational Church, worried that secret societies were diverting money from personal savings and "from more useful channels."[49]

Beyond the practical education in politics, lodge affiliation also provided a psychological training in leadership. As Betty Kuyk notes, "the benevolent society became an institution for belonging and a badge of status. It served the black American psyche through the trauma of Reconstruction and through the disillusionment of disfranchisement and Jim-Crowism."[50] Moreover, the benevolent societies provided a proving ground for leadership within the African American community just at the time when it was becoming increasingly clear that, on both the federal and state levels, the civil rights of black citizens were being infringed upon or withheld entirely, and that they were being deprived of voice and power in municipal affairs. Over time, however, their leadership experiences in secret societies undoubtedly aided black males in their approach to Republican Party politics. In the private world of male fraternal orders, black men who worked to transform themselves into "the best sort" experienced electoral politics, oratory, and negotiation. Just as "the club movement among black women owed its very existence to the groundwork of organizational skill and leadership training gained through church societies," black fraternal orders were the proving ground for hundreds of black politicians and social activists.[51] African Americans, faced with employment opportunities circumscribed by white racism, by low wages, lack of access to businessmen's clubs, libraries, restaurants, and dance halls, formed fraternal and other benevolent societies to provide some form of social network and financial security for themselves and their neighbors.

The ideology of white supremacy determined many of the options available to African Americans after Reconstruction. Though not formalized in Atlanta until the 1890s, the customs of Jim Crow, nevertheless, made for de facto segregation in employment and social relations. The African American community was effectively marginalized and denied access to capital and investment opportunities, though not completely isolated from white society and the marketplace. On the other side of the wall of segregation, African Americans built a community on traditions they knew, adapting them to fit their new circumstances. Black Atlantans understood and acted upon larger market values, sharing a desire for, as Eric Foner has argued, "self-ownership, family stability, marketplace equality, political participation and economic autonomy" with white Americans. Yet African Americans, who had "a vision very much of their own," also engaged the marketplace from the context of their own ideals of community and mutual cooperation.[52] Fraternal orders and mutual aid and benevolent societies were formed with an eye toward racial unity, cooperative support, and the production of capital.

The hierarchy of status conditioned social networks in Atlanta's working-class communities. While individual fraternal orders or benevolent societies expanded the social life of the community as a whole, they also served as spaces for status competition. Lodge members' comments about "the best sort of people" and "the finest caliber of colored citizens" are indications of their acceptance of status hierarchy.

There is an irony in the role that cooperative efforts played in the development of what became the economic elite in Atlanta during the first two decades of the twentieth century. These organizations came into existence to provide mutual support and were second only to the churches as community builders. The solidification of economic resources in the confines of these organizations was in part the base of business development within Black Atlanta. Ultimately, African Americans, mostly male, at the highest status levels in the black working class became entrepreneurs, investing capital in business concerns that were connected to the needs and goals of the community as previously embodied in fraternal orders, mutual aid, and benevolent societies. Business concerns fed off the monopolies established by these cooperative groups. Secret society purchases of plots in the Oakland Cemetery, predating the establishment of South View Cemetery and the Georgia Real Estate Trust and Loan Company, provide more than evidence of a market demand. They supplied would-be entrepreneurs with a "lead list," a solid "customer base" for sales.

The commitment of the administrators of the Atlanta Benevolent Protective Association to selling their organization to other African Americans underscores their larger commitment to race solidarity. The association did maintain its "race" character after it was purchased by Herndon and company. Commitment to cooperative support or mutual aid faded, however, as the association gave way to a business with a concern for profit. An African American who secured insurance from Atlanta Life continued to interact with other African Americans but was no longer solely an insuree, pooling his resources with fellow workers who shared his anxiety about unemployment or sickness; rather, he was a consumer who purchased a more expensive policy from a salesman.

The extra cost of the policy represented the firm's profit margin. The salesman was, by necessity, interested in generating profit both for himself and the stockholders of the firm. Private profit, then, became the rule of the day, superceding concerns with "mutual aid."

The interjection of profit into the arena of mutual aid helped to change the dynamics of the black community. On one level, black business successes meant race progress or uplift. On another, it became the basis for a more intense stratification within the black community. Increases in material wealth meant greater distance between the various strata in Black Atlanta. Wealth in the hands of entrepreneurs put more physical distance between the elite and the plain folks, as the former began to move away from the old working-class enclaves and acquire more property. This "flight" was of course circumscribed by segregation in the housing market. Still, "elite" neighborhoods grew in direct proportion to increased wealth. Further, and more importantly, the social distance also grew. The insurer and the insuree were less likely to be social peers after the development of business concerns like the Atlanta Mutual Life Insurance Company.

Distance developed in other spaces too. In the last decade of the nineteenth century, the elite more frequently socialized in "institutional" organizations—literary societies, the YMCA, the National Women's Clubs, or the Epworth League—rather than traditional black fraternal organizations. Although blacks in Atlanta continued to share a racial orientation, less and less did they share a social or cultural one based on common life experiences.

To gain insight into the circumstances of the developing class stratification in Atlanta's African American community at this time, we might telescope forward to the period shortly after the 1906 riot to examine the ways the elite positioned itself in the broader context of American society. A number of Atlanta's most prominent black leaders were in attendance at the 1908 national Clifton Conference held in Massachusetts. These included Wesley J. Gaines, pastor of Bethel AME, Alexander D. Hamilton, general contractor and director of the Atlanta YMCA (Colored), Henry H. Proctor, pastor of First Congregationalist Church, and W. B. Matthews, principal for eighteen years of Atlanta's Gate City Public School for Colored Children.[53]

W. N. Hartshorn, director of the International Sunday School Association and sponsor of this sixth Clifton Conference, drew together seventy participants from seventeen states—including educators, ministers, doctors, lawyers, publicists, and activists—from some thirty-four black schools, nine missionary associations, and twelve denominations. The subject of the conference was "the development of the American Negro since his emancipation," and among those speaking was Atlanta's W. B. Matthews.[54]

Matthews was an 1890 graduate of Atlanta University, having worked his way through the evening educational program. He was an active member of Proctor's First Congregational Church and president of the local colored chapter of the YMCA. In 1906, he had chaired the Atlanta committee in charge of preparing for Booker T. Washington's National Negro Business League Conference.[55] His paper for the Clifton Conference, "The Present Needs of the Negro," was one of several dozen such papers and addressed what he believed to be the central housing-related problems for the black community and their potential solutions.

Matthews called local whites to task for building poor quality tenements for Negroes to live in, noting that "Negroes must live there. They are forced to do so by the cheap labor system. Men are compelled to live there for shelter." He further observed that these tenements bred crime and vice: "[N]ot a single week . . . have I failed to see the police officers of that section arresting somebody, hunting down and taking away somebody for stealing, drinking or wife beating. They foster criminals and from them come some of the worst types of Negro we have." Matthews argued that the children who lived in such tenements, including the one positioned immediately behind Gate City School, were "poorly fed and dirty" and given to disorder, mischief, and bad language. Children from these tenements, built by whites with no thought to home life or sanitary conditions, did not attend Sunday school nor did their parents attend church. Instead, they spent Sundays "relaxing and giving and serving big dinners" for family and friends, all of which discouraged the proper "development of the race."[56]

Matthews contrasted this description of tenement dwellers with that of black homeowners in Atlanta. On blocks where Negroes owned their own homes, he argued, there was order, peace, and stability. Everyone attended church and Sunday school. There was no fighting or crime and no need for Atlanta policemen to visit such neighborhoods. Children from these families conducted themselves with proper decorum and were proud of themselves and their race. He concluded by arguing that the present need of "the Negro" was "sympathy from Southern whites." This sympathy should encourage the city of Atlanta to provide a greater number of public school facilities, better salaries for Negro schoolteachers, and better equipment in the buildings. In addition, there should be a law preventing whites from building poor quality tenements and encouraging the development of home ownership for all Negroes. These measures would ensure substantial change and were, in fact, the "key to uplift."[57]

Matthews's analysis of the problems facing Atlanta's Negroes at the turn of the century reflects his adherence to the "politics of respectability" as envisioned by historian Evelyn Brooks Higginbotham. She notes that the politics of respectability as it relates to African Americans "emphasized reform of individual behavior and attitudes both as a goal in itself and as a strategy for reform of the entire structural system of American race relations." Black Baptist women, argues Higginbotham, "emphasized manners and morals while simultaneously asserting traditional forms of protest, such as petitions, boycotts and verbal appeals to justice." In the final analysis "respectability" "combined both a conservative and a radical impulse[;] . . . [it both] reflected and reinforced the hegemonic values of white America, as it simultaneously subverted and transformed the logic of race."[58] This vision assumed, at least in part, that the solution to the "Negro problem" was cultural and social refinement on the part of African Americans themselves.

Much of the social reform activity of African Americans in Atlanta prior to and in the aftermath of the 1906 race riot lends itself to this model. Matthews's analysis castigated whites for economically exploiting the black working class by paying low wages and providing inadequate housing; he also chastised the Atlanta city government for not providing proper public school education to aid in the uplift of black children. But he, simultaneously, condemned "the worst types of Negro" for their lack of piety and clean living. This double-edged strategy had a status bias. Internalization of the dominant culture's vision of correct behavior and the linking of "proper" behavior by the black elite to citizenship rights spoke of their aspirations to middle-class status as well as their commitment to race uplift.

Matthews's rhetoric also echoed that of Proctor, Davis, and Carter in the weeks and months following the violence of the 1906 riot. These community leaders, recognized spokesmen for "the Negro race," continued to engage in the politics of respectability as the riot faded into memory. They regularly discussed the need for sobriety, cleanliness, thrift, and virtue within the black population. Their appeals for proper behavior, however, were concurrent with their condemnation of racial discrimination, prejudice, and violence on the part of southern whites, all of which were barriers to black self-help and progress.

As presented in his Clifton Conference lecture, Matthews's analysis of the "Negro problem" in Atlanta reflected the hopeful strategy of a desperate black leadership. The analysis assumed that middle-class blacks, those that owned their own homes, would lead the way in social uplift. By setting the example of proper behavior and dress, they would serve as guides for those who lived in tenements and who failed to live up to the moral and social standards of ladies and gentlemen. Self-styled members of Atlanta's black elite with degrees from Yale, Brown, Morehouse, and Howard, professional men—doctors, lawyers, teachers, contractors, and ministers—increasingly perceived themselves as role models for the black working class and examples of the "best sort of Negro" for white society. Respectability and an emphasis on manners and morals, or so it was hoped, would create a bridge linking the emerging black middle class to the dominant culture. This would allow the black middle class to assume, in turn, the mantle of paternalistic leadership vis-à-vis the black working class. The black elite understood the cultural development of the race to be the necessary first step on the road to racial uplift. This acculturated population would then be charged with building progressive social relations with their southern white peers, part of the duty of the "Talented Tenth." Speaking in the chapter "Of the Sons of Master and Man" in the *Souls of Black Folk,* Du Bois pointed out "the increasing civilization of the Negro . . . the development of higher classes . . . increasing numbers of ministers, teachers, physicians, merchants, and independent farmers who by nature and training are the aristocracy and leaders of the blacks." The responsibility of this new breed of black aristocrats, according to Du Bois, was, for the sake of "friendliness and philanthropy of broad-minded sympathy," to make common cause with members of the white elite such that they could, together, uplift the Negro race.[59] Rising Black Atlantans embraced this vision.

The church and the school were two of the strongest mechanisms for the transmission of social and cultural values in Atlanta, and black fraternal organizations represented a third lever in the machinery of uplift. Teachers, preachers, and fraternal elders also supplied lessons in mainstream culture and values. Educators, as historian Stephanie Shaw notes, emphasized the need for graduates (especially female graduates) to practice exemplary moral and social behavior believing "the more upright they were . . . the more likely it was they could break down the prejudice of white people."[60] Arguably, African American internalization of these "middle-class" values and standards was assimilative, and upward mobility went hand in glove with assimilated values and behaviors. Yet black aspirations to rise upward, toward the dominant culture, were also rooted in their desire to improve the quality of their lives and hopefully gain access to rights of citizenship and social equality.

This uplift strategy was layered over the black social institutions that had developed in early postwar Atlanta, institutions that had grown from freedmen and -women's commitment to racial solidarity. African American values laid the groundwork for post–Civil War communities before the arrival of external aid. African Americans, using their own meager resources, worked to provide education, tend to their sick, and raise their children before Fireside Schools for Mothers and Atlanta University. Political organization and economic development also revealed dedication to the idea of community. This was especially true before large numbers of African American men and women began their climb up the ladder of social mobility through pursuit of higher degrees and professional status.

The strength of community in Black Atlanta was rooted in the shared commitment to improving the quality of life for African Americans in the face of white repression. The transformation of this community, from postwar enclaves marked by cultural and social connectedness to a twentieth-century community defined by nascent class conflict and tensions, was a lengthy one. Black Atlanta was much less stratified by class in 1875 than in 1890, less so in 1900 than in 1920. And the culture and worldview of Black Atlantans was not frozen in a slave past; it shifted, adapted, and grew as the circumstances of life for black people changed. Access to education and the growth of fraternal and mutual aid societies contributed to that change. Still, while the form and style changed over time, the black commitment to racial solidarity and progress did not waver. The political activism of African Americans in Atlanta, as discussed in the next chapter, was fostered by that commitment.

CHAPTER SIX

Citizenship Denied

Blacks in Atlanta City Politics

Photographs are a valued part of the cache of archival materials that are the tools of the trade for historians. They seem to reanimate men and women long since dead by putting a face on the names found in written documents. Yet historians must be careful not to assume the documentary realism of photographs; they do not always tell the whole story. Consider the photograph of Jackson McHenry, captain of the black militia corps, the Governor's Volunteers, who graced the front page of the February 13, 1904, issue of the *Atlanta Independent* in full military regalia. The caption beneath his photo heralded McHenry as "the invincible—a political Napoleon who has done more for the elevation of his race, and the young men in particular[,] than any man in Georgia—A political tug who has brought safely into the political harbor many disabled ships." The occasion for the celebration of McHenry was the selection of the Fulton County delegates to the 1904 Georgia state Republican convention. McHenry along with fellow black Republicans Henry Rucker, C. C. Wimbish, and John M. Reeves had been chosen as delegates. A working man of modest means, Captain McHenry was a passionate speaker, who just two days earlier had held his audience in Friendship Baptist Church in thrall with his answer to the question "Is Roosevelt the proper man to be reelected as President of the people of the United States? If so, why?" Yet despite the media fanfare and McHenry's loyalty to the Republican cause, the man with the sharp, clear-eyed gaze, immortalized in the *Atlanta Independent* newspaper photo, never held office in Atlanta or anywhere else in Georgia. Like dozens of other black activists and thousands of black voters, McHenry's political career was constrained by the pervasiveness of white supremacy and the effectiveness of Jim Crow.

The date of the McHenry photo and the accompanying article is a significant one, since it can serve as an index of the actual political progress African Americans had been able to achieve against an active and hardening white opposition. Citizenship rights, tied to concepts of independence, manhood, and uplift, were central to the efforts to build a free black community. African Americans in Atlanta welcomed their freedom, embraced the rights of citizenship granted in the passage of the Reconstruction-era amendments to the Constitution, and cultivated political activism from the end of the Civil War through the 1906 riot and beyond. Members of the community organized, petitioned, protested, and ran for office. Ministers, teachers, newspapermen, and members of fraternal orders and women's clubs encouraged their fellow African Americans to stay abreast of the issues and to do everything within their power to register and to vote. Determined to use their citizenship to their best advantage, blacks in Atlanta negotiated a space between the desires of whites and their own hopes for the future. Invoking concepts of democracy and justice, while appealing to the lingering paternalism of their white peers, blacks struggled to keep a foothold in the world of politics. They cultivated the spirit of the New Negro, identifying themselves as men and women of "good character" in a strategy designed to thwart the increasingly virulent racism that threatened their civic freedom.

The political and racial infighting in Atlanta in the last decades of the nineteenth century and most of the first decade of the twentieth was a result of the efforts of African Americans to secure and maintain their civil and voting rights in the face of pressure exerted by the larger white community to restrict those rights. Even as blacks worked to hold on to the political tools of freedom, marshalling their economic, moral, and political resources to defend their cause, shifting allegiances within the white community frustrated black efforts. White supremacists mounted an effective campaign to disfranchise African Americans through attacks on alleged black immorality and criminality. This campaign, which got underway in the earliest days of Georgia's Reconstruction, blossomed in the wake of Atlanta's prohibition battles of the 1880s, and within two years of the 1906 riot succeeded in disfranchising most blacks in the state.

Reconstruction was uneven in the American South. In some states, the great nineteenth-century experiment in democracy was over almost before it had begun. It was "a splendid failure" in Georgia, where advocates of Reconstruction did not have sufficient power to withstand the conservative onslaught that "redeemed" the state by 1871.[1] Black politicians, expelled from the George state legislature in September 1868, never recaptured power or momentum, despite their December 1869 reinstatement at the hand of the U.S. Congress.[2]

Georgia's black population was eager to participate in the reconstruction of the state and began early to prepare for the rights of citizenship. A Freedmen's Convention held in Augusta in 1866 brought together blacks from all over the state to discuss political rights, responsibilities, and goals.[3] The Georgia Equal Rights and Educational Association, an outgrowth of the convention, played a pivotal role in black political as well as educational activism. The association established chapters statewide to educate blacks about their rights and the workings of government. Such lessons in liberty proved fruitful; black Georgians organized and voted for thirty-seven of their number to serve at the Georgia state constitutional convention in Atlanta in December 1867.[4]

Active and outspoken black delegates to the state's constitutional convention formed a coalition with white Republicans, most notably ex-Union officer John Emory Bryant, former New Yorker and businessman Rufus Bullock, and former Confederate captain and organizer of the Blodgett Volunteers Foster Blodgett, as they struggled to secure political rights for freedmen.[5] Given the voting strength of African Americans, a greater proportion of the constitutional delegates should have been of African descent. Blacks made up 46 percent of all eligible and 90 percent of all Republican voters. Instead, only 22.4 percent of the delegates to the convention were black. Historian Lee Drago has argued that the reduced number of delegates was linked to the "self-conscious" feelings of "inferiority" on the part of black voters. According to Drago, this sense of inferiority, tied to their history as slaves, led black leaders to encourage whites to stand for election to the convention in their stead. African Americans were quite familiar with the racism of their white peers, regardless of political party, and would certainly have recognized the difficulties facing black delegates to the convention. Yet I would argue that the issue of literacy played a more significant role in the decision not to promote blacks as delegates than did free-floating feelings of inferiority. Illiteracy was a serious limitation for many would-be black politicians of the Reconstruction era. Black voters, seeking the "best men" for the job, sought out literate men who they believed could best represent their interests. Black Georgians who had been slaves were less likely to be literate, or familiar with the workings of government, than either white carpetbaggers like John Emory Bryant or local whites like Benjamin Conley.

Henry McNeal Turner, Tunis Campbell, and Aaron A. Bradley were among the most assertive delegates to the 1867 constitutional convention and later won offices in the state legislature. All three black men had experienced freedom before the war, were educated, and had been previously employed with the Freedmen's Bureau. Henry McNeal Turner had a long career as a black political activist and social reformer. An itinerant minister for the AME Church, Turner was educated at Trinity College and went on to serve as a chaplain for black troops during the Civil War. He was assigned to the Freedmen's Bureau in Georgia but left it as a result of "not receiving the respect I thought was due me."[6] Aaron A. Bradley returned to Savannah in 1865, having escaped slavery, studied law, and developed his own practice in Boston. An outspoken activist, Bradley remained engaged in the battle for black civil and political rights in Georgia through the final Republican defeat. Tunis George Campbell had been born free, but unlike his compatriot Turner, had spent his childhood in New York State rather than the South. Campbell was also an AME minister but earned his living as a hotel steward. Active in the "negro conventions" of the antebellum period, Campbell came south to work at Port Royal and, in 1865, joined the Freedmen's Bureau. He would later settle in McIntosh County, Georgia, where he would lead the black community in its efforts to resist political "redemption" by white planters. Like Turner, Bradley and Campbell also left the bureau when their efforts to help Georgia freedmen hold on to the lands granted them by Sherman's Field Order Number Fifteen put them at odds with federal policy.[7] These three men and their black colleagues, who organized the black Republican Party in the spring of 1867, helped to produce a new state constitution that had some promise but offered Georgia blacks few guarantees.[8]

The obstacles to civil rights for blacks in post–Civil War Georgia were formidable. Immediately after the war, black freedoms and rights were constrained by white political maneuvering and questionable uses of the framework of law. The Georgia state legislature had, while convened in winter 1865–66, reinstated a series of restrictive racial codes that tied political rights to citizenship status. As only white persons were identified as citizens, blacks were deemed ineligible for all rights of citizenship, including the right to vote and hold public office.[9] Such actions contributed to a political climate hostile toward black freedmen and were therefore part of the motivation for the U.S. Congress to pass, in March 1867, the First Reconstruction Act. Unfortunately for African American freedmen in Georgia, the racism of their white fellow Republicans would prove to be as much a barrier as the animosity of southern Democrats.

The Republican-dominated constitutional convention met in Atlanta in December 1867. White Republican George Burnett boldly summarized the feeling of many Georgians, irrespective of their party affiliation, when he proposed a resolution declaring the state first, last, and always a white man's country. Black Republican delegates were thus put on notice as to the nature of their upcoming fight to secure political rights in Georgia. Indeed, black Republicans had only limited success in their efforts. Their greatest achievements were the measure establishing a system of public education, laws supporting the rights of agricultural laborers to obtain a lien against their employer's property, and the abolition of public whipping. Unfortunately, black activists were unable to prevent some of the most restrictive measures proposed by conservatives from becoming law. The new constitution contained no specific language concerning the rights of African Americans to hold office, nor did it directly address the issue of blacks on juries. Black delegates could not prevent the retention of Irwin's Code, the set of antebellum restrictions that identified blacks as falling outside the category of citizen. They were also unsuccessful in their efforts to bar language that permitted racial discrimination and segregation in public transportation.[10]

White delegates, using charges of immorality that prefigured later struggles between black and white Republicans, challenged black citizenship rights and the legality of black participation. Black delegates argued against repressive measures by highlighting their new status as citizens of the nation and emphasizing the power of the federal government. Aaron A. Bradley, whose antidiscrimination proposal had aroused the ire of conservative whites, argued that Burnett's racist resolution was in opposition to the tenets of both the Civil Rights Act of 1865 and the Fourteenth Amendment.[11] Bradley's outspoken commitment to political equality for African Americans provoked his white colleagues at the convention to take radical action. He was charged with being morally unfit to hold his seat, and, in a foreshadowing of things to come, delegates voted to expel him from the convention.[12]

Despite the limits of the new constitution, African Americans in Georgia flocked to the polls and elected thirty-two of their peers to the state legislature in the April 1868 elections: three to the senate and twenty-nine to the house. State senators Tunis G. Campbell and George Wallace and many of the twenty-nine black legislators elected had also been delegates to the constitutional convention. Bradley, despite his earlier expulsion, was also elected to the senate. Unfortunately, this black election victory did not hold. African American legislators in the George state house of representatives were expelled from that body September 3, 1868. The Georgia state senate followed the action of the lower house and voted out the black senators nine days later. Less than a year after his first expulsion, A. A. Bradley was again driven from office.[13]

Georgia's white politicians made it clear that black legislators had been expelled, charged with illegally holding office, on the basis of their race. Black legislators vigorously protested their dismissal on constitutional and moral grounds, but their reasoned arguments did not sway their white peers, nor did Henry McNeal Turner's impassioned speech in defense of African Americans' right to serve. In a corrupt marriage of whiteness, Republicans joined forces with Democratic conservatives to vote in favor of the dismissal of black officeholders. Defeated, the men filed out of the state house as one body.[14]

Expelled legislators and more than a hundred other black voters and politicians met in Macon the next month to plan strategy to reverse the decision. Turner and Representative James M. Simms carried a full report of the episode to the U.S. House of Representatives Committee on Reconstruction. Their protest and testimony helped persuade Congress to refuse to readmit Georgia to the Union unless the state formally endorsed all the provisions of the Fifteenth

Amendment granting blacks voting rights. The expelled black members of the original 1868 Georgia legislature were reinstated in December 1869 by an act of the U.S. Congress.

They returned, in January 1870, to a state legislature where Democrats and rogue Republicans, including John Emory Bryant, had formed a powerful conservative alliance that ended any potential for radical Reconstruction in Georgia. Violence and intimidation by the Ku Klux Klan marked the legislative elections of 1868–72. William J. Walker, a member of Atlanta's First Congregational Church, was murdered by Klan members in Blakeley, Georgia. Though the *Atlanta Constitution,* reporting on the U.S. Congressional investigations into Ku Klux Klan outrages in 1871, mocked the proceedings and denied the existence of the terrorist organization, thousands of blacks were denied access to the polls or coerced into voting for conservative white candidates by nightriders.[15] Southern Democrats, along with conservative white Republicans, dominated the legislature and were at the helm of the ship of state when Georgia rejoined the Union. The diminishing strength of the Republican Party, coupled with the consistent and ultimately successful efforts to disfranchise Georgia's black voters, limited blacks' civil rights and diluted the political power of the African American community. Yet despite the steady decline of black officeholders and elected officials, African Americans remained active in, and sometimes crucial to, political battles in the state for the remainder of the nineteenth century.

The failure of Georgia's brief Reconstruction undermined the political aspirations of African Americans. Blacks remained active and politically viable in urban centers where they were a majority and in rural counties where they were well represented. The city of Savannah, with an established black elite and a flourishing church network before the Civil War, contributed 11 percent of the African American officeholders in Georgia during Reconstruction and remained a center of black political activism through the 1890s.[16] By contrast, blacks in Atlanta had less of a base on which to build a successful political machine and less political success than blacks in Savannah.

Atlanta's black community did organize and pursue politics during and after formal Reconstruction. Blacks in the city of Atlanta were very involved in Republican Party politics, though Fulton County failed to elect a black Republican to the Georgia state legislature during Reconstruction. Black Republicans from Atlanta elected black delegates to attend district, state, and national Republican conventions from the 1860s to the 1920s, and Republican rallies and ward politics helped elect two African Americans to municipal offices in Atlanta in 1870.[17]

The 1847 city charter of Atlanta, which prohibited African American men, either as slaves or as free people of color, from exercising the rights of citizenship or the franchise, was revised in 1868 to extend such privileges to freedmen. As the original wording of the charter allowed for ward-specific elections, African Americans, with a majority in two city wards, had a political advantage. Black voters organized and elected black Republicans William Finch of the third and George Graham of the fourth ward to the Atlanta City Council two years later.[18]

Conservative white Democrats, stunned by black success in the 1870 election, were determined to limit African American access to the franchise. The Atlanta City Council, outraged that two black men had been chosen to serve in their body, voted to establish a policy of citywide elections in 1871, thus watering down black voting strength. This was but the first step in the sustained effort to disfranchise black voters. The white primary, the 1877 state law imposing a cumulative poll tax, and the 1908 Felder-Williams Amendment to the state constitution further limited and then effectively eradicated the black vote in both Atlanta and Georgia at large.

The Democratic white primary debuted in Atlanta in 1872 and remained in effect for three years. Only white males registered in the Democratic Party were allowed to vote in the primary elections that determined the final candidates for offices.[19] The white primary invoked racial loyalties and provoked racial tensions. The process not only excluded African American voters from participation in the selection of candidates but also allowed the Democratic Party to represent itself as *the* political voice of the white race. In conjunction with citywide elections, the white primary meant that Republicans, the majority of whom were African Americans, could hope to gain office only if they won support of their candidacy from whites in the rival party and then captured the majority of all votes cast in the city.

The decline in popularity and power of the Republican Party in the 1870s and 1880s and consequently of its political threat led to a corresponding decline in the use of the white primary by Democrats. The fact that it became very unlikely that black Republicans would be elected encouraged internal competition between factions of whites in the city's Democratic Party after 1875. Black voters remained active in Atlanta, negotiating in the political space between white conservatives and independents. Independent Democrats courted African Americans, using the black vote as a tiebreaker on specific issues and candidates. The black vote proved crucial on the issue of prohibition in the 1880s. It was the activism of black voters that inspired the city's executive committee to reinstitute the white primary in 1892. It remained in force for the bulk of city elections in that decade.[20]

Georgia's 1877 poll tax law further diminished black voting strength in Atlanta. The 1868 poll tax legislation required males ages twenty-one to sixty to pay an annual tax on all real and personal property. Revenues raised by the tax were to support public education in the state.[21] Black delegates, desperate to finance education for newly freed adults and children, had accepted the poll tax at the 1867 constitutional convention. Unfortunately, the majority of freedmen in Georgia were unable to pay the election year tax, and Democratic registrars were delighted to disqualify them as voters in the 1868 fall elections. Despite black legislators' attempts to nullify the law two years later, the poll tax remained law in Georgia for the duration of Reconstruction. However, historian J. Morgan Kousser argues that Republicans, aware of the limits the poll tax law placed on would-be black voters, did act to suspend the tax until 1871. The passage of the 1877 cumulative poll tax law served as a further deterrent to blacks acting on their voting rights. The new law necessitated payment of the previous twelve years' poll tax as prerequisite to voter registration. The legislation, as written, applied to all male voters in the state regardless of race and limited access to the franchise for most working-class blacks and whites. Registration officials sometimes exempted poor whites who were unable to pay their tax on condition that they register and vote for the "white man's party," the Democratic Party.[22] Across the state, however, even black registrants who were able to pay their tax faced other barriers in the form of voter intimidation and harassment, though blacks of means in Atlanta continued to register and vote after the change in the law.[23]

African Americans in Georgia faced the greatest threat to their voting rights with the passage of the Felder-Williams Bill in 1908. The bill sought to incorporate a number of requirements for voter eligibility that reflected the hostility white Georgians harbored toward the idea of enfranchising a population deemed "unquestionably inferior" by most of them. Felder-Williams required Georgia voters to be literate or propertied and of "good character." In order to "register in accordance with the requirements of the law," would-be voters were required to pass a literacy test (with certain exceptions noted below) that demonstrated the ability to "correctly read in the English language any paragraph of the Constitution of the United States or of this State and correctly write the same in the English language when read to them by any of the registrars."[24] The authors of the bill undoubtedly recognized the threat that literacy tests posed to the vast majority of white voters and made several provisions to address this problem. Felder-Williams carried two clauses that secured the voting rights of illiterate white males: owners of forty acres of land valued at five hundred dollars or more were exempt from the literacy test, as were Civil War veterans, at least those whose grandfathers had been able to vote before the conflict. Ironically, this clause would have enabled black veteran Roderick Dhu

Badger and other black males with white fathers and grandfathers to register and vote in Georgia, though there is little evidence that blacks made an effort to take advantage of this racial blind spot.

"Good character," a euphemism for whiteness, proved to be as detrimental to black voters as the literacy portion of the law. Those individuals of good character, as judged by white registration officials, could register to vote despite failure to pass the literacy test.[25] But the qualities of "good character," ostensibly properties of manhood such as Christian faith, diligence, honesty, and general moral uprightness, were in actuality considerably less important than the race of the prospective voter. Black men, according to the radicalized reasoning of the day, were by definition lacking in good character. African American men, deemed "ignorant," "vicious," and "lascivious" by whites, were understood to be a lesser breed, capable of mimicking proper behavior but not truly possessing moral fortitude or reason. It was the failings of such black men, argued southern conservatives, that necessitated the "purification" of politics by the elimination of the black vote. By contrast, most if not all white men, by virtue of their race, met the "good character" qualification for registration. Race was thus an essential loophole in the legislation; it allowed for disfranchisement of most of the state's black population while protecting white males who would have otherwise been disqualified.

Black Atlantans struggled to circumvent the barriers to voting imposed from the 1870s through the turn of the century. They organized into political caucuses to address issues of public education, prohibition, police brutality, and sanitation. African Americans politically organized themselves in conjunction with black churches, fraternal organizations, and the local black press. African Americans at the forefront of political activism in this period were distinguished by possession of "good character," a solid reputation, and commitment to the black community. Economic status was less a concern than literacy in the early years of political activism; however, as members of the community began to accumulate more wealth, candidates and activists were more likely to possess greater assets. The development of black institutions of higher education, passage of the Civil Service Act, and the development of black-owned businesses in the city improved the standard of living for a small number of Black Atlantans. By the turn of the century, activists were wealthier and better educated than most other Black Atlantans.[26]

City Councilmen William Finch and George Graham were the first and only African Americans elected to city government until the middle of the twentieth century.[27] Nevertheless, African Americans continued to organize, campaign for office, and vote when they were able. Black candidates ran for city offices in the elections of 1871, 1877, 1878, 1880, 1881, 1886, and 1887,[28] and the black community produced an all-black ticket comprised of ten affluent community members in 1890.[29] African Americans engaged in political activism as participants in Republican Party politics through petitions, proposals, and protestations to city government and through appeals to the court of public opinion in both the white and the black press.

Together, Finch and Graham provide a profile of African American males involved in politics in Atlanta in the post–Civil War period. Neither man was affluent at the time of his election to office. Both were migrants to the city. Neither man had a formal education, but both were literate. Both men resided in predominantly black areas of the city—Finch in Shermantown and Graham in Summerhill. This profile suggests that African American political activists in Atlanta in the last quarter of the nineteenth century were most likely to be working-class males who were literate, recent arrivals, and based in the black community. Men active in politics in Atlanta in the 1870s and 1880s who fit this profile include Moses Bentley, Hampton Hall, Ransom Montgomery, George McKinney, and Jackson McHenry.

William Finch, at the elite end of the working-class scale, was a craftsman, a skilled tailor who learned his craft in slavery and opened his own business shortly after moving to the city.[30] Finch had no formal schooling but was taught to read and write while a slave in the home of Georgia Supreme Court Justice Joseph H. Lumpkin.[31] At the close of the war, Finch was elected as a delegate to a Freedmen's Convention in Augusta. Serving in that capacity, he was part of the group of black political activists who formed the Georgia Equal Rights Association in 1866. After a brief stay in Augusta, Finch and his family relocated in 1868, becoming part of the great stream of migrants into Atlanta.

George Graham represents the less privileged end of the spectrum of the city's black working class. Much less is known of Graham, who left little official record beyond his brief service as city councilman. He was a Georgia native though not a resident of the city before the war and not involved in politics in the 1860s. Unlike Finch, Graham left slavery with no specific trade. He was identified as a carpenter on the 1876 census. Graham is one of the handful of black property owners with at least one thousand dollars in property as of 1876 (as indicated by the Fulton County Tax Record of 1876). He was also one of the six charter members of the South View Cemetery.[32] Graham was at least marginally literate, though certainly not on a par with Finch.

Political activist Jackson McHenry, like Finch, arrived in Atlanta sometime in 1868 and settled in the fifth ward. He was employed alternately as a blacksmith, a porter, and, through political appointment, a janitor for the financial committee of the Georgia state legislature and the U.S. Customs House. McHenry was involved in Republican Party politics at every level. He ran for city council

William Finch, one of two blacks
elected to the Atlanta city council.
(Courtesy of the Atlanta History
Center.)

in 1870 and the state legislature in 1876. He repeatedly served as a delegate to
Republican district conventions and was elected a delegate to the state conventions in 1888 and 1904.[33] McHenry had no formal education and was not a man
of letters. The "King's English," reported E. R. Carter, was "not at all safe when
it falls into his mouth."[34]

McHenry made at least two less-than-successful forays into the business
world. He sold sewing machines on commission as an agent for the Wheeler
and Wilson Sewing Machine Company in the 1880s, and at the turn of the century he was operating a horse and buggy shop.[35] Carter claimed that McHenry
paid taxes on "between two and three thousand dollars' worth of property" in
1894. However, McHenry did not break the thousand-dollar mark prior to 1890.
The 1890 Tax Digest documented his ownership of $1,050 in property. In 1895,
he paid taxes on eight hundred dollars in property. Five years later, his total
worth was $875.[36] Obviously, in this early period that one was politically active
did not necessarily mean that one was wealthy.

Black political activists rose to the fore on the basis of their ties to the community. Most activists lived in predominantly black areas of the city, though
developing ties to the black community involved more than merely residing
in the third, fourth, or fifth ward. African American political activists had extended social relationships and interaction with a broad spectrum of the black
community through churches, fraternal organizations, social activities, and employment. Connections within the community gave activists name recognition
with black voters. Their interaction also gave them contact with and insight into
the needs of their would-be constituents.

Finch's early political activities stood him in good stead in his pursuit of office in Atlanta, but his membership and status as an elder of Bethel AME church

Republican activist Jackson
McHenry. (Courtesy of the Atlanta
History Center.)

gave him a necessary moral stamp of approval and the greater cachet with black
voters in the city that was even more typical of black political leaders. Mitchell
Cargile, one of four black men on the Republican Party ticket in the city elections of 1871, was a superintendent at Bethel AME, a member of the Crystal Fount
Lodge, and a shareholder in the South View Cemetery. Career politician C. C.
Wimbish, a leader in a black militia company, was active in the First Congregational Church, as was his wife, teacher and seamstress Ida Wimbish. Businessman Floyd H. Crumbly ran for city council in 1890. He was familiar to members
of the black community through his profession as retail grocer. Crumbly was
also one of the organizers of the Georgia Real Estate Loan and Trust, a member
of the Grand Lodge of Freemasons, founder of the Negro Historical Society, and
the secretary of the Board of Trustees of the Carrie Steele Logan Orphanage.[37]
Grocer James Tate was a Republican candidate for the state legislature in 1870
and 1886. His career as an activist began with him teaching at a school for black
children in 1865 and his participation in the Augusta Freedmen's Convention
the following year. Tate was also a member of Bethel AME and served as a delegate to the 1886 Knights of Labor convention in Richmond, Virginia.[38] Finally,
E. R. Carter was a prohibition activist. In addition to being pastor at Friendship
Baptist, he was also a member of the Freemasons, the Colored Co-operative
Civic League, and the Evangelical Ministers' Union.[39]

The development in Atlanta of several institutions of higher education gave
black political activists increased opportunities to obtain a formal education
as the century drew to a close. Indeed, from the 1870s on, having a formal education joined the list of necessary qualifications for black political activists.
Mitchell Cargile, C. C. Wimbish, and E. R. Carter pursued their educations at
Clark College, Atlanta University, and Atlanta Baptist Seminary, respectively.

Education facilitated Cargile's move from cabinetmaker to undertaker in the early 1870s. Wimbish's education prepared him for his 1875 appointment as a black letter carrier in Atlanta and his three decades of political activism in the Republican Party. Carter entered Atlanta Baptist Seminary in 1879 and pursued a course in theology. He would later argue that his liberal arts education, which included foreign languages, stood him in good stead as he traveled to Europe and the Middle East, and it certainly helped him negotiate the political landscape of Atlanta.[40]

The character of African Americans involved in political life in Atlanta changed over time. Working-class and poorly educated blacks who owned only small amounts of property gave way to established businessmen with normal school or college degrees and more substantial property holdings. Community involvement remained a constant, as did the commitment to expand opportunities for members of the black community. The capriciousness of white society also remained a constant in the last three decades of the nineteenth century. Barriers to political participation created by the restoration of the Democratic Party and the corresponding decline in the influence of the Republican Party curtailed the rights of citizenship for African Americans despite their best efforts.

The fight for access to education had consumed a major part of the political energy of black activists in Atlanta in the 1870s and 1880s. Educators, working men, ministers, businessmen, doctors, and newspaper editors all worked to secure public school education for black children in Atlanta. From the 1880s through the turn of the century, prohibition inspired similar activism within the black community. African American leaders—newspapermen, ministers, and educators—committed time and energy to ending the hold "world-dooming" liquor had on the black community.

The prohibition battle made for unlikely alliances. Concerns about the impact of "demon rum" and the evils of whiskey cut across the racial divide. Black and white ministers preached against the sins of alcohol. Black and white newspapers editors warned of the ruin and degradation that awaited men and women who spent their hard earned wages in local dives, nursing glasses of the devil's own brew. Diverse opponents of prohibition also joined hands. Black and white politicians, previously at odds, made overtures toward one another. Shared social goals united blacks and whites on both sides of the prohibition conflict, producing, as John Hammond Moore noted, "the strange phenomenon of Atlanta Negroes being cheered lustily by whites in the 1880's, participating in scores of integrated meetings and marching off to the polls by the thousands."[41]

Atlanta's white clergy supported prohibition, as did a significant portion of the white elite. White antiprohibitionists included businessmen whose livelihoods were in service industries and working-class whites who presumably were the customers in the city's drinking establishments. Northern-born entrepreneur and hotel owner Hannibal Kimball stands as important exception. Identifying himself as an advocate of a "dry" Atlanta in November 1885, Kimball was confident his establishment, the Kimball House Hotel, would thrive despite prohibition.[42] African American leaders in the prohibition camp argued that by supporting the cause, they were aligning themselves with the "best people" in Atlanta and demonstrating their own high moral standards. Some black elites shared concerns with white elites about the moral condition of Atlanta's citizenry, especially black citizens. Yet they differed in their analyses of the problem and in their strategy for ending the crisis. The black community described the battle for prohibition in moral and status terms. It was, in the eyes of black advocates, a battle to save the soul of the African American community, to keep blacks on the path of moral uplift and civilization. More specifically, it was part of the black elite's struggle to raise the moral standards of their low-status peers. Indeed the black elite implied that the establishment of prohibition in the city would lead to a reduction in black arrest and imprisonment. "If prohibition prevails," argued black minister C. N. Grandison, "the convict lease system is doomed to extinction."[43]

The white population in Atlanta also addressed prohibition as a moral issue, at least initially. In the brief interlude of interracial cooperation that marked the earliest prohibition battles, reform-minded whites joined with morally conservative blacks to push for temperance in Atlanta. The members of the WCTU, the Ladies Prohibition Association, and the Young Men's Prohibition Club all emphasized the "Christian love" and values that undergirded their political efforts. Yet, by the 1890s, increasingly conservative whites were far more inclined to frame the prohibition conflict in racial terms. Many whites, including supremacists, used prohibition as an excuse to further circumscribe the political and social conduct of blacks. The later prohibition battles exacerbated the growing status tensions within the black community and strained points of connection to the white community.

Prohibition concerns surfaced in Atlanta in the mid-1880s. African American civic leaders, ministers, educators, and political activists all weighed in on the question. Community activists were divided. Ministers to a man endorsed prohibition, but some businessmen and political activists were strongly antiprohibition. Religious leaders focused on the danger posed by vice to both the moral and cultural evolution of the race. Businessmen and politicians focused on the idea of equality before the law and black access to the alcohol market both as entrepreneurs and as consumers.

Fulton County went "dry" by referendum in November 1885 when seven of ten precincts voted for prohibition. Morally conservative black voters were instrumental in the victory. E. R. Carter, minister and First Ward Club president, and other men of the cloth had rallied their parishioners and fellow ward residents for the prohibitionist cause. Despite the role blacks played in securing prohibition, not all members of the black community had favored the ordinance. While black prohibitionists had met in October 1885 at the Lloyd Street Methodist Church to cheer temperance, other blacks, including employees—mostly service and domestic crew—at Kimball House participated in an antiprohibition rally later in the same month.[44] Neither were all white Fulton county residents happy with the outcome of the election. Businessmen in the city had opposed prohibition fearing it would hurt Atlanta's service industry. City liquor retailers, restaurateurs, and others in the hospitality industry would lead the challenge to the county's prohibition policy in 1886 and in a second referendum battle in 1887. Black political activists on both sides of the prohibition issue used the conflict to reinsert themselves into city politics.

African American AME Bishop Henry M. Turner, then editor of the *Southern Recorder*, used his paper to rally fellow ministers to the cause of prohibition. The *Recorder* stressed the inherent conflict between consumption of alcohol and the "upliftment of the race." Black female church activists encouraged young black women to enroll in the local chapter of the WCTU (Colored) that was organized in the city in 1887, placing emphasis on the link between femininity, virtue, and racial uplift. Young black women were warned that the female purity and moral "uprightness" necessary to redeem the race were inconsistent with the consumption of alcohol.

Young black men were also cautioned about the lack of temperance. Virtue did not play the same role in defining black masculinity as femininity, yet black men were warned of the dangers of the "high life." Strong drink and corresponding lapses in judgment would lead black men to ruin, financial as well as moral, and their hard-earned savings would evaporate as they sat upon the tavern stool. Intemperance represented a lack of discipline, a failure to sublimate passions to reason, and as such was in opposition to the idea of civilized masculinity that black elites cultivated in fraternal orders, Republican clubs, and their struggle to maintain political access. E. R. Carter and William Finch joined Turner and Bishop Gaines in their call for temperance. They urged black men to set aside pursuit of physical pleasures and use their political power to ensure the progress of their race. In their eyes, striking a blow against "demon rum" by voting for prohibition was evidence of racial progress and civilization. Rev. Grandison was perhaps most severe in his admonitions against drink: "Any negro man who throws up his hat for whiskey is not fit to be a negro man."[45]

Moses Bentley, Jackson McHenry, and Alonzo W. Burnett were black activists who were sometimes in the antiprohibition camp. "Wets" were less concerned with moral issues, focusing more on pragmatic economic and political issues. McHenry challenged the vision of his more conservative black peers, questioning the wisdom of endorsing a vision of African Americans that suggested a link between blacks consuming alcohol and a complete lack of morality on their part. He and other "wets" highlighted the role the alcohol trade played in the city's important service industry, which employed blacks as porters and domestics. Barbershop and grocery owner Moses Bentley undoubtedly argued in favor of the economic opportunity that the direct retailing of liquor offered the black community. H. W. Williams operated a saloon at 16 West Alabama Street, less than three doors down from Bentley's barbershop at 13½ West Alabama. Williams and fellow black saloon keepers Stephen Hightower, Robert Stevenson, Thomas Stafford, and William M. Gaines maintained their saloons in the central business district in the late 1870s and early 1880s. While a far greater number of blacks in the same area owned and operated lunchrooms and restaurants catering to a black clientele rather than saloons, business-minded African Americans were reluctant to close the window of opportunity on their peers. Editor Benjamin Davis, who agitated for "the manhood and the equal political and civil rights of the race," expressed similar concerns as black businessmen about temperance and business opportunity. A staunch capitalist, Davis condemned the city policy that prohibited black men from receiving licenses to own and operate shops that dispensed liquor.

The concerns of business-minded "wets" were not without merit. And the city itself must have seen the virtues of the "wets'" reasoning, since Atlanta's dry status was, for the most part, more apparent than real. The November 1885 law was modified in the summer of 1886 by an ordinance that allowed for the sale of certain wines, locally produced beer, and liquor sold by the quart with the purchase of special one hundred–dollar licenses from the city. To the dismay of both prohibitionists and black liquor retailers, large-scale white-owned establishments—such as the Kimball House and the Atlanta Brewery—continued to engage in the sale of alcohol to white patrons under the modified guidelines, while smaller black establishments were forced to close. As reported by Moore, some Black Atlantans gave voice to the common understanding that "prohibition merely took whiskey and beer from Decatur Street to the silver soda fountains on Whitehall."[46]

Not all "wets" were part of the black political elite. Lower-status men and women demonstrated their opposition to prohibition by continuing to visit the city's dance halls and dives. The term "dive" covered any and all establishments in the city that served alcohol to blacks and were depicted in the press and messages from the pulpit as dark places of sin and vice. It was alleged that black vagrants, "criminals," and other "enemies of society" frequented these "dens" to indulge in the consumption of liquor, games of dice, and other forms of loose living. Much of this talk was hyperbole. Many customers of such drinking establishments were working-class men and women who stopped in the bars, restaurants, and "jooks" adjacent to the central business district on Decatur, Peter, and Ivy Streets after long days at tedious, low-paying jobs to meet with friends and enjoy a bit of relaxation. Historian Tera Hunter argues that despite the efforts of the black elite to dissuade their lower-status peers from partaking in "Hurtful Amusements," working-class blacks visited saloons and barrooms in pursuit of both alcohol and relaxation. They continued to gather and to imbibe despite lectures from the black elite.[47]

African Americans pushed for representation on campaign tickets in the elections of 1886 and 1888, and weighed in on prohibition in 1887 as city voters organized to revisit the question. The white-dominated Democratic Party was divided against itself on the issue of prohibition. In addition the presence of white candidates who expressed Populist leanings, such as Walter Brown who identified himself as "the poor man's friend," complicated the prohibition fight. Black activist William Finch, noting that he was "a natural born citizen of the United States," reminded white prohibitionists that the black vote had the previous year "helped win the prohibition battle." "The colored people," continued Finch, as he spoke at an October 26, 1886, political rally for prohibitionists, "want to be good citizens. The better element of the colored people, when they see anything which promises well for the city, are ready to cooperate to push it." Finch concluded his comments by reiterating black citizenship rights and black commitment to "good government," and by expressing his "hope that there . . . [would] be some representation accorded" blacks on the nominating committee for the prohibition ticket.[48] In separate forums, Carter and Turner celebrated the black clergy's protemperance stand, reminding their white peers that they had been resolute since the end of slavery. All three men agitated for an African American presence on city ballots. Black activists Moses Bentley and A. W. Burnett along with ministers E. R. Carter (representing the first ward) and W. J. Gaines (representing the fourth ward) served on the 1886 Committee of Fifty, which nominated candidates for the Citizen's Fusion ticket. The Citizen's Fusion ticket, made up of influential city businessmen, journalists, and reformers, the "best men" of the city, who were themselves divided on the issue of prohibition (hence "Fusion"), accepted blacks as part of the platform committee but offered blacks no positions as candidates. Neither did the (antiprohibition) People's ticket select blacks to serve as part of the slate of candidates. Nevertheless, the majority of the 562 black eligible city voters, encouraged again by black ministers and other members of the black elite to support the "best men," gave their electoral support to the Citizen's Fusion ticket.[49] The Citizen's Fusion ticket carried the day and modified prohibition remained the law of the land, but blacks earned little in the way of either social or political gains for their continued support of the city's white conservative elite.

The following fall, despite the efforts of black and white clergy, Fulton County voters reversed their 1885 prohibition ordinance and "demon rum" was once again fully legal in Atlanta. It is easy to envision Rev. W. J. Gaines's dismay upon discovering the majority black fourth ward had produced the greatest number of antiprohibition votes. Clearly, black "wets" had been unmoved by the moral suasion of black conservatives. Outspoken black voters had challenged the wisdom of black elites in 1886 in reaction to the modification of the previous year's prohibition ordinance: "I know the negroes have been tricked. I know they can't buy liquor and I know white men can. I ain't going to have my civil rights imposed on, and if there's any law in Atlanta I'm going to have my liquor as long as a white man has his. Prohibition is a put up job by the democrats and those high hat preachers."[50] In the wake of the defeat of prohibition in the fall of 1887, some blacks were even more direct in their dismissal of the black elite strategy of casting their lot with white conservatives. The *Savannah Tribune* reminded black readers that "like 'our good friends' always do when elections are over," white elites who had cultivated the black vote in 1885 had failed to support black leadership in either their quest for political office or their efforts toward community development.[51]

A year later, black activists would again negotiate with both the "wet" and "dry" factions, the "Peachtree silkstockings," and the working-class "People" in an attempt to gain access to political power in the city. Eighteen black activists were elected as part of the Committee of Seventy organized to establish the political platform for the 1888 election. Walter Brown who ran for mayor on the People's ticket that year encouraged blacks to participate in the election by voting for his working-class man's ticket, which remained antiprohibition. Brown's "People's ticket" was supported by working-class whites and the Knights of Labor–affiliated Mutual Aid Brotherhood that had long sought to overturn prohibition in the city. He was also supported by blacks who were lured in by his concern with the development of infrastructure in the city (streets and water lines) as well as schools for black children and his interest in the possibility of black policemen.[52]

Brown, whose working-class politics would led him to resurface as a full-fledged Populist in the 1890s elections, was defeated by the more mainstream Democrat John T. Glenn. Glenn had also garnered the support of blacks in the city, including Moses Bentley who warned Brown supporters that "the men who are trying to array ignorant Negroes against the best white people would throw dynamite in the dark, if they had a chance."[53] Jackson McHenry, who was somewhat wary of Brown's white working-class supporters, also supported Glenn. Historian Clarence Bacote, citing the perhaps hyperbolic reportage in the *Atlanta Constitution,* argues that once black activists understood that their demands for "two clerkships in the county courthouse, two detectives to handle Negro cases, two drivers day and night for the police wagon, four members on the Board of Education, a Negro fire company, one member of the City Council, and a school house for Negro children in the Fifth Ward" were not going to be forthcoming, they withdrew their support from Brown's camp.[54] It must be remembered, however, that Glenn's "Peachtree ticket," supported by elites such as city promoter Henry Grady, had made no effort to offer black voters any political concessions. Indeed, in his most patronizing fashion, Grady had encouraged black voters to "work with conservative men for the good of the whole city" rather than agitate for representation as candidates for office.[55] Glenn's victory did nothing to assist black elites in their struggle to provide basic social services for their community. What is more, Brown's defeat, one of many for Populist-leaning politicians in Atlanta, would contribute to a weighing of the values and dangers of the black vote, and contribute, ultimately, to Populist support of black disfranchisement (see chapter 7).

The 1880s prohibition battles demonstrated African Americans' limited access to political rights in Atlanta. White politicians were willing to cultivate the black vote when it suited their purposes. White moral reformers had celebrated the black contribution to the passage of the 1885 prohibition ordinance, literally rewarding E. R. Carter's First Ward Club with a cash prize for getting out the black reformist vote.[56] However, neither reform-minded prohibitionists nor city-building-minded "best people" were willing to extend support of black voters to the idea of black candidates or to aid the black community in the effort to secure needed city services. Equally significant, the volatile energy generated by the battles over prohibition did not dissipate, despite the overturn of the county referendum. Passionate denunciations of the moral character of African Americans and commentary focused on the dangers that blacks with access to alcohol posed to a "civilized" society lingered and were linked to racial tensions and incidents of white mob violence in Atlanta in the years preceding the 1906 riot.

Despite their less-than-satisfactory experience with electoral politics, their being limited to appointment to committees to select candidates and design the platform, blacks remained involved in the political process in Atlanta. African Americans, frustrated with both "the best men" and "the people," organized an all-black ticket and ran, unsuccessfully, ten black candidates in the municipal election of 1890. Undaunted, black political activists in Atlanta continued to meet and discuss local and national political candidates and policies. Debate societies, social clubs, and the colored YMCA provided forums that helped African Americans, male and female, remain abreast of the affairs of state and keep their political skills sharp. Despite being marginalized politically, activists and organizations within the black community worked to foster political awareness and engagement.

Accordingly, Charles Grier organized Black Atlanta's Lincoln Memorial Society eight years after the repeal of prohibition. A gentlemen's debate and social club, the group drew members from the city's black colleges. Young, "patriotic," and forward-thinking men gathered for monthly meetings to discuss political concerns that affected their community. On the occasion of attorney W. R. Gray's election to the presidency of the organization, the members of the Lincoln Memorial Society invited Peter James Bryant to lecture on the merits of "the new Negro." Jackson McHenry's lecture in February 1904 had been sponsored by the Central Star Society, a women's charitable and mutual aid organization. McHenry shared the stage with Mrs. S. E. Harper, who spoke on "the Negro problem and his progress since emancipation." Similarly, the chapters of Atlanta's colored YMCA met to debate whether "the national government should educate the descendents of freedmen." This sort of activity remained a constant in turn-of-the-century Black Atlanta and fed mainstream political activism in the community.

Insurance executive William Driskell, who was a member and chairman of the Frederick Douglass Literary Society, known for public debate on social issues, also served as secretary of the first ward Republican committee. The Republican Party retained the loyalty of African Americans in Atlanta, although they received little in the way of reward for their faithfulness save some local patronage. Jackson McHenry, as noted, held his position as a janitor as a result of political patronage. Charles William Thomas, who served as chairman of the Republican state central committee in 1889, was also rewarded with an appointment as record clerk to the federal court in Atlanta and later as private secretary to the U.S. marshal. The most significant patronage appointment in Atlanta was President William McKinley's appointment of black Republican Henry A. Rucker as collector of internal revenue. Historian Gregory Mixon notes that Rucker had, in fact, worked his way up the ladder, having previously served in several lesser government positions. Nevertheless, Mixon also points out that, despite winning the plum collector job, Rucker was unable to reap the full reward of his appointment. The racial etiquette of Jim Crow deprived him of the right to fill positions beneath him with men (presumably black men) of his own choosing—a perk normally afforded the man chosen as collector.[57] The limit of Rucker's patronage power was lost on whites in the city. Rather than Rucker acting to replace whites with blacks, change in the population of workers at the tax collector's office was facilitated by whites themselves, including the half-dozen white clerks who quit their jobs in protest of Rucker's appointment. The *Atlanta Constitution,* determined to fan the flames of racial antipathy based on the supposed black encroachment of white employment opportunities, published an editorial cartoon on August 10, 1897, in which Rucker's appointment was portrayed as driving respectable white civil servants from the tax collector's office as tackily clad, cigar-smoking, and thick-lipped (as well as presumably unqualified) blacks entered.[58]

Some federal legislative changes, at least in theory, offered the promise of advancement to enterprising black men. African American men who had pursued higher education as part of a program of upward mobility believed the passage of the 1883 Pendleton Act would open the doors of opportunity, or at the very least improve their chances of securing positions irrespective of patronage. The Pendleton Act reformed the nation's civil service by linking employment in the U.S. Civil Service to successful completion of the newly instituted exam. The civil service exam did not, however, take southern racial etiquette into account. In practice, black men who pursued civil service positions quickly discovered that, in Atlanta, the racial customs of Jim Crow carried far more weight than federal policy.

The aborted civil service careers of two Black Atlantans, C. C. Penney and William Allen, exemplify the gap between stated federal policy and local practice. Both men were employed in the Atlanta Post Office by appointment of Postmaster General John R. Lewis. In June 1889, Lewis, a white liberal and long-term Republican, was made Postmaster General in Atlanta via patronage appointment by President Benjamin Harrison. Lewis's term began with racial controversy when in July 1889 he hired C. C. Penney, a recent black graduate of Atlanta University who had successfully passed the civil service exam. Although Penney was qualified for the job, his employment entailed working in close proximity to a white female postal employee, A. V. Lyons. Indeed, her father, Nathan Lyons, was the supervisor of the registered mail department in which both Penney and the young Miss Lyons were to be working. The furor was predictable. According to the *Atlanta Constitution,* Lewis's actions were in violation of established southern etiquette as young Miss Lyons "was brought into intimate and direct association" with a "greasy black."

Penney's appointment gave conservative whites in the city reason to grumble about black expectations of equality and the dangers of white Republican appointments. The grumbling increased in the weeks following Penney's hiring and the resignation of both members of the Lyons family from the postal service. A mob of disgruntled white Atlantans gathered in the downtown area early in

August 1889 to vent their frustrations at Lewis's breach of white supremacist etiquette by burning the postmaster in effigy. The situation calmed down by mid-August, but not before Lewis, a former Union officer, was called before the public and made to declare verbally his unwavering support for white supremacy in all things.[59]

Given his public humiliation, it is somewhat surprising that Lewis was willing to make a second unpopular hiring decision on the basis of federal civil service policy only two years later. Shoemaker and Atlanta Baptist Seminary graduate William M. Allen had served as a mail clerk in the Athens, Georgia, post office in 1884. After passing the civil service exam in June 1891, he applied for the position of letter carrier. Although previously chastised by the mob for hiring an African American, Postmaster General John R. Lewis nonetheless hired the thirty-one-year-old former shoemaker. Like many other upwardly mobile black men and women in Atlanta, William Allen was slow to heed the ominous message of an increasingly bold white racism. He undoubtedly believed that the passage of the Pendleton Act, in conjunction with his university degree, would improve his economic opportunities in the Gate City. Yet Allen was to remain in the employ of the postal service for less than a month; he filed his letter of resignation on June 22, 1891, and returned to shoemaking in the shop of A. J. Delbridge.

E. R. Carter, who chronicled this tale of Allen's brief sojourn with the U.S. Postal Service in his history of the African American community in Atlanta, *The Black Side*, put a positive spin on this sudden turn of events. Of Allen's departure Carter reports, "other duties were so urgent upon him that he found it necessary to return to them. He received a very flattering letter from the postmaster who regretted his [Allen's] hasty action." It is far more likely that Allen's "duties" had less to do with his departure than did the palpably deteriorating racial climate of the city. College educated as well as a skilled violinist who had organized the first black orchestra in Athens, Allen had also taught school in that city prior to his relocation to Atlanta in pursuit of better opportunities. His retreat to skilled labor suggests much about the increasingly violent nature of the racial tensions in Atlanta and the limits imposed by Jim Crow.

In the intervening two years between the appointments of Penney and Allen, white Atlantans had grown less tolerant of black actions that suggested social equality or progress and more accustomed to the use of violence to maintain white supremacy. The actual lynching of Warren Powell in September 1889, less than a month after the mob's dramatic "virtual" lynching of Lewis, reinforced the marginality of blacks' civil rights. Warren Powell was accused of sexual assault on a white woman and a white mob in East Point, Georgia, pursued and "arrested" him, hanged him by the neck, and burned his corpse.

Powell's lynching in East Point, a suburb of Atlanta, is neither as well known nor as well publicized as the brutal murder and mutilation of Sam Hose outside of Palmetto, Georgia, in April 1899, a decade later. There were not thousands of spectators, and the national press did not report the story of the murder of Warren Powell. Yet, as in the case of Hose, the significance of Warren Powell's lynching extended beyond his death. The Hose lynching outraged African Americans, most notably W. E. B. Du Bois, who cites the news of the lynching of Sam Hose as the turning point in his own consciousness about the value of reasoned dialogue in the face of violent racism, but Hose's April 1899 murder did not generate the same response from whites in Atlanta.[60]

Historians of racism and the Jim Crow South have documented the horrific April 1899 lynching of Sam Hose. Indeed, many scholars have emphasized the link between the white blood lust evidenced in the Hose murder and the deteriorating race relations in Atlanta. While I have chosen not to detail the events of the Hose lynching, it is important to mention here as it was a very significant event in the history of race relations in Georgia. The execution was attended by thousands of white spectators and was widely documented by local and national newspapers. Du Bois relates the tale in *Dusk of Dawn,* highlighting the fact that blacks in Atlanta were traumatized both by the lynching itself and by the fact that Hose's body parts were put on public display. My point here is not to diminish the impact of the Hose lynching, but to stress the effect of the lynching of Warren Powell, which gave blacks in Atlanta, at a much earlier date, a glimpse of rampaging mobs of armed white men. Whites from Atlanta did travel to Newnan to witness the Hose lynching, but their direct participation in the 1889 violence of East Point, a decade before, was considerably more pronounced. Further, East Point had a larger black population and was physically more proximate to Atlanta than Palmetto where the killing of Alfred Crawford that precipitated the Hose arrest occurred, or to Newnan, the site of the Hose lynching. Following the 1889 murder of Warren Powell, armed white men from Atlanta, private citizens and city policemen, traveled the few miles from the city center to East Point to help ensure that blacks in that area did not rise up against white authority. White Atlantans roamed the streets of East Point dragging black men from their homes onto the streets, where, without provocation or protection from local law enforcement, they were beaten with gun butts and whips.[61] The aftermath of Powell's lynching was a foreshadowing of things to come; *seventeen years* before the race riot of 1906 the white citizens of Atlanta resorted to extreme mob violence to reinforce supremacy and control over blacks in the region. Warren Powell and Sam Hose were just two of the hundreds of black men lynched in Georgia in the last two decades of the nineteenth century. The number, though far below Rebecca Felton's "a thousand a week," was nevertheless more than sufficient to reinforce white Georgians' commitment to white supremacy.[62]

If politically active members of the black community were somehow in doubt as to their assigned status, no less a personage than Governor Allen D. Candler hastened to make it clear. Historian Leroy Davis notes that Candler's speech at the Fourth Annual Atlanta University Conference on Negro Problems was "unprepared and hurried" and "revealed no new thinking in the New South of the late 1890s."[63] Indeed the language of Candler's May 1899 address (just a month after the Hose lynching) was not new, and the racist sentiments he expressed would have been familiar to those who had attended the 1867 constitutional convention, but there was nothing unrehearsed or haphazard about the theme of his talk. The governor was direct and precise. Negroes, he argued, became "*in the eyes of the law,* the equals of the other races of the Republic [only] as a result of the unfortunate experience of Reconstruction"(emphasis added). He continued, "they were clothed not only with all the privileges, but all the responsibilities of citizenship," but, unprepared for these duties, they had proved to be "unsatisfactory citizens of the country." The solution to this problem, according to Candler, was to be found in education—but not education for the purpose of becoming a skilled political actor or "a third rate member of the American Congress." Rather, Candler encouraged "training in arts and science and literature, and morality, especially morality," so as to create "a successful merchant or . . . a useful intelligent mechanic."[64] For the governor and thousands of white Atlantans and other Georgians, the situation was plain. The window of opportunity forced open by Reconstruction was closed. The sooner blacks recognized this fact and truly understood their place in the social order, the better.

African Americans in Atlanta and across the state did not heed Allen Candler's advice. To the contrary, in the face of increasing white radical agitation aimed at excluding them from the body politic, high-status blacks came together in 1905 and 1906 to plan and agitate for their liberty. Du Bois, having already penned *The Souls of Black Folk* in 1903, joined with other black academics and race leaders for a closed meeting in Buffalo, New York, in July 1905. The Niagara movement was born in that July meeting and formalized in January 1906 with the expressed goal of securing political rights for blacks and ending racial segregation.[65] The Georgia Equal Rights Convention, which took place in Macon in February 1906, was organized with similar goals. Some two hundred black Georgians gathered to assess the status of race relations in the state and to develop strategies to counter the increasingly negative rhetoric on race emanating from whites at both the municipal and state level. William J. White, long time political activist, educator, journalist, and associate of both Hope and

Du Bois, called the Macon meeting both to protest the antiblack rhetoric that was beginning to heat up in the governor's race and to make plain black commitment to civil rights. *Atlanta Independent* editor Ben Davis spoke out against the meeting warning "agitators" that the event was useless and, more important, that the racial climate of the state was not conducive to the success of such an event. "We may have as many conferences as we please but the line of demarcation is eternally fixed and we can not rise any higher than the estimate our neighbors place upon our worth and usefulness as American citizens. Conferences are not the places to begin our fight for civil and political independence. Self is the fertile field in which to begin operation."[66]

Davis was partially right, though for the wrong reasons. It was true that neither the passionate speeches of William White and Henry McNeal Turner nor the editorial endorsement of *New York Age* editor Thomas T. Fortune could hold back the rising tide of white supremacy. Still, the Macon convention left an important record of black commitment to civil and political rights and, equally important, of the collective agitation to protect the rights of universal manhood suffrage. While southern whites envisioned the black "place" as beneath their heel and did much to make that nightmare a reality, black men and women were committed to an alternative vision.

Tensions grew in Atlanta as Jim Crow and the white commitment to exclusion countered black efforts at betterment and progress. Whites had some success in containing and restraining Black Atlantans in politics, employment, and law. But the slow steady progress of the black community still posed a threat to white Atlanta's ultimate supremacy and control. The goal of disfranchising the black community was, as Michael Perman reminds us, "intended to reassert a 'white supremacy' that had proved elusive since the end of the war with a firmness and rigor *unattainable since slavery*"[67] (emphasis added). Though the success of the black community had been tempered by racial restrictions prior to the 1906–8 drive to disfranchise African Americans, it had not been eradicated. Black freedom and progress flew in the face of a white society that remained committed to returning southern society to as close to a pre–Civil War status quo as was possible. Disfranchisement was envisioned as the final post in the fence built to corral and control black people. The black strategy of acculturation that emphasized the internalization of Victorian values as a means of transforming and "uplifting" the African American community must be understood against this political backdrop. Unfortunately it proved unsuccessful as a solution to the threat of white racism and Jim Crow segregation. Instead, black political and civic activism in Atlanta forced to the fore tensions between the desire of whites to limit black society and the desire of blacks to live fully as free citizens and prepared the ground for a turn toward violence.

CHAPTER SEVEN

The Turn toward Violence

The Atlanta Race Riot and

Progress Curtailed

African Americans remained committed to creating a space in which the members of the black community might live and act as full citizens of the republic and as independent people. Their efforts were constrained by political exclusion, limited upward mobility, and increasing social segregation. Despite these barriers, the additional burden of unjust criminal prosecution and confinement, and the growing threat and use of violence, much of the black community remained engaged in the process of building a life. African Americans continued to pursue their education, join social clubs, support their churches, and engage in politics. Most Black Atlantans would keep at these activities after the violence of the 1906 riot, though as many as a thousand Black Atlantans would flee the Southland, convinced that there was a disjuncture between their community building and white supremacy.[1] Black entrepreneurs would increasingly relocate their businesses to within the confines of Sweet Auburn Avenue and their residences into all-black neighborhoods on the western and eastern sides of the city. The black elite would also pursue the strategic use of uplift ideology even after the violence of the 1906 riot, clinging desperately to a much-needed tool of defense. Yet violence would take a toll on uplift ideology as surely as it destroyed black lives and property. In the end, the black community would turn in on itself, focusing even greater attention on internal needs and goals.[2]

The misuse of law, specifically the manipulation of the legal code and the rules of sentencing, was yet another method by which whites corralled members of the black community. The hostile rhetoric that emanated from whites in response to black social and economic activism paled in comparison to the violence leveled at African Americans by Georgia's justice system. Black Atlantans were, through the state's penal system, subjected to forced labor that came as close to reinstating the conditions of slavery as was possible within a purported framework of legality. Georgia's system of convict lease benefited from racial discrimination in black arrests and criminal prosecution and was responsible for the exploitation and death of thousands of African Americans. Established in 1866, formalized and revised by the legislature in 1876, convict lease provided white businessmen and subcontractors with hundreds of thousands of dollars in nearly free labor until the system was abolished by an act of the legislature in 1909.[3]

Atlanta's white elite was heavily involved in Georgia's leasing program. Two members of the city's political "ring," Joseph Emerson Brown and Alfred Holt Colquitt, along with the long-term member and chairman of Atlanta's Board of Police Commissioners (1883–1905) James Warren English, advanced their fortunes on the backs of black convict laborers. Brown and Colquitt, who both served as U.S. Senators from Georgia (Brown 1880–91, Colquitt 1883–94) and took turns as governor (Brown 1857–65, Colquitt 1877–82), were partners in the Dade Coal Company in northwest Georgia. The coal company was the lynchpin of an empire that included the Western and Atlantic Railroad (of which Brown was president) and four iron companies. The mining empire was based upon convict labor. Controlled labor costs of less than a nickel per worker per day facilitated a tremendous post–Civil War increase in wealth for both men. "Captain" James W. English, former Confederate soldier and laborer turned real estate mogul turned banker, moved into city politics in the late 1870s. English was elected mayor in 1881 and would remain a fixture in Atlanta politics through the turn of the century. Powerful and wealthy, English, like Brown and Colquitt, moved to grow his fortune by taking advantage of the state's convict lease program. English joined Brown (whose Dade Coal Company became Penitentiary Company One in 1876) in bidding for convict lease contracts as part owner of Penitentiary Company Two and Three.[4] The three penitentiary companies leased convicts from the state, often releasing them, at substantial profit, to other firms. While Brown's convicts slaved and died in his infamous mines, English's toiled in his Chattahoochee Brick Company in Fulton County. The firm was notorious for English's employ of a brutal "whipping boss," James Casey, and English himself faced corruption charges in 1887 for his convict lease dealings. Yet English, like Brown, was affluent and well connected, and so escaped any serious consequence from the trial. He continued to benefit from convict leasing until the system was abolished.[5]

The state convict lease system and the local chain gang, though not exclusively black, drew heavily upon the African American population. Blacks in Atlanta, like their peers around the state, found themselves arrested for minor charges of "vagrancy," petty theft, or assault, then tried, convicted, and sentenced to heavy jail terms. Alex Lichtenstein observed that "Georgia was known for its lengthy prison sentences."[6] Historian Matthew Mancini is more emphatic, noting that the length of jail terms for the same level of crime escalated considerably over the course of the lifetime of the convict lease system, with a life sentence becoming the most common. The number of African Americans arrested in Atlanta was disproportionate to their percentage of the population. Of the more than 150,000 arrests made in the city in the ten years preceding the riot, in excess of 80,000 were of blacks. Black men aged fifteen to thirty represented the lion's share, though the number of black children under the age fifteen arrested increased tremendously after 1900—more than a thousand in 1904, four times the number of children arrested seven years before. Disorderly conduct and drunkenness, "suspicion," and idling were the most common causes of arrest. Most arrests in the city resulted in the assignment of fines rather than jail time, but low-status blacks were often incarcerated because they were unable to pay the fines.[7]

The myth of the menacing black vagrant was tied to whites' belief in their "legitimate right to command Negro labor."[8] Convict lease and other forms of forced labor were natural outgrowths of white racial stereotypes about black "fitness" for slavery. Yet as Lichtenstein notes, "Unlike antebellum slaveholders, however, postwar beneficiaries of the convict lease had no 'way of life' bound up with dependence on convicts, no particular commitment to forced labor, other than that of the capitalist's balance sheet of investment, production and profit." Whether on not one accepts arguments about paternalism, reciprocity, and loyalty on the part of slaveowners in the antebellum slave system, it is clear that whites in the postemancipation era, who had neither a substantial financial investment nor a "social" connection to black convicts, had even less reason to care for forced laborers than they had had for caring for their slaves.[9] The consequences of this new reality were the brutal treatment, abuse, and often death of black convict laborers.

Southern lawmakers incorporated vagrancy laws into the black codes that were established in most states at the close of the Civil War and then struck down by the 1866 Civil Rights Act. Variations on those laws were restored after the Democratic "redemption" of the former Confederate states. Policemen regularly harassed black men who gathered in public places; those who could not prove employment (and sometimes those who could) faced arrest and assignment to the chain gang. Thousands of black Georgians were forced into this system of pseudoslavery. The city of Atlanta used such forced labor to lay and repair roads at little cost to municipal government.

The level of arrests and the accompanying violent treatment by city police outraged Black Atlantans. Black journalists condemned convict lease, the chain gang, and police brutality. A. P. Nella, black columnist for the *Atlanta*

Independent, wrote of the anguish and frustration he experienced while watching black men paraded through the streets of Atlanta, shuffling along with the peculiar gait that was a product of ankle chains. "Under the very shadow of Atlanta University may be seen during any week day[,] digging away[,] a half hundred Negroes in chains and stripes. We never pass them but that our sense of pride is made to trail in the dust. Our streets and highways must be kept in repair, but it is anything but a pleasing spectacle to respectable black people to see it done after this manner by blacks exclusively."[10]

Columnist Nella went on to ponder the effectiveness of the black elite efforts to secure "the right of franchise" or uplift the image of the race in the face of legions of black men in leg irons in the streets of the city. Nella was, no doubt, aware that the city did not reallocate the savings made by exploiting imprisoned black labor for the construction and maintenance of roads into efforts to ameliorate the living conditions in black areas of Atlanta by addressing the lack of sidewalks or, more critically, open sewers.[11]

Members of the black elite, whose criticisms of the system fell on deaf ears, attempted to address the issue of convict labor by reducing the number of black arrests. Though they were unsuccessful in their efforts, African American residents organized and petitioned the city for black police officers from the mid-1860s through the turn of the century. Petitioners, believing that black policemen would be less likely to engage in acts of brutality or arrest members of the community without due cause, attempted to use the logic of Jim Crow in their request. Addressing the white community, African Americans argued that black officers, who shared the culture of the residents, would be better suited to police African American neighborhoods. Undoubtedly, members of the black elite also hoped that black police officers would be better able to recognize status distinctions within the community, thereby reducing the chances of elites suffering the indignities associated with police harassment.

Jim Crow segregation in Atlanta proceeded apace in the last decade of the nineteenth and first decade of the twentieth century. A new city in the old South, Atlanta had neither de jure segregation nor traditional patterns of housing segregation prior to the war. However, as the period progressed, and the black population of the city continued to expand, new patterns of social exclusion based upon race developed. The black population in the city grew from roughly nine thousand in 1880 to thirty-five thousand by the turn of the century. This growth put pressure on the black neighborhoods of Summerhill, Shermantown, Jenningstown and Mechanicsville as there was increased competition for housing. Though the city would not pass the first residential segregation law until seven years after the riot, population pressures, exorbitant rents, and segregationist attitudes saw working-class blacks pushed to the outskirts (excluding the northern borders) of the city.[12] In addition, de facto segregation denied blacks access to local public parks and libraries, hotels, and white-owned restaurants. Racial segregation of the state's transportation system was instated after the passage of Jim Crow legislation in 1891. Local streetcar companies implemented racially restrictive policies that met with resistance from the black community at various times over the course of the following fifteen years. High-status black women participated in an 1896 boycott of the Atlanta Traction Railroad to protest Jim Crow policies. Similarly, Henry McNeal Turner agitated for a black boycott of the city's streetcars "after the city council passed an ordinance that colored people should take back seats and let the white people occupy the front seats." Wrongly attacked by *Atlanta Independent* editor Ben Davis in the January 23, 1904, edition of the paper for "breaking the streetcar boycott," Turner fired back in a letter, published in the paper on February 6, 1904. Noting that he had been unsuccessful in convincing fellow blacks in attendance at a meeting at the Central Avenue ME Church to participate in a general boycott of the streetcar line, Turner reported returning his newly purchased horse and reconciling himself to riding "just where the white man tells me."[13] Despite Rev. Turner's experience, boycott would remain a tool of black resistance throughout the Jim Crow era.

The spread of Jim Crow policies in Atlanta was attached to the supposition of black inferiority and the need to control black behavior in freedom. Arguments about black inferiority were layered over commentary concerning the "morally inadequate" black raised by the 1880s prohibition battles. The ideology of the immoral/criminal black did not disappear as African Americans struggled with Jim Crow exclusion or issues of arrest and police violence in the 1890s and 1900s. Indeed, arguments about black vice and depravity were imbedded in the racial justifications for vagrancy laws that undergirded the system of convict lease. Old tensions concerning the link between black immorality, black voting rights, and political corruption were revived and highlighted as part of the racially charged 1906 gubernatorial race. *Atlanta Constitution* editor Clark Howell and career politician Hoke Smith waged campaigns that utilized hatred and fear of the political, social, and economic presence of blacks. Both candidates asserted their desire to curb the "nigger threat" to southern (i.e., white) society, which was manifest in black access to the political process and black "pretensions" to social equality.[14]

Lawyer, journalist, and reform candidate Hoke Smith began the battle for governor with the hope of curtailing the influence of corporations and monopolies—specifically railroads—in the political life of the state. A solid Democrat, he was selected to serve as Secretary of the Interior (1893–96) in the administration of Grover Cleveland during his second term as president. Smith, with the aid of his newspaper, the *Atlanta Journal,* approached the gubernatorial race highlighting the need to purge state politics of corrupting influences. The decision to include black political participation in that category was, as argued by Michael Perman, a result of Smith's relationship with white supremacist Thomas W. Hardwick and Populist Tom Watson.[15] Watson, who had faced the crushing defeat of the Populist Party, joined forces with Thomas W. Hardwick to support Smith's run for governor (despite their ideological differences), having become convinced that Smith was the most viable candidate. Watson shared Hardwick's vision that the well-being of southern society required the formal disfranchisement of the black population. As early as 1892, Tom Watson had moved away from what had been the Populist Party's commitment to a biracial alliance between working-class blacks and whites. Arguing that the defeat of the party was tied to the presence of black voters, specifically that Populist involvement with blacks had left the party open to accusations of race disloyalty and deterred whites from voting for Populist candidates, Watson began to campaign for the exclusion of African Americans from the body politic.[16] Smith, who was well aware of the power of the racial stereotype, agreed in exchange for Watson's support to spearhead a campaign for the elimination of the black vote. Reviving old charges of black political corruption based on rumors of African Americans selling their votes for rum or money, Smith challenged white voters to eliminate the black vote. Black disfranchisement, argued Smith, would remove the threat of "Negro domination" and "corruption" from the state of Georgia and leave the political field open to its rightful players: white males.

Clark Howell challenged Smith's proposed policy by arguing that additional disfranchisement measures were unnecessary, and would more importantly also limit white males' access to the vote. Using his own paper as a bully pulpit, Howell stressed the fact that existing methods—the Democratic white primary and the poll tax—both sufficiently limited the voting strength of African Americans. He deflected charges from the Smith/Watson camp that he was soft in his white supremacism by calling his opponent's own race loyalty into question. By joining forces with Watson, charged Howell, Smith risked fracturing the Democratic Party, *the* white man's party in the south. For extra measure, Howell also used the pages of the *Atlanta Constitution* to expose past political dealings between the newly minted "radical" Smith and black activists.[17]

Smith and Howell worked to "outnigger" each other in campaign rhetoric once race had been overtly introduced to the contest. Howell worked to keep Smith's history of interracial political cooperation before the voters. On the defensive, Smith intensified the racist rhetoric of his campaign, highlighting white fears about black "regression into barbarism." Enfranchising the naturally inferior black had been a tragic mistake, argued Smith. "Bad niggers," no longer under the control of the slave master's lash, were wandering vagrants who frequented bars and were the cause of the South's growing problem with crime. Equally as problematic were educated "uppity" blacks who provided direct competition to white workers. Disfranchisement, therefore, was a necessary step in reasserting control over this unstable and dangerous population. Smith urged voters to consider the alternatives to exterminating the black vote: "Shall it be ballots now or bullets later?"[18]

Hoke Smith won the August 1906 gubernatorial race by a wide margin. The campaign's racially charged rhetoric had generated fear and anger in the white population, and white Georgians had been easily convinced of the need to control and "purify" the political process through the elimination of blacks. Smith made good on his campaign promises, acting on issues of reform during his term. In the spirit of reform, Smith provided Georgians, especially African Americans, with an unqualified good by ending the state's convict lease system. Unfortunately, Smith also acted on his promise to limit black political participation. Smith, negotiating with white legislators who were anxious about the possibility of inadvertently disfranchising poor whites along with blacks, was engaged in shepherding the proposed Felder-Williams amendment to the state constitution for two years. The amendment was finally ratified in October 1908 in the state election.[19]

Blacks across the state and in Atlanta had rallied in an effort to defeat the 1908 amendment. Just as they had organized in 1866, blacks organized in 1907, forming the Georgia Suffrage League, to combat yet another effort to deprive them of their political rights. Henry Proctor, Alonzo Herndon and John Hope lobbied the state legislature to stop their deliberations. Journalist Ben Davis and others urged all eligible African Americans to register so that they might vote to protect their rights. Thousands of black voters who might have registered did not—this no doubt owed to the climate of fear that had been created as well as to the economic burden of the cumulative poll tax. And the success of the 1908 amendment further reduced the numbers of black voters on the registration rolls in Georgia.[20]

In reality, "Negro domination" was never a threat in Georgia. Reconstruction had been short lived and ineffective and early measures had, as Clark Howell suggested, diluted black voting power. Blacks in the capital city of Atlanta, though slowly rising, remained politically marginalized and were hardly an economic threat to the white population. Despite this reality, whites in Georgia sought an extreme solution to the slim threat blacks posed to white supremacy and found it in the idea of pushing the society backwards to what it had been "prior to the introduction of black suffrage."[21] The *Atlanta Constitution* (Howell's paper) and Smith's *Atlanta Journal* had repeatedly sounded the alarm during the campaign. These papers, along with the *Atlanta News* and

Atlanta Georgian, had focused attention on Atlanta's allegedly large population of black "vagrants" who frequented "dives" and terrorized the city's law-abiding white population.

In the spring and summer of 1906, "dives" were the second issue taken up in the newspapers' diatribes concerning the threat of black "brutes" after the issue of black vagrancy. The presence of "nudes" (suggestive depictions of white women common in saloon "art" in the late nineteenth and early twentieth century) on the walls and on liquor bottles, it was asserted, augmented the danger posed by dives. Lurid portraits of white women, according to the racist logic of whites, easily inflamed drunken "low-life" blacks. The power of drink, combined with the images of white women, allegedly drove black men, scarcely removed from the wilds of Africa, to acts of beastly savagery. Proof of the truth of these startling allegations was found, so the papers claimed, in the series of "rapes" and "sexually motivated assaults" upon innocent white women in the city and surrounding areas.

Atlanta newspapers covered several cases of alleged rape or sexual assault by black males between April and September 1906.[22] "The Reign of Terror" and "The Way to Save our Women," two editorial series printed in August 1906 by the *Atlanta Georgian,* detailed the vulnerability of southern white women and the viciousness of their black attackers. (Attacks involving white males were not similarly highlighted in either paper.) The stories were very descriptive, with no consideration given to the privacy of the supposed victims. Reports of such assaults were placed in the context of the continued discussion concerning black criminality and patronage of local dives. The editor of the *Georgian* demanded that black elites concentrate less on supposed racial injustice and more on controlling black riffraff.[23]

The concern over danger and lawlessness of the "lower sorts of Negro" in the city prompted local white leaders to political action. The *Atlanta Constitution* reported on a "Meeting of Citizens to Suppress Crime" that took place on September 1, 1906. A group of "the best known and most influential citizens of Atlanta" met at the YMCA to present to the public and the press a resolution aimed at curtailing future repetitions of "outrages recently committed by negroes in the country in which white women were assaulted." The paper printed the resolution, which was to be presented to the city council, in full, along with significant editorial commentary from white men involved in the citizens' council. The resolution contained the "severest condemnation" of black assaults upon white women and demanded speedy enforcement of the law, the "summary breaking up of all low dives in the city," and an increase in the size of the city police force. The council recommended that "tramps and vagabonds" be driven from the community by legitimate police authorities. The resolution rejected the idea of the formation of "any white cap organization or Klan, like or similar to the Ku Klux Klan," to deal with black violence; the council objected to such organizations not on moral principle but on the grounds that "such organizations cannot be controlled."[24] Plans were made to pursue the issue of separate trolley cars for black and white passengers with the Georgia Electric Light and Power Company.

Some five hundred Atlantans signed the resolution of the citizens' council. District Court Judge George Hillyer, *Atlanta News* editor Charles Daniel, Rev. J. H. Eakes, City Councilman E. W. Martin, W. H. Kreigshaber, Captain W. D. Ellis, and other business and church leaders were members of the council and signatories. Even F. L. Seely, publisher of the sensationalist *Atlanta Georgian*, signed the rather mildly worded document.[25]

African American community leaders responded to the media-driven frenzy. Black ministers who had previously denounced the sin of alcohol consumption once again joined whites in condemning dives, pool halls, and gambling dens. Educators, businessmen, and political activists held meetings at local churches to express their desire to rid the city of such places. High-status blacks expressed their disapproval of assaults against white women, emphasizing the low status and moral character of the alleged perpetrators. The members of the "better class" in the race stressed their desire to live as "law-abiding citizens" in peace and harmony with the city's white population. They were also quick to reassure all concerned that they had no pretensions to social equality. The black elite understood that the entire race was being indicted for the actions of a few. They expressed anxiety about and fear of white retribution. They also expressed a sense of responsibility toward the black lower class.

A letter to the editor printed in the *Atlanta Constitution* demonstrates the attitudes of the black elite. G. A. Ballard, Clark University graduate and then teacher at the Teacher Cookman Institute in Jacksonville, Florida, assuming that the newspaper reports were all true, began by condemning, as did "other law-abiding members of my race," the rash of assaults in the city. Noting that the "class of brutes" who had committed such acts of violence against white women had little education and failed to attend church regularly, Ballard argued that during his schooling at Clark he had never been taught "social equality or race domination." Instead, he had learned the "righteous principles" of honesty and race uplift through education. Ballard closed by expressing his belief in the "law-abiding white man" who would "stick by and protect the faithful and law-abiding negro." He also voiced his hope that the entire black race not be painted with the same brush and that "the young be given proper instructions, and the hardened criminals be put where they will not affect human society."[26]

AME church officials also wrote the *Constitution* to express their concerns and to suggest plans of action. L. A. Townsley, former pastor of St. Paul's AME and then elder in the Griffin district, suggested the establishment of a vigilance committee composed of "law-abiding citizens, preachers, and teachers" who would "clean up and close up every den and dive and whiskey shop and beer saloon in the city." Townsley argued that a squad of black undercover officers would allow the police department to better apprehend "the negro loafing and gambling element." He also endorsed the white citizens' council recommendation of segregated streetcars, noting that "the present system is breeding each day much bitterness which could be avoided."[27]

The Antioch AME Church of Decatur penned an open letter to the "white citizens of DeKalb and Fulton Counties" in which Rev. J. G. Robinson rejected the implied accusation of Sheriff Nelms concerning black criminals finding refuge within the community.[28] Robinson asserted, to the contrary, that "under no circumstances would we shield, or sympathize with, the perpetrators of these hellish deeds . . . that we do not give shelter nor bread to suspicious characters and further, that we notify officers of the law of the whereabouts of any suspicious characters." Robinson acknowledged "too much crime amongst us as a people" but also condemned the white media's agitation and the failure of whites to distinguish between the "criminal element" of the race and those African Americans with a sound "family life and home-loving habits."[29]

Baptist preachers, too, weighed in on the issues. Pastors of the six largest black Baptist churches in the city—E. R. Carter of Friendship Baptist Church, Peter James Bryant of Wheat Street, H. R. Harrison of Frazier Street, E. P. Johnson of Reed Street (and president of the Evangelical Ministers' Union), W. W. Floyd of Zion Hill, and A. P. Dunbar of Mount Olive—all signed an open letter to "fair-minded white people of Atlanta and vicinity," which was printed in the *Atlanta Independent* on September 22, 1906. Like other such public letters, the declaration from the Baptists drew attention to the distinction between "Negro preachers, teachers and editors" and "vicious rounders, loafers and grossly ignorant" criminals. The former were "humiliated by and disgraced because of the recent fiendish and inexcusable outbreaks." In contrast, the latter "do not read our papers, do not and have not attended our churches and schools, but frequent the barrooms, poolrooms, gambling dens, dives and restaurants," where they [take] "lessons in bestiality, criminality and deviltry and have their unbridled passions stirred by mean liquor." The ministers urged the closure of restaurants, especially those along Decatur, Ivy, and Peter Streets, noting that they were "barroom annexes . . . for colored women to gather and drink." The group called attention to their efforts to provide a home for wayward youths and their attempts at ridding their communities, especially the fourth ward, of "questionable places." The Baptists closed their letter by placing themselves firmly in the "law and order brigade of this community, first, last and forever."

Rev. Proctor also joined the clamor concerning dives and the lower classes. Speaking on the eve of the National Negro Business League Conference being held at Bethel AME, he condemned the continued existence of dives in the city. Proctor's speech, titled "The Dives Must Go!," stressed the sin and criminality inherent in the low-class dives and saloons of the city and demanded that the city close up such places, thereby ensuring the public safety of all citizens.[30] He had addressed the white public on these issues earlier in September in an open letter to the *Atlanta Georgian.* He too had drawn a line between low-status blacks, who lacked proper moral training, and community leaders. Proctor concluded that the bad influence of dance halls, liquor, and poolrooms, combined with unemployment, created the black criminal. The answer, then, was to enforce vagrancy laws and eradicate the centers of vice from the community.[31]

Black newspaper editor Benjamin Davis offered commentary on the issue of crime, vices, and dives as well. He stressed the importance of stamping out "lawlessness" as a prelude to full acceptance into southern society. Davis shared with other high-status community activists the belief that dives, dance halls, and clubs were the "cess pools that breed criminals." He urged black ministers and teachers to go into the tenderloin district of the city and clean up such establishments rather than preach to the converted on Sunday mornings. Davis went so far as to suggest a curfew to "clear the streets of women and children not employed after 9 P.M."[32]

The *Atlanta Independent,* did not, however, place all responsibility for vice on the shoulders of low-status blacks. Davis reminded Black Atlantans that "the city council absolutely refuses to sell a man of color a license to run a bar." Dives, barrooms, and clubs existed, and "the mean and poison liquor" was available, because "white men" received licenses "to open rendezvous and asylums for the idle and criminal." Davis noted that "a bar was a legitimate business concern . . . no more harm for a Negro man to walk into . . . than it is for a white man." The crime lay in the willingness of licensed white vendors to "sell minors whiskey, operate a joint in connection with the bar proper or dispense beer and whiskey to disreputable women and keep their joints packed with idlers all day." Davis urged African Americans to begin a letter-writing campaign to convince the city's police force to close the "pools of immorality now existing and operating in the city."[33] Davis joined others of the black community in trying to make clear the distinction between the members of the black elite (and for that matter, all law-abiding black citizens of Atlanta) and the few reckless individuals whose actions provoked violent response from whites. Yet he did not lose sight of white responsibility in creating the circumstances prevailing in the black community.

Ministers, teachers, and editors alike may have had hopes that whites would recognize divisions of status and accomplishment among Atlanta's blacks, but their idealism and optimism were misplaced. As 1906 advanced, it became increasingly clear that the entire black community would suffer for the actions of a few, and that when racial hatred erupted in the city, it would, as in East Point, be violent and indiscriminate.

The public discourse concerning black crime and dives continued in the press. The *Constitution* added its own particular touch of humor to the discussion in a series of cartoons that appeared in the paper under the title "Police Matinee—Pen Shots" written and drawn by Gordon Noel Hurtel. The cartoons showed gross caricatures of African Americans and were written in a supposed black dialect. Black vagrants and washerwomen were targeted as ignorant objects of humor. The *Atlanta News* carried forward the conversation on a much more deadly note, calling in late August for the formation of a White Protective League. The paper urged white men in Fulton County to come together to protect white womanhood from black attackers, suggesting that a thousand men serve as citizens' auxiliary to the local police force. League members would patrol the city and surrounding area, ready to defend white civilization against black criminality. The paper thus prepared the city's white population for direct, violent action, if need be, in response to black crime.[34]

The *News*, the *Constitution*, and the *Georgian* all took part in a discussion aimed at the political and social control of the black population in the city of Atlanta. The 1906 electoral campaign was based in large part on hatred and fear of African American participation in the body politic as full citizens. Part of a discourse of violence in a spectrum that encompassed employment discrimination and exclusion at one end and lynching and riot at the other, the media and white civic leaders stoked the fire of racial and sexual tensions, preparing the city for the conflagration that would follow. While the outside world was shocked by the disorder in this "model" New South city, the violence and destruction of the 1906 riot were the predictable conclusion to two decades of hate mongering.

The riot unfolded in a violent two-act drama. White assault upon African Americans and their property began Saturday evening, September 22. The local white population, tense and primed by the ongoing rhetoric concerning prohibition, disenfranchisement, and attacks on white women, was pushed over the edge by the evening editions of the *Atlanta Constitution* and the *Atlanta News*. "Father Begged to Settle Case with Negro" was the front-page headline in the *Constitution*. The two-column article reported with great detail and pathos the courtroom drama of distraught father Thomas L. Bryan, whose daughter, Miss Orrie Bryan, had been the victim of attempted assault by a black man,

"Playing Perlice," "Charlie's Change," and "Darktown Cherubs." These racially stereotyped images mocked black "vagrants," washerwomen, and the black community's wish for black policemen. ("Police Matinee: Pen Shots," cartoon by Gordon Noel Hustel, *Atlanta Constitution*, 2 September 1906.)

Luther Farzier. Speaking "with a tone in his voice and a look in his eye that made the recorder and all others in the courtroom understand [his] terrible earnest," Bryan asked that he be allowed with "only these hands and fingers that God gave me . . . [to] settle this case in a few minutes."[35]

This news story and others of its kind, along with the series of five extras run by the *Atlanta News* and disseminated through the city by newsboys, were the final catalyst for the riot. Around 9:00 P.M., a crowd of whites began chasing black men through the streets of the city and beating them senseless . The crowd grew into a mob of over a hundred and fanned out, up Decatur, Broad, Forsyth, Fair, and Marietta Streets and up Pryor and along Peachtree toward Church Street.

The dives, the supposed cause of black criminality, were relatively unscathed by mob action. Only one saloon, Campbell and Poole on Broad Street, was entered and destroyed during the riot. The mob focused its attention instead upon the destruction of black-owned businesses.[36] Toward that end, rioters threw bricks and stones through the windows of businesses along Marietta and Forsyth Streets. Alonzo Herndon's Peachtree barbershop was entered and pillaged by the mob. Two other black barbers working in their shop across from the federal building were beaten and killed, their bodies dragged outside and stripped, and the shop destroyed.[37]

Local officials did not sound the alarm bell until midnight, at which point the riot in the central business district was in full swing. Consequently, Georgia Electric Light and Power had not stopped its evening trolley service, and more than a half a dozen blacks were beaten and injured as their trolley car, traveling through the central business district, were attacked by angry mobs of white men, shouting "Save our women!" and "Kill the niggers!" An African American woman aboard the trolley "fought like a savage wildcat with an umbrella," and another fended off her attackers with a hatpin. Local police and the trolley conductor managed to get the car away from the crowd, but not before three black male passengers had been beaten to death. The attacks on trolley cars continued until the transportation company discontinued service several hours later.[38]

The growing crowd raided and emptied a pawnshop and hardware store along Peters Street. Now armed with looted knives, guns, metal rods, and wooden planks, the mob was even more dangerous and unruly. Mayor James Woodward ordered fire hoses turned against the crowd, a tactic that had little impact. Sheriff Jennings was attacked by the crowd, as were other white citizens who counseled calm and order. Ultimately, nature succeeded where man could not; heavy rain around 2:00 A.M. helped the local police force clear the streets well before dawn.[39]

The mob rested on Sunday, providing an interlude in the action. The arrival of the Fifth Regiment of the state militia encouraged white rioters to remain indoors. Blacks who had not taken shelter at home were rousted by local and state police and arrested. The dives were raided and all "idle negroes" were "corralled." Most of the city's black population was not on the streets; however, African Americans in the ravaged Darktown and in the East Side area spent Sunday smuggling guns into their neighborhoods and working on plans for defense. On Sunday and Monday evenings residents of Darktown doused their streetlights, armed themselves, and waited for the return of the mob. Blacks in this area allegedly fired on trolley cars passing through their neighborhood Sunday evening. Young Walter White, who lived with his family in the Darktown area, recalled the riot in his autobiography written years later. He highlighted the lingering fear and apprehension in the days following the mob's visit to his neighborhood.[40]

Black college professors and administrators armed themselves and patrolled the grounds of Morehouse and Spelman. Other men from the West Side ordered their wives and children to the safety of the brick walls of the colleges while they remained at home, armed and waiting.[41] But the mob neither returned to Darktown, nor ventured to the black men's and women's colleges. Instead, in a move chillingly reminiscent of the East Point incident, a company of nine county officers and two civilians journeyed to a community south of Atlanta known as Brownsville to disrupt an "incendiary meeting" and to disarm blacks rumored to be plotting revenge against whites in the city.

Blacks in Brownsville had anticipated the worst and were in fact armed to defend themselves. Hundreds of blacks had fled central Atlanta and sought sanctuary in this prosperous black neighborhood that was home to Clark University and Gammon Theological Seminary. White officers advanced on Brownsville after dark, arresting any armed blacks they encountered on the streets. Blacks, either unable to distinguish the arresting officers from the anticipated "mob" or perhaps more realistically anticipating the sort of violent police action demonstrated in 1889 in the aftermath of the Powell lynching, opened fire. Officer Jim Heard was killed in the first exchange of gunfire. Retreating, the policemen left Brownsville with their prisoners. Two black men were shot to death in the process.[42] The mayor imposed martial law and state militiamen placed Brownsville under watch the next morning. Soldiers invaded homes and schools under the pretext of searching for weapons. Three black men were killed during this search; a fourth was killed the next day en route to his place of employment.[43]

The rioting was over by Tuesday morning. Five of the twelve companies of militia were dismissed from the city. The city's newspapers reported between fifteen and forty African Americans killed, although in fact the number was much smaller. The city coroner reported the official death toll as twelve people: ten blacks and two whites.[44] Thousands of dollars' worth of property had been damaged or destroyed. Yet, with amazing rapidity, the city began to restore order. The Fulton County Grand Jury enjoined the press from publishing "all sensational and inflammatory new matter . . . in short, to use conservatism and discretion in the treatment of all facts relating to the conditions now confronting us." Both the black and the white press were soon calling for a return to harmony. Conservative white elites, who had tolerated rabid racial dialogue in the weeks prior to the riot, now engaged in a paternalistic discourse on the need to take care of the *"good negro,"* as opposed to the vagrant. Black elites joined them in an equally paternalistic discourse on the need for sobriety and industry among the black lower class.

The question of prohibition was once again raised in the aftermath of the riot. Local dives, saloons, poolrooms, and dance halls were closed. The city council passed an ordinance revoking licenses of all such establishments until October 1, 1906. Licenses were then reissued with the understanding that establishments serving alcoholic beverages should exclude black customers; those establishments that continued to serve alcohol to African Americans would be closed immediately.[45] The city also continued its ban on granting liquor licenses to blacks.

Militiamen at rest, Atlanta, 1906. Inset photo: lawmen and private citizens surround a home in Brownsville, 1906. (Courtesy of the Atlanta History Center.)

Local whites, including the editor of the *Constitution,* reminded African Americans of the cause of the violence: crimes against white women. And the media continued their conversation concerning the need for "the better class of blacks" to control black undesirables. The press also called for a cessation of unnecessary provocation and a return to "law and order." Thomas Dixon's play *The Clansman,* scheduled to run in the local playhouse from October 1 to November 3, was canceled to facilitate the fragile racial peace.[46]

The riot also precipitated the development of civic organizations designed to open a dialogue between blacks and whites. Members of the black elite, including Proctor, Herndon, Murphy, and McNeal Turner, requested a meeting with the mayor in the wake of the Brownsville riot. The group was invited to meet with Mayor Woodward, former police commissioner, now Fourth National Bank president, James W. English, and director of the state militia Colonel Clifford L. Anderson.[47] African American leaders met with these officials on Tuesday, September 25, and expressed concerns regarding the violence toward and protection of black citizens. Specifically, black activists reported complaints about police harassment and mistreatment on streetcars.[48]

Later that same day, a meeting attended by a thousand Atlantans denounced the violence of the mob and called upon local police authorities to protect the sanctity of white womanhood and to act swiftly to punish would-be attackers.[49]

The Committee of Ten grew out of this mass meeting. A select group of key figures in Atlanta city politics, the Committee ostensibly ran the city in the immediate aftermath of the riot. The group called for the restoration of harmony and
established a fund to help pay for "the sick and wounded of both races and to
bury the dead."[50] Spokespersons for this group of citizens counseled a return to
work as the ultimate panacea. In the spirit of New South booster Henry Grady,
committee members recommended "the resumption of all business, and urge
that it [sic] be run, even at a loss." Black leaders urged black workers to return
to their places of employment, trying to reassure thousands who had refused to
leave their homes following the weekend of violence. *Independent* editor Benjamin Davis was outrageous in voicing his commitment to work as the cure.
"The Negroes committed no rape in slavery because their masters kept them
busy, and the best preventative now for crimes of all characters . . . is to keep
the Negro busy. If he won't keep busy on his own initiative, make his [sic] stay
busy by force."[51]

African American religious leaders called a second mass meeting at Wheat
Street Baptist Church on September 30, 1906. Black and white ministers, including Peter James Bryant of Wheat Street and Dr. David Marx, rabbi of the He-
brew Benevolent Congregation, addressed their concerns regarding the riot.[52]
This meeting produced the Christian Civic League, a hybrid of the white Gospel
Union directed by W. J. Northern, former governor, and the black Evangelical
Ministers' Union.[53] Members of the latter believed that worship and the practice of fundamental Christian principles would restore positive relations in the
community. Specifically, they argued that weekly prayer meetings held at the
YMCA (Colored) and monthly lectures on the need for obedience to the law
would facilitate the return of harmony.[54]

Also established to ensure understanding between the races was the Atlanta
Civic League. Charles T. Hopkins, white lawyer for Atlanta University, organized the league by invitation. He was careful to specify its nonpolitical nature:
members would encourage peace through moral rather than political means.
Two thousand Atlantans responded to Hopkins' suggestion to form an organization to promote racial harmony in the city. White businessmen, including all
the members of the Committee of Ten and *Atlanta Georgian* editor F. L. Seely,
made up the bulk of the Atlanta Civic League's membership, but the group also
had a "Colored Co-operative" composed of black community leaders. The Colored Co-operative League formalized the pattern of intraracial paternalism and
status distinctions within the black community.

Individual, presumably low-status, African Americans were encouraged to
bring their social and legal concerns to the pastor of their black church. The
pastor would funnel those concerns to the high-status members of the Colored

Co-operative League who would investigate the complaint and then, theoretically, ensure that legitimate concerns received a proper hearing and resolution. These procedures were designed to provide low-status members of the community a collective ombudsman as a potential shield from the great vagaries of the white justice system. By limiting the numbers of blacks who had direct contact with the courts or law enforcement, high-status blacks reduced the opportunity for high-status whites to intervene directly in the black community. The policy revealed both white acceptance of the capriciousness of the judicial system's treatment of low-status African Americans and black desperation in the face of the shredding of their civil rights.[55]

The Atlanta Civic League, the Christian Civic League, the Businessmen's Gospel Union, and the Committee of Ten combined to restore the phoenix city to its previous working order. Black civic leaders identified by whites as "good negroes," ministers, businessmen, and newspapermen were essential to the process of recovery and restoration of order following the riot. The rhetoric of such men suggests, in part, acceptance of black responsibility in the riot. High-status blacks agreed with arguments concerning the danger of black vagrants, low-class dives, alcohol, and sexual assault. Black community leaders came forward time and again to stress the differences between the better classes and the lower classes. Accepting these arguments did not, however, translate into a wholesale capitulation to white paternalism and racism. The experience of the riot confirmed for *all* African Americans the maliciousness of southern racism. The same white elites who stressed the importance of the "good negro" and the need for "law and order" in the aftermath of the riot were in fact responsible for having stirred the white community to violent action.[56] The riot encouraged African Americans to further retreat into their highly stratified social enclaves.

Black civic leaders regularly linked the undesirable aspects of working-class life with the structural conditions that maintained them. Proctor reminded the editor of the *Constitution* that "the criminal element is not so from any inherent reason, but is the inevitable resultant of poverty, ignorance, and vice."[57] Blacks who frequented dives and dance halls were, according to community leaders, most often unemployed, uneducated, and spiritually unredeemed. Their behavior was the result of lack of exposure to the righteous path in life rather than of some innate inferiority. The existence of a criminal class of blacks was not caused by the failure of black elites to control low-status blacks. The failure lay instead in the limited resources of the community. The lack of facilities rather than of effort was at the heart of the matter. Black leaders, such as Proctor and Neighborhood Union founder Lugenia Burns Hope, reassured themselves and white society that if enough additional resources were made available, they could reconstruct the black community in such a way as to severely reduce the black criminal class.[58]

Black elites, in the aftermath of the Atlanta riot, highlighted the efforts they were making to provide for the upliftment of their race, including the establishment of kindergartens, playgrounds, Sunday schools, the YMCA, and a home for "wayward youths." All of these efforts had grown out of commitments and decisions made within the black community. The commitment to interracial cooperation in the wake of the riot, however, allowed blacks to appeal for aid to concerned whites. If, argued black elites, black criminality was a result of improper training, then it was incumbent upon the white community to help blacks provide facilities for better training. If whites were committed in thought to improved racial relations, they could express that commitment in deed by supporting the efforts of elite blacks to build necessary social and religious institutions in the city.

Proctor, who had established a pattern of appealing to whites for contributions to First Congregational Church well before the riot, expanded his appeals at each Tuesday meeting of the Christian Civic League. He asked for contributions to pay the mortgages of the colored YMCA building and the new church building for First Congregational. Similarly, E. R. Carter appealed to white elites in the city for contributions to the Baptist Center for Wayward Youths and sought the governor's endorsement for his efforts to uplift his race.

The strategy had its limits. It was effective only so long as whites were convinced that their acts of noblesse oblige were not too costly, economically or socially. Blacks were not able to parlay appeals to white responsibility into more public schools or even more teachers for their children. The Atlanta public school system was unwilling to provide increased support for African American children, despite the persistent rhetoric concerning the link between ignorance and the development of a criminal class.

The actions of black civic leaders immediately after the riot (and as late as the 1908 Clifton Conference) suggest that they were unwilling to absorb or else slow to recognize the deeper messages of the riot. Rising levels of achievement, of uplift, visible in the black community did not reassure whites in the city. On the contrary, an upwardly mobile black community that agitated for civil liberties and equal access was resented and perceived as a threat by local whites. Even before the riot, all blacks had been subject to harassment on the streetcars and first social, then legal, segregation in public spaces. During the violence, the white mob, if not the elite whites who had encouraged them, had been unwilling to distinguish between the black elite, the "good negroes," and the lower classes or "dangerous negroes"; Darktown and Brownsville had both been attacked. Both a small black-owned barbershop and the plush shop belonging to Alonzo Herndon were damaged in the lawlessness of September 1906.

The 1906 riot exposed the conflicts inherent in the uplift model. Black political activists and civic leaders were confronted with the limits of their power and the ineffectiveness of the uplift strategy. They had committed themselves to working with "the better class of whites" for the improvement of race relations. Black leadership had joined whites in their attacks on "low-class" blacks, and continued after the riot to lecture the black working class about proper values, morals, and lifestyle. But they could no longer, postriot, be comforted by the rhetoric of their white peers. Despite the interracial dialogue that blossomed on the heels of the violence, few members of the black elite could completely forget the political betrayal of white leadership following the prohibition battles of the 1880s, the violence of 1889, the increasing Jim Crow segregation in employment and social services, and the political campaigns of 1905–6. Regardless of the potent appeal of the idea of a class hierarchy, the riot revealed that race was the definitive mark of division in the New South.

The Atlanta riot had a transforming effect on the black community. The limited degree of interracial détente and cooperation that followed on the heels of it could not supersede the intraracial efforts of the black community. In the wake of the riot, African Americans focused even more on developing their own resources, driven to build their own institutions and find social satisfaction in their own circle. Though it had been made clear that once white mob violence was unleashed, it struck out with little recognition of distinctions of class and respectability, the gap between the black working class and the black elite nonetheless became ever wider in the postriot era. Educated, high-status blacks and their illiterate, low-status peers recognized that life inside their racial circle had become increasingly stratified. Black communalities—commitment to church, social clubs, education for their children, and even the fading hope for the rights of citizenship—remained but the two groups had fewer spaces of direct contact in which to investigate or actualize experiences of shared identity.

EPILOGUE

The 1919 departure of Henry Hugh Proctor from the pulpit of First Congregational Church is illustrative of the changes within the city and the disenchantment of those who had previously placed their hopes for progress in the hands of the black community's "best sort." Proctor, who had been one of the most outspoken proponents of the politics of respectability and uplift, who had worked tirelessly at fund-raising and championing interracial cooperation to "bring peace to the tortured city," resigned his position. Proctor had expanded upon his domestic work of racial reconciliation, going on to serve as an Army chaplain overseas during World War I. Although he returned to Atlanta after the war, in the fall of 1919 he answered the call of Nazarene Congregational Church in Brooklyn, New York and left the South forever.

Proctor's intended departure caused a sensation in the city. Mayor J. L. Key wrote First Congregational Church arguing that the congregation "should not permit" the relocation of its pastor. James Morton, executive secretary of the Committee on Church Co-operation, also protested the move. "With full sense of the importance of your work in the past, and of the increased demand for calm and courageous leadership at this time, we feel impelled to express the hope that you may be led to remain in Atlanta." By December, Clark Howell, editor of the *Atlanta Constitution,* was more resigned to Proctor's move. In a letter to the city editor of the Brooklyn paper, *The Eagle,* Howell extolled Proctor's "conservative" counsel, describing him as "a tower of strength to his race, a splendid citizen of Atlanta" who "leaves here with the friendship and confidence of not only his race but of the white people of the city."[1]

Black Atlantans too were distressed at the impending departure. The members of the executive committee of the Carrie Steele Orphanage, Henry A. Rucker, E. H. Oliver, and R. H. Singleton, wrote of their "regret" at Proctor's decision and praised him as a "staunch friend and most loyal supporter." E. M. Martin Jr. of the Atlanta Mutual Insurance Company likewise regretted Proctor's departure but also "rejoiced, for a mind so great as yours should not be circumscribed or confined to a small territory but should be national and international in its functionings [sic], for the needs of the world are incessant and great and yours is the master-mind."[2]

For his part, the good reverend argued that he was not forsaking the Southland; rather, he could do more for his "people in the North than in the South." Neither was he abandoning his belief in interracial cooperation, for "the black man and the white are contrasts, not contraries; complementary opposites, not

irreconcilable opponents. Their interests are identical, their destinies insepara-
ble." Instead his plan was simply to move his efforts north to "New York, the
United States in miniature," where he would have "the opportunity of working
out on *American soil* the new ideal of brotherhood in black and white"[3] (emphasis added.)

The pastor was not the first black man who returned from foreign shores
only to find he could no longer reconcile black patriotism with white racism.
African American men had hoped that bravery and sacrifice on the battlefield
would translate to equality and opportunity at home. They came home, strid-
ing proudly in their uniforms, men and American citizens in the fullest sense,
expecting some reward for their efforts. They were quickly disillusioned by the
discrimination and violence that greeted them. Certainly the city of Atlanta,
which had imposed work or fight laws on African Americans, had no interest
in entertaining discussions of social equality with black veterans.[4]

Proctor's departure from Atlanta was connected to the disillusionment
shared by many black veterans who left the South for more progressive climes.
Yet, I would argue, there was additional motivation for Proctor's move. World
War I, the great conflagration that marked the end of innocence for many
Americans, marked, for Henry Hugh Proctor, the end of the illusion of racial
uplift through interracial cooperation with white elites in the South, the end of
optimistic hopes that Atlanta's whites, or at least the "best sort" among them,
would recognize, applaud, and support the achievements of Black Atlantans.
As the preceding chapters have documented in detail, Proctor had worked long
and hard in the days both before and after the riot to win the support of the
white elite in building understanding and cooperation between the races.

He had not, as he himself argued in "The Dawn of a New Day," the last chapter of his memoir *Between Black and White*, abandoned his ideals of cooperative
love or brotherhood. But he was abandoning a place that held on to "old delu-
sions," including "the idea that one race may be down," and "another may be
up." After twenty-five years at First Congregational Church, struggling to uplift
his black brothers while his white ones demurred or ignored his efforts, Proctor
was convinced his ideas could not bear fruit in southern soil. The work of uplift
could move forward only if whites made room for black progress. Proctor, and
many of his status group, had been slow in coming to that understanding in
the aftermath of the riot. But in the face of the heroic sacrifices of the war, and
the postwar lynching of black men who were still in military uniform, many of
Atlanta's black elite were forced to the conclusion that entrenched racism was
an insurmountable barrier to black progress in the American South, including
the Gate City.

The community building efforts of African Americans in Atlanta in the first decades of freedom reflect a powerful desire to reorder their world, to craft their vision of liberty and society, but through their own raced understandings. For, as Lawrence Levine notes, "there was desire for things the whites possessed— freedom, power, mobility, luxuries," yet these were to be obtained by Black Atlantans embracing their own ideas of progress, rather than merely following white teachers, social reformers, and politicians.[5] They were confident that by working together, they would be able to build a strong and free community based on a common history and a shared vision of the future.

The combination of black status competition, the black desire for economic development, and white repression enabled mainstream culture to infiltrate and influence the African American community in Atlanta. Education played an important role in this process. Financial access to industrial and liberal arts education in Atlanta was the springboard for the economic and social mobility of some African Americans. Assimilation of mainstream values was a logical if not entirely predictable response to hegemony. Yet no system of hegemony is total. African Americans exiting slavery in 1865 did not leave behind the cultural traditions and values learned in bondage. They sought to build social systems based on their own belief systems. The values of community, including a sense of racial solidarity, survived the transition from slavery to freedom.

While class did not markedly stratify early Black Atlanta, the community became increasingly differentiated by status. Status conventions determined points of affiliation within the community. African Americans made choices about the groups they joined and the functions they attended, at least in part, on the basis of status. Status tensions were exacerbated as the community developed economically. Economic growth provided some improved job opportunities and necessary physical development in the black community. Expanding interaction with the market and corresponding growth of personal wealth gave African Americans pursuing high social status the economic leverage to improve their station. Over time, this process produced distinct class divisions in the black community, magnifying points of difference and minimizing, but not entirely eliminating, points of communality. Fraternal lodges, social clubs, and churches remained places of social diversity where some high-status and "lower-class" blacks mingled. At the same time, economic and cultural development nurtured seeds of division within the black community. The process began to accelerate in Atlanta in the last decade of the nineteenth century. By the end of the first decade of the new century, class was an increasingly divisive factor.

Negative attitudes and behavior of whites further intensified the energy of division within the black community. Whites in post–Civil War Atlanta focused their efforts on the control and containment of the African American population. They blocked full access to the political process, to education, and to economic advancement. White elites also recognized the growing status divisions and hierarchy within the black community. Highlighting these divisions, white elites cultivated a paternalistic attitude towards the black working class in the black elite as part of the larger effort of social control. Indeed, the black elite was persuaded to act increasingly as caretakers/overseers of the black community, maintaining order and compliance with rules of behavior dictated by the white elite.

This method of social control generated inconsistent results. The "best sort" of blacks did not have the necessary power to completely control the black working class, any more than did the white elite have the ability to dominate completely political and social relations with working-class whites. Neither did the black elite consistently follow the mandates of the ruling whites. Black leadership in Atlanta had its own agenda for the community. Black elites did internalize some dominant cultural values and belief systems. They did criticize their less affluent brethren for lacking either the self-direction or self-discipline to move forward, to progress on all fronts. Nevertheless, Atlanta's African American community leaders also recognized their own responsibility to uplift, to improve the material and social conditions of the race. Uplift included pushing to acquire fair and equal treatment before the law and the full rights of citizenship, social and economic. Black leaders were willing to accept the mantle of paternalism because it was the only effective game in town and because they hoped to leave a proper legacy for the race. Their drive to gain equal access to southern society for themselves and their progeny brought them into conflict with the white leadership's vision of the world. Their efforts at reason and persuasion, at demonstrating respectability and civic responsibility, availed them little in the face of adamant white racism. Ultimately, what they could rely on was the spirit of black community. The work of black solidarity, the work of uplift inside the community, proved more effective and longer lasting than efforts to reach across the lines of power and race to achieve equality.

APPENDIX

Table 1. Affluent African Americans in Atlanta, 1880

Name	County and Town Property	Total Worth	Notes
Allen, Luke	$1000	$1090	carpenter
Badger, Robert	$1000	$1085	dentist
Badger, Roderick Dhu	$4500	$5850	dentist
Baldwin, Rosa	$1800	$1810	seamstress
Beall, Courtney	$2000	$2000	trader
Bird, Mitchell	$1600	$1655	grocer
Cargile, Mitchell, Sr.	$1300	$1510	undertaker
Craig, Jane (estate)	$1200	$1255	
Darden, Wesley	$	$2675	drayman*
Delbridge, Allen J.	$	$1040	shoemaker*
Eskridge, Peter	$1200	$1270	blacksmith
Fain, Henry	$1000	$1100	tailor
Finch, William	$ 500	$ 645	tailor
Gaines, W. J.	$ 800	$ 800	minister
Graham, George	$1200	$1490	carpenter
Herrington, Alfred H.	$	$1090	*
Howard, David T.	$	$2120	messenger*
Johnson, Annie	$ 900	$1077	
Love, Jordan	$	$1525	bricklayer*
McHenry, Charles	$1000	$1255	grocer
McHenry, Jackson	$ 300	$ 332	blacksmith
Monroe, Crawford	$	$3000	drayman*
Morgan, Charles	$1800	$1840	carriage trimmer
Norris, Homer V. M.	$	$2801	carpenter*
Peck, Francis	$ 450	$ 466	minister
Perdue, John	$1600	$2175	drayman
Perkins, Henry	$1200	$1300	blacksmith
Quarles, Frank	$ 500	$ 500	minister
Rivers, Joseph	$	$1202	blacksmith*
Swanson, Mary	$1200	$1300	
Tate, James	$2700	$3500	grocer
Turner, William F.	$	$1045	porter*
Ward, Thomas M. D.	$	$2100	minister*
Wood, Joseph	$1500	$1555	minister

Compiled from the Fulton County Tax Digest, 1880; Atlanta city directories; E. R. Carter, *The Black Side*; and Thornbery, "Black Atlanta."

*Data taken from Thornbery, "Black Atlanta," p. 327.

Occupations are provided when they can be identified.

Table 2. Affluent African Americans in Atlanta, 1885

Name	County and Town Property	Total Worth	Notes
Allen, Luke	$	$1225	carpenter*
Badger, Robert	$1200	$1400	dentist
Badger, Roderick	$7000	$8000	dentist, on white list
Beale, Courtney	$2000	$2020	grocer
Bird, M. H. (estate)	$1000	$1000	grocer
Bradford, James	$1500	$1500	butler
Brewster, Annie	$1500	$1500	
Brown, Felix	$1600	$1610	cook
Brown, Martha	$1000	$1000	
Bryce, Smith	$1200	$1225	telegraph lineman
Calhoun, Moses	$3000	$6300	grocer and manages a boarding house; $3000 in household
Cargile, Mitchell, Sr.	$1300	$2025	undertaker; $1100 = ¾ acre land in district 14
Carter, Henry	$1500	$1510	carpenter
Cary, Mary	$1100	$1150	nurse
Casey, W. M.	$2000	$2100	shoemaker
Clark, Henry	$1350	$1375	railroad worker
Conyers, Joseph F.	$1300	$1400	contractor
Cooper, Rufus	$1000	$1100	tailor
Copeland, Willis	$1000	$1020	carpenter
Curry, Hardy	$1000	$1035	shoemaker
Darden, Hillard (Iylard)	$2000	$2925	drayman; $500 = 50 acres in district 14
Delbridge, Allen J.	$3200	$3585	shoemaker
Dixon, Ayna	$1200	$1300	laundress
Eskridge, Peter	$2500	$2800	blacksmith
Finch, William	$ 800	$ 885	tailor
Ford, Annie	$1300	$1350	grocer
Fowler, Joseph M.	$1700	$1700	carpenter
Good Samaritans	$2000	$2000	fraternal order
Graham, George	$1500	$1525	carpenter
Graines, Dr. W. J.	$3000	$3000	bishop AME
Grosby, Thomas	$1000	$1030	clerk
Hall, Elder Robert	$1000	$1070	laborer
Hamilton, Alex	$1000	$1050	contractor
Henry, Richard J.	$1500	$2000	porter
Herndon, Alonzo F.	$ 500	$ 610	barber
Hill, Lena	$1000	$1025	laundress
Hill, Molly	$1000	$1010	

Table 2. (*continued*)

Name	County and Town Property	Total Worth	Notes
Holmes, Nick	$1400	$1500	shoemaker
Howard, David T.	$2000	$2420	undertaker
Hutchins, Dougherty	$1800	$1900	barber
James, M. Vernan	$1500	$1600	hackman
Johnson, Savannah	$1000	$1075	laundress
King, Rufus M.	$ 750	$1495	laborer; $100 = ½ acre in district 14
Latham, Adam	$1500	$1580	shoemaker
Lewis, Isham	$1300	$1375	janitor
Love, Jordan	$1500	$1525	mason
McHenry, Charles	$2000	$2360	grocer
McHenry, Jackson	$ 400	$ 850	hackman
McKinley, Jacob	$5400	$6800	grocer
McMichael, Hattie	$1200	$1275	
Miller, Berthenia	$1000	$1050	
Mitchel, Mick	$1000	$1100	harness maker
Monroe, Crawford	$4900	$5450	drayman
Morgan, C. H.	$2900	$3730	grocer
Moyer, Issac	$1300	$2620	grocer
Murphy, Willis, Sr.	$2000	$2200	grocer
Nichols, Wm.	$1000	$1000	mason
Ogletree, Baltimore	$1100	$1110	driver
O'Neil, Hiram	$2500	$3690	contractor; $1000 in horses
Parks, Fanny	$1000	$1000	
Peck, Fanny	$1000	$1060	
Perdue, John (estate)	$1050	$1160	wood and coal dealer
Perkins, Henry	$1200	$1265	laborer
Phillips, Harvey	$1000	$1015	cook
Pitts, Taylor	$1300	$1300	laborer
Pledger, William A.	$ 900	$ 940	Republican activist
Price, John W.	$2000	$2000	
Reese, Robert	$1950	$1950	hackman
Reeves, Jo M.	$1200	$3200	$2000 = land unspecified in location and amount
Richardson, Charles	$1900	$2000	postal clerk
Rivers, Joseph	$2700	$2810	blacksmith
Rogers, James	$1850	$1850	railroad worker
Rucker, Henry	$ 300	$ 300	porter
Ryalls, Jefferson	$1100	$1100	grocer
Scott, Charles	$1000	$1050	carpenter

Table 2. (continued)

Name	County and Town Property	Total Worth	Notes
Short, James	$1200	$1250	carpenter
Smith, Annie V.	$1200	$1250	dressmaker
Steele, Carrie	$1600	$1800	listed as a confectioner in city directory 1880, no listing 1885; $200 in household goods
Steele, Samuel (Robert)	$ 600	$ 650	porter; Carrie Steele's son
Swanson, Mary	$1200	$1260	
Tate, James	$3800	$5720	grocer; $1000 = 50 acres in district 17
Thompson, Tracy (estate)	$1000	$1000	
Todd, Henry	$3000	$3000	
Turner, H. McNeal	$3000	$3200	bishop AME
Turner, W. T.	$1000	$1225	porter
Underwood, Henry	$1500	$1550	carpenter
Vaughn, George	$1000	$1010	mason
Washington, George	$1400	$1400	minister
Watts, Henry	$1000	$1000	blacksmith
Williams, Henry H.	$1100	$1110	postal clerk
Wimbish, Christopher C.	$3000	$3075	postman
Wood, Joseph	$1200	$1200	minister
Wyly, Emmett	$1200	$1200	

Compiled from the Fulton County Tax Digest, 1885; Atlanta city directories; E. R. Carter, *The Black Side*; and Thornbery, "Black Atlanta."

*Data taken from Thornbery, "Black Atlanta," p. 327.
 Occupations are provided when they can be identified.

Table 3. Black Churches in
Nineteenth-Century Atlanta

AME
Bethel AME Church
Lloyd Street Church
Shiloh AME Church
St. Paul's African Church
Union Church
Wood's Chapel

AME *Zion*
Shaw Temple

Baptist
Antioch Baptist Church
Bethlehem Baptist Church
Ebenezer Baptist Church
Friendship Baptist Church
Macedonia Church
Mount Calvary Baptist Church
Mount Olive Union Church
Mount Pleasant Church
Mount Zion Church
Pleasant Grove Church
Primitive Baptist Church
Providence Church
Springfield Church
Wheat Street Baptist Church
Zion Hill Baptist Church

Congregational
First Congregational Church

NOTES

Introduction

1. Lawrence Levine has observed that while freedom "opened up unprecedented opportunities for acculturation and accommodation, the freedmen did not necessarily exploit them either uniformly or immediately. Indeed, one of the first results of emancipation in a number of areas in black life and culture was the intensification of black separatism" (*Black Culture and Black Consciousness,* 140). In addition, Eric Foner reminds us that "slavery negates both individual rights and community self determination and as free people, blacks sought both the personal liberties of whites and *collective* empowerment ("The Meaning of Freedom in the Age of Emancipation," 458; emphasis added).

2. McMath, *A Southern Pilgrimage,* 3.

3. My discussion, which ends in the immediate postriot period, focuses on high-status blacks more than on Black Atlanta's poorest residents. Tera Hunter's work offers an excellent treatment of black labor relations and gender issues as manifest across the Southland through the period up to and including World War I in *"To 'Joy My Freedom."* Hunter details the myriad ways working-class black women in Atlanta and other southern locales struggled to break free of an existence constrained by the necessity of domestic labor and the presumptions of their employers to create lives in which they might pursue some pleasure, and some economic independence.

4. Williamson, *The Crucible of Race,* 189. In this chapter, entitled "In Violence *Veritas,"* Williamson argues that violence was a natural outgrowth of the white radical obsession with the Negro problem—that being how to contain the "negro" who was regressing into barbarism in the absence of the necessary social control of slavery.

5. Hunter, *"To 'Joy My Freedom,"* 98.

6. Walker, *Deromanticizing Black History,* xvii.

7. Benedict Anderson's celebrated text addresses the ways members of a given society create community in the act of imagining. As he notes in the introduction, "all communities larger than primordial villages of face to face contact (and perhaps even these) are imagined. Communities are to be distinguished, not by their falsity/genuineness, but by the style in which they are imagined" (*Imagined Communities,* 6).

8. Foner, "The Meaning of Freedom in the Age of Emancipation," 458.

9. Even when the ideology of race as physical evidence of innate difference, of superiority (white skin), and of inferiority (yellow, red, brown, and black skin) was in vogue in the late nineteenth and the early twentieth century, it was often a slippery concept. U.S. immigration policy reminds us that various groups were alternately raced or deraced over the decades. The Irish were identified as a different (inferior) "race" from the British in the 1800s and then transformed into a "white" (superior) race to the "brown" or "dark" Italians and Greeks in the 1900s.

10. Fields, "Slavery, Race and Ideology in the United States of America," 96. For a critique of Fields, see Roediger, *The Wages of Whiteness*, and Winant, *Racial Conditions*.

11. In *The Mismeasure of Man*, Stephen Jay Gould offers a cogent analysis of Louis Agassiz's vision of the hierarchy of race and his brutally racist analysis of African Americans and their place in the evolution of man (62–104).

12. Higginbotham, "African American Women's History and the Metalanguage of Race," 268–69.

13. See Chafe, *Civilities and Civil Rights*, 8–10.

14. Rouse, *Lugenia Burns Hope*, which offers up the life of a high-status black female as an example of uplift in action. While most of Hope's life work lies beyond the confines of my study, her philosophical outlook and actions reflected those of Henry Hugh Proctor and reinforced the complicated and paternalistic dynamic of racial uplift in Atlanta.

15. For a detailed discussion of the issue of the "underclass" and its role in American history, see Katz, ed., *The "Underclass" Debate*. Eric Foner, in "Reconstruction Revisited," addresses concerns of presentism in post–Civil War literature.

16. Lewis, "Connecting Memory, Self, and the Power of Place in African American Urban History."

17. Nell Painter's brutally titled article "Soul Murder and Slavery" reminds readers to consider the pain inflicted and the scars that remained as men and women exited slavery. W. E. B. Du Bois, too, though he committed himself to the struggle for the future, wrote of the damage that violent oppression had inflicted upon those enslaved. Readers should not mistake any discussion of the harm of slavery for a revival of what should be long-dead discussions of postslavery pathological disorders, sexual or otherwise, and historians must be careful not to downplay the impact of slavery on black consciousness.

18. See Ransom and Sutch, *One Kind of Freedom*, Jaynes, *Branches without Roots*, and more recently, Jones, *The Dispossessed*.

19. Thomas Holt, in *Black over White*, critiqued the mulatto elite of South Carolina for their less-than-complete support of legislation that would have been of use to working-class and poor blacks.

20. Stevenson, *Life in Black and White*, 258–59. Also see Berlin, *Slaves without Masters*. Mark Shultz argues for a new examination of "the social roots of the mulatto elite" in his discussion of interracial families in rural Georgia. However, Shultz also acknowledges the wisdom of Frederick Law Olmsted's observation that "the great majority of mulatto children born to Virginia slaveholders were neither emancipated nor given special consideration" ("Interracial Kinship and the Black Middle Class," 143).

21. Johnson and Roark, *Black Masters* and Gatewood, *Aristocrats of Color*. Mulattos of privilege, as varied in their political worldview as in the experience of their origins, for the most part cast their lot with the African American community, though Gatewood details their penchant for enforcing color bias and engaging in elitist behavior vis-à-vis their darker skinned peers.

22. Friendship Baptist Church Centennial Program, 1962, Friendship Baptist Church file (hereafter FBC file), Atlanta University Archives. Frank Quarles was the only black

pastor in the city whose ministry began in the antebellum period and extended into and beyond Reconstruction.

23. Carter, *The Black Side* (original in Atlanta University Archives, Woodruff Library).

24. Weber, *Theory of Social and Economic Organization*, 425.

25. Ibid., 348.

26. Collins, *Weberian Sociological Theory*, 14.

27. Of course, racism limited the space into which African Americans could move with this status-based training. The white community rarely allowed black access to the wider market, access that would have provided greater diversity in the economic base of the black middle class or increased options for the working class.

28. The historiography of slavery, nearly a century long and hundreds of volumes deep, continues to challenge and alter our understanding of the experience of bonded labor in the United States. Numerous scholars, in articles and monographs, have assessed the literature and commented on the future of the field. The study of slavery is anything but static; successive generations of scholars have radically challenged if not completely overturned the assertions and assumptions of their forerunners. The 1918 work of Ulrich B. Phillips *(American Negro Slavery)* and other scholars trained in that tradition was revised by the works of the post–World War II generation led by Stampp *(The Peculiar Institution)*. Recent twenty and twenty-fifth anniversary celebrations of the works of Gutman *(The Black Family in Slavery and Freedom)*, Genovese *(Roll, Jordan, Roll)*, Blassingame *(Slave Community)*, Ransom and Sutch *(One Kind of Freedom)*, and Engerman and Fogel *(Time on the Cross)* are a testament to the way these scholars and their works dominated the field, offering revisions and challenges unimagined by either Phillips or Stampp. Other scholars (Leon Litwack, John Boles, Ira Berlin, Deborah Gray White, and Peter Kolchin, among them) continue to tweak and fine-tune our understanding of the slave past. Yet while many arguments have been rejected altogether (Stampp's assertion that slaves were but "white men in black skins" or Elkins's concentration camp analogy come to mind), some arguments continue to be supported by new research and new interpretations. The slave community thesis articulated by Blassingame and reinforced by the work of Stuckey *(Slave Culture)* and Levine *(Black Culture and Black Consciousness)* continues to influence the work of scholars such as Norrece Jones, Brenda Stevenson, and Whittington Johnson. Contemporary scholars do not apply the argument in an uncritical fashion; rather, the community thesis is seriously reconsidered in light of new evidence. Jones draws upon the slave record to document both a lack of paternalism on the part of owners and a corresponding lack of deference on the part of slaves. Stevenson's discussion of the black family details shared responsibilities and commitments that extended to the greater black community.

29. Stevenson, *Life in Black and White*, 254.

30. See Jones, *Born a Child of Freedom*, and King, *Stolen Childhood*.

31. All three men appear sporadically within this study but are not treated in depth. For biographies and more detailed discussion of the activism of the three men, see David Levering Lewis, *W. E. B. Du Bois: Biography of a Race, 1868–1919* and *W. E. B. Du Bois:*

The Fight for Equality and the American Century, 1919–1963; Leroy Davis, *A Clashing of the Soul: John Hope and the Dilemma of African American Leadership and Black Higher Education in the Early Twentieth Century;* and Gerald Horne, *Black Liberation/Red Scare: Ben Davis and the Communist Party.* Horne's text begins with a discussion of Ben Davis Jr.'s Republican father—Atlanta journalist Ben Jefferson Davis.

One. An Island in the Up-country

1. See Johnson and Roark, *Black Masters.*

2. Garrett, *Atlanta and Environs,* 1:124. Russell, *Atlanta, 1847–1890,* 17. For details of the lottery, see Land Lottery 1821 Records, DeKalb Historical Society.

3. Hahn, "The Yeomanry of the Nonplantation South," 42.

4. Hahn, "The Roots of Southern Populism," 29.

5. Garrett, *Atlanta and Environs,* 1:129–30. Garrett notes that "a whiskey barrel was kept on tap in the rear of the store, where cash customers were entitled to drinks 'on the house,' but it was considered good etiquette for strangers or occasional visitors to leave a nickel or dime on the barrel head after imbibing."

6. Ibid., 147–62. Sparsely populated, the area provided good terrain for the junction of the proposed Western and Atlantic and Georgia Railroads. The latter was to bisect the state from the coast to the Alabama border; the former came south from Chattanooga. It took the state of Georgia a dozen years to complete the building of the railroad system designed to move goods from the western farmlands to the eastern shore.

7. *Atlanta, 1847–1890,* 41–42.

8. Eighth U.S. Census, 1860.

9. The Seventh U.S. 1850 Census does not enumerate the population of the city by wards.

10. Russell, *Atlanta, 1847–1890,* 71.

11. Eighth U.S. Census, 1860; Ninth U.S. Census, 1870. Thornbery, "The Development of Black Atlanta," 3.

12. Atlanta City Council Records, February 19, 1848, 1:9, Atlanta Historical Society (hereafter City Council Records).

13. City Council Records, March 5, 1852, R (Rough Sections):77.

14. Atlanta City Ordinance Book, 107, Atlanta Historical Society (hereafter Ordinance Book).

15. *Plain Folk and Gentry in a Slave Society,* 5–6. See also Morgan, *American Slavery, American Freedom.*

16. City Council Records, July 29, 1851, 1:169.

17. The slave was to be held until the following morning, whereupon his owner or employer would pay the arresting officer one dollar. A variation of this law remained on the books and was enforced until the 1880s, when African Americans in the city protested that it gave policemen incentive to harass and arrest innocent members of the black community (City Council Records, January 28, 1853, 1:198–99).

18. Ordinance Book, May 20, 1853, 139–45. Two Atlantans, I. F. Peacock and a Mr. Lin, were fined in June 1854 for allowing slaves to live in violation of this ordinance.

19. Reidy, 62, 102; Hudson, 79. Also see Berlin and Morgan, eds., *Cultivation and Culture,* and Loren Schweninger, *Black Property Owners in the South.*

20. *Plain Folk and Gentry in a Slave Society,* 45.

21. The link between urban hiring out and slave independence has been long noted by scholars. As John Boles points out, "their owners' efforts notwithstanding, urban slaves were able to meet, share ideas, and shape their own world beyond their masters' walls" (*Black Southerners,* 127). Addressing the issue of independent movement by slaves despite Atlanta City Council restrictions, Tera Hunter writes, "Slaves took advantage of the lax patrol to move around the city, to participate in a rich if still limited communal life, almost as if they were free" (*"To 'Joy My Freedom,"* 13).

22. Ordinance Book, July 21, 1855.

23. "Slavery as Seen through the Eyes of Henry Wright—Ex slave." Rawick, *American Slave, Georgia Narratives,* vol. 13, pt. 3, 196–97.

24. In reaction to the efforts of white laborers to strengthen the case against hiring out, five slaveowners petitioned the council in March 1858, asking that the mayor's power to grant permission to hire out in individual cases be restored. The petition was tabled, as were most petitions concerning hiring and living out after January 1856.

25. "Slavery as Seen through the Eyes of Henry Wright—Ex slave," Rawick, *American Slave, Georgia Narratives,* vol. 13, pt. 3, 197. Harris, *Plain Folk and Gentry in a Slave Society,* 74–75.

26. City Council Records, January 1, 1861, 3:477.

27. Poole, "On Borrowed Ground." Also see Johnson, *Black Savannah,* 4.

28. The 1853 ordinance stated that failure to pay the two hundred–dollar retainer would result in the arrest of the person of color in default who would remain under arrest until such time as the fine was paid. Revisions of the law in 1859 specified that the individual was to be arrested and held for five days, during which time the city marshal was to advertise that the individual was to be hired out "at public outcry, at the city hall" and contracted to work until such time as his or her wages allowed for payment of the two hundred–dollar retainer. The reporting officer was rewarded with one-fourth of the retainer. If not hired, the free person of color was to receive thirty-nine lashes "each and every morning he or she may remain within the corporate limits of the city."

29. Ordinance Book, June 23, 1852 and May 20, 1853.

30. Ibid., 79–80, 93, 139–45. Violations of these restrictions were punished by the application of thirty-nine lashes "to the bare back of the offender."

31. Seventh U.S. Census, 1850, Free Schedules, DeKalb County, City of Atlanta, 432–67. Blacksmith Ruff was the only member of the group of nineteen to have an occupation listed on the census rolls. Ruff was also the only one of the group to be identified as literate. E. R. Carter, in *The Black Side,* notes that one of the first free people of color in the city was a female property owner, Miss Mary Combs. Combs sold her property at the juncture of Wheat and Peachtree Streets in Terminus and used the profit to buy her husband's freedom. Edward Sweat, in "Free Blacks in Antebellum Atlanta," notes that county records document the sale of Combs' property for five hundred dollars in 1861. There is no Mary Combs listed on the Free Schedules in 1850 or 1860; however, single thirty-year-old Laura Combs may be the woman to whom Carter and Sweat referred.

32. William Gifford and his family entered the city in early 1855. A. W. Stone, acting as Gifford's guardian, petitioned the city to allow Gifford to reside within the city limits (City Council Records, February 1855, 2:50).

33. Eighth U.S. Census, 1860, Free Schedules, Fulton County.

34. Sweat, "Free Blacks in Antebellum Atlanta," 65.

35. City Council Records, July 15, 1859, and February 8, 1861, 3:230, 515. Badger remained in the city and continued his practice. He was required to pay both the five-dollar tax on his person and the five-dollar tax on professionals. Despite this burden, he was the wealthiest African American in the city, owning more than five thousand dollars' worth of taxable property by 1873. Given the minute free black population and the lack of financial resources of slaves, it is reasonable to assume that Badger had a large white clientele.

36. City Council Records, March 3 and June 6, 1856, 2:141, 159. Ransom Montgomery stands as the exception to this rule. The city granted Montgomery, as a reward for extinguishing a fire on the Chattahoochee Railroad Bridge, permission to sell pastries at the passenger depot (Carter, *The Black Side*, 10–15).

37. City Council Records, September 27, 1852, R (Rough Sections):139–40.

38. City Council Records, February 22, 1856, O (Rough Section):162.

39. City Council Records, October 3, 1856, 2:190. The council decided not to pass a separate ordinance further restricting the African American right to assemble; instead its committee on ordinances voted to require permission and a license for each group that planned gatherings. The council did not refund license fees if permission to gather was revoked.

40. There is some confusion as to the founding date of Bethel AME Church. Carter's *The Black Side* suggests that the church was organized between 1843 and 1846. Other records from that time period, however, suggest 1848.

41. Much has been written about the distinctions in color and caste made by free mulattos and blacks in South Carolina and/or New Orleans. Douglas Egerton addresses the "African American disunity in the Palmetto state" made all the more clear by the 1790 establishment of the Brown Fellowship Society which "existed for the purpose of drawing biologically constructed lines of demarcation between the wealthy browns and Charleston's sizeable black community whether bond or free" (*He Shall Go Out Free*, 92). The pattern of interracial dynamics of the Badger family reflect Mark R. Schultz's discussion of blacks in Hancock County, Georgia. Hancock County, southeast of Atlanta, was home to numerous families distinguished by "interracial kinship ties" in which white patriarchs either acknowledged and/or offered assistance to their black children. Schultz notes that "most of the socially significant postbellum interracial relationships seem to have been constructed between wealthy planters living in rural areas and mulatto domestic servants." The white Badgers, Murphys, and Candlers, all men of wealth and affluence who chose black/mulatto women from within their own households as concubines and both recognized and assisted their mixed race offspring, fit into this model. However, this model was not the norm for Atlanta ("Interracial Kinship Ties and the Emergence of a Rural Black Middle Class," 153).

42. Book of Remembrance, DeKalb County, Badger Family Records, DeKalb County Historical Society.

43. Irish railroad laborer Barney Riley, who may in fact have been the father of Rhonda Map's three children, would not have been able to provide his family with the kind of privileged connections and protection that Badger afforded his sons. Without the advantages of class and status, Riley and Map's children would have been forced to navigate through the sea of restrictions that circumscribed the lives of the majority of free people of color in the area.

44. Thornbery, "The Development of Black Atlanta," 200–201 and Caroline Bond Day Papers, Family Histories note cards A10, Peabody Museum.

45. Schweninger, *Black Property Owners in the South*, 97–141.

46. "Concluding Reflections," in Hudson, ed., *Working toward Freedom*, 236.

Two. Phoenix Rising

1. Author's telephone interview with South View Cemetery sexton A. H. Watts, grandson of Albert Watts, August 16, 1994.

2. The generalities of Reconstruction-era employment and the specifics of employment for working-class black women in Atlanta have been addressed in other academic treatments of the city. My purpose here is to address the employment opportunities blacks created for themselves in the face of limits imposed by the larger white society. See Ransom and Sutch, *One Kind of Freedom*; Jaynes, *Branches without Roots*; Hunter, *"To 'Joy My Freedom"*; and McLeod, *Workers and Workplace Dynamics in Reconstruction-Era Atlanta*.

3. Schweninger, *Black Property Owners in the South*, 5.

4. William Tecumseh Sherman's siege and occupation of Atlanta played an important role in the transformation of the city. The war isolated Atlanta from both northern suppliers and would-be trade partners in Europe, forcing residents to rely on their own limited resources. The destruction of much of the city gave municipal elites—councilmen, entrepreneurs, and small manufacturers—new opportunities to push their agenda for economic development forward. Indeed Henry Grady's vision of a New South took root in the scorched earth left by Sherman's troops. For a discussion of the part the war played in moving the southern society from the Old to the New South, see Dan T. Carter, "From the Old South to the New," in Fraser and Moore, eds., *From the Old South to the New*, Clarence Mohr, *On the Threshold of Freedom*, and James M. Russell, *Atlanta, 1847–1890*. White supremacy was perhaps not the inevitable outcome of the social and political experiment of Reconstruction. Yet, as Williamson explains in *The Crucible of Race*, the early defeat of southern white liberals who envisioned alternatives to white supremacy and the rise to power of white racial radicals set the tone for southern race relations from the late 1880s through the first quarter of the twentieth century.

5. Russell, *Atlanta, 1847–1890*, 102–103.

6. Mohr, *On the Threshold of Freedom*, 193.

7. Castel, *Decision in the West*, 464.

8. Rawick, *The American Slave, Georgia Narratives*, vol. 12, pt. 2, 95; Mohr, *On the Threshold of Freedom*, 126–33.

9. Mohr, *On the Threshold of Freedom*, 164–67.

10. Russell, *Atlanta, 1847–1890*, 110–11.

11. *On the Threshold of Freedom*, 208.

12. Castel, *Decision in the West*, 488.

13. *Personal Memoirs*, 2:118–20.

14. Ibid., 118.

15. Ibid., 179.

16. The unpublished census list provided a space for the notation of place of birth for all members of the family. Most parents and children identified Georgia as their place of birth; many adults listed South Carolina as the birthplace of their parents.

17. Rawick, *The American Slave, Georgia Narratives*, vol. 12, pt. 1, 319–25, pt. 2, 79–90, 91–96, 295–302.

18. See Rabinowitz, *Race Relations in the Urban South*; Robinson, "Plans Dat Come from God" in Burton and McMath, eds., *Toward a New South?*; and Mohr, *On the Threshold of Freedom*.

19. Cimbala, *Under the Guardianship of the Nation*, 120.

20. Russell, *Atlanta, 1847–1890*, 174–75.

21. Cimbala, *Under the Guardianship of the Nation*, 84.

22. American Missionary Association Papers (hereafter AMA Papers), letter from Jeannie Barnum to Hunt, January 27, 1866, and letter from Rebecca Craighead to Hunt, March 5, 1866.

23. Cimbala, *Under the Guardianship of the Nation*, 91–2, and Hartshorn, *An Era of Progress and Promise*, 372–8.

24. AMA Papers, letters from Frederick Ayers to Hunt, February 3 and April 30, 1866. The state of Georgia passed legislation mandating racial segregation in the early 1890s. Still the city of Atlanta did not pass an official residential segregation ordinance until the second decade of the twentieth century.

25. Ninth U.S. Census, 1870, Fulton County; White, "The Black Sides of Atlanta," 199–225.

26. AMA Papers, letter from Ayers to Rev. George Whipple, February 15, 1866.

27. AMA Papers, letter from Craighead to Hunt, January 15, 1866.

28. AMA Papers, letter from Craighead to Hunt, February 15, 1866.

29. *Atlanta Constitution*, Mortuary Report, Internments for December 1868, January 3, 1869. The paper attributes the disproportionate number of African American deaths to smallpox.

30. Another outbreak of smallpox occurred in the city in the spring and summer of 1882 with similar results.

31. McLeod, *Workers and Workplace Dynamics*, 7. Dittmer, *Black Georgia in the Progressive Era*, 13.

32. Rawick, *The American Slave, Georgia Narratives*, vol. 12, pt. 2, 96.

33. Thornbery, "Development of Black Atlanta," 191–224, 317–22. Hopkins, "Occupational and Geographic Mobility in Atlanta," 1870–1896," 201–13.

34. AMA Papers, letter from Ayers to Whipple, February 15, 1866.

35. McLeod, *Workers and Workplace Dynamics,* 5.

36. Ibid., 32–35 and 24–26.

37. Ibid., 3.

38. Registers of Signatures of Depositors in Branches of the Freedmen's Savings and Trust Company (hereafter Freedmen's Savings and Trust), Rec. No. 82.

39. McLeod, *Workers and Workplace Dynamics,* 34–36. Black railroad workers appealed to army officials during Reconstruction, protesting job discrimination—an action that, McLeod notes, resulted in a separate wage scale formalizing higher wages for whites and lower wages for their black peers. Similarly, when black workers went on strike rather than sign documents releasing the railroad from responsibility for work-related injuries, officials at the Western and Atlantic simply replaced them with white workers.

40. Kuhn, *Contesting the New South Order,* 11, 20–21. Kuhn notes "nearly 700" workers were employed at the Fulton Bag and Cotton Mills in 1896.

41. Freedmen's Savings and Trust, Rec. No. 91.

42. McLeod, *Workers and Workplace Dynamics,* 113–16.

43. Thornbery, "Development of Black Atlanta," 323, Fulton County Tax Digest, 1885, Georgia Department of Archives and History.

44. Flipper, *The Colored Cadet at West Point;* Atlanta City Directory 1870, Atlanta Historical Society (hereafter City Directory); Freedmen's Saving and Trust, Rec. No. 11.

45. Ordinance Book, 1851–1860. Council members charged that the merchandise was often stolen from the homes of white masters or employers.

46. City Council Records, January 16, 1869, 5:491

47. Carter, *Biographical Sketches of Our Pulpit,* 143.

48. City Directory, 1859. Thornbery, "Development of Black Atlanta," 323.

49. McLeod, *Workers and Workplace Dynamics,* 86–87.

50. Kuhn, *Contesting the New South Order,* 28–29. Kuhn notes that in addition to their racism, white workers objected to the black female laborers in the mill because their presence resulted in lower wages for white female workers.

51. Thornbery, "Development of Black Atlanta," 322; Hunter, "Household Workers in the Making," 293–94; Gretchen Maclachlan, "Black Women's Work in Atlanta," 16.

52. Hunter, *"To 'Joy My Freedom,"* 52. There are no formal statistics on wages for black female servants and washerwomen. Wages are estimates, at best. Hunter offers an insightful analysis of the work life of black women in Atlanta in the five decades after the Civil War. Her discussion of the 1881 washerwomen's strike and black women's denial of the accusation that they were "disease carriers" highlights the role lower-status women played in creating community and in claiming their own definitions of freedom.

53. Sholes and Weatherbee, Directory of the City of Atlanta, Georgia, 1881, New York State Library, Albany. In "The Development of Black Atlanta," Thornbery discusses the harassment faced by Baulden and suggests that Dr. Ashley failed to earn sufficient income as a physician.

54. See Tables 1 and 2—note the changes in their wealth in the last two decades of the century.

55. Fulton County Tax Digest, 1895.

56. Thornbery, "Development of Black Atlanta," 221–23.

57. Fulton County Tax Digest, 1900.

58. Both texts outline the history of black economic activity in America. Walker includes a brief discussion of pre-colonial economic activity among African slaves, while Schweninger begins in the post-Revolutionary era. Both scholars argue that blacks embraced a capitalistic ethos even as slaves, often working to acquire wealth so as to ameliorate the material conditions of their lives and, when possible, to purchase themselves or loved ones. Blacks encountered resistance to their efforts at economic mobility in antebellum legal statutes and in white social custom. Schweninger and Walker each detail economic strategies, such as the forming of mutual aid societies, employed by African Americans, enslaved and free, to circumvent prohibitions that denied access to credit, including laws against black bank stock ownership.

59. "Negroes Making Money," *Atlanta Journal*, April 28, 1894; "Thrifty Negroes Who Are Rich," *Atlanta Constitution*, August 31, 1890. Crumbly joined the Army as a young man and after serving five years joined Charles H. Morgan in the grocery business.

60. Rabinowitz, *Race Relations in the Urban South*, 85. John Dittmer identified Howard as "the son of a white lawyer, as well as the half-brother of a congressman." It has been suggested that David T. Howard was the half brother of Pierre Howard Sr. and therefore the son of U.S. Congressman William Schley Howard. T. S. Howard was born in 1875 and served in the U.S. Congress from 1910 to 1919—which excludes him as the possible father of David T. Howard, who was an adult prior to the close of the Civil War. However, T. S. Howard's father, Thomas Cook Howard, lived in Atlanta's fifth ward in 1860. In residence in that household was at least one male slave child old enough to be David T. Howard, which would make T. S. Howard and David T. Howard half-brothers (Dittmer, *Black Georgia in the Progressive Era*, 43). Sociologist Caroline Bond Day documented Howard's mixed-race heritage in her 1932 work, *A Study of Some Negro-White Families in the United States*, but she provided no specifics as to the identity of his parents.

61. *Atlanta Independent*, full-page advertisement by Howard, February 10, 1904.

62. John T. Schell shared his life story with E. R. Carter, who published a four-page biography of the grocer in his text, *The Black Side*. Schell, who took the last name of his stepfather (a man his mother married after the Civil War), did not provide Carter with his mother's name. He did, however, identify his white father by name and attribute his own business acumen to him. See Carter, *The Black Side*, 142.

63. In the midst of the Great Depression, Badger's daughter, Aradicia (Arrie) Darling Badger, would ask sociologist Caroline Bond Day to downplay her privileged family's link to white ancestors: "When I gave you information I thought that it would help in your study but none of us want either information or pictures used in book form or publication in any form . . . Just put in some other family." Letter to Caroline Bond Day from A. D. Badger, July 29, 1930, Caroline Bond Day Papers, box 1, letter 1.

64. Although the deposit records have been lost to fire, the surviving signature cards offer much to historians of the era. Data drawn from signature cards filed in the Atlanta branch from January 1870 to July 1874 contain information concerning age, sex, occupation, place of birth, place of residence, and location of family members of the

depositor. The signature cards also reveal the devastating aftereffects of the system of slavery on the black family. Most depositors identified the names of both parents, yet dozens reported fathers, mothers, siblings, and spouses lost to slavery by sale. Cook Willis Mitchell's mother, Viva Mitchell, drowned in Harris County and he lost his father, Henry May, to sale.

65. The registers of signatures of depositors for the period 1865–74 contain over four thousand signatures for the Atlanta branch from January 15, 1870, to July 2, 1874. The signatures are not alphabetized but ordered by date. My sample consisted of 420 depositors—slightly less than 10 percent of the total. Where possible these names were cross-listed with the names of Black Atlantans found in tax digests, newspapers, and church records. The large number of students enrolled as depositors reflects both the numbers of educational institutions in the city and a link between the pursuit of education and commitment to economic development.

Significantly, the vast majority of the depositors at the Freedman's Bank in Atlanta were not identified as either light skinned or mulatto. To the contrary, most depositors were either "black" or "dark brown," which highlights the absence of a significant community of affluent light-skinned blacks in post–Civil War Atlanta. Of the 420 depositors in my sample, 410 were identified by race based on observations of the bank clerk. Of that number 5 were actually white men and identified as such, 12 were identified as almost white, 22 as light brown, 3 as very light brown, 83 as brown, 58 as dark brown, 48 as very dark brown and 178 as black or almost black. A single depositor was designated as mulatto.

66. Rabinowitz, *Race Relations in the Urban South*, 82.

67. Fleming, "The Freedmen's Savings Bank," 2:137. The level of embezzlement from the Atlanta branch was also lower. White Congregationalist member Philip D. Cory was tried and convicted of embezzling eight thousand dollars in bank funds but he avoided serving time for his crimes by taking a post as an Indian agent in the West. C. S. Johnson, a black cashier who had previously served in the Augusta branch, replaced Cory.

68. Fleming, "Freedmen's Saving Bank," 1:55.

69. Mark Schultz, who emphasizes the connection between the financial success of members of the post–Civil War black middle class and their affluent white relations, notes that the face-to-face credit relations of the postwar South undermined the ability of black entrepreneurs to gain access to credit and contracts without the patronage of white "individuals of wealth and authority." In addition, the "free market" of the post-bellum South was as raced as every other element of the society. For black men who did gain access to credit in the private (read white) sector, access to capital did not necessarily translate to access to prosperity because southern blacks were regularly denied sales without the benefit of a white patron who could vouch for their "good character." ("Interracial Kinship and the Black Middle Class," 150). As previously noted, only a handful of successful black men in Atlanta moved into the middle class with a "leg up" from white relations. African Americans did transact financial business with at least one white-owned bank in Atlanta. The Fourth National Bank, also known as the Merchants Bank, owned and operated by banker William Lowry, one-time mayor James W.

English, and merchant Robert Maddox, hired Wesley Redding as porter and teller for black patrons. See Mixon, "The Atlanta Riot of 1906," 218, 398–99.

70. Education costs were low at Clark, though Atlanta's lowest-status blacks would have had difficulty securing money to pay even Clark's college fees, given their desperately low wages. Tuition and board costs for the calendar year were ten dollars per month or seventy-seven dollars per year if paid in advance. Day students paid a monthly tuition of sixty-five cents per month in the 1870s. Fees increased in the 1880s: tuition was raised to one dollar per month, and room and board was six to eight dollars per month. Black contractor Harrison Coles opened the first black mortuary in the city. He expanded his contracting and building firm to include undertaking in the 1870s.

71. Garrett, *Atlanta and Environs,* 609.

72. Fulton County Tax Digest, 1900.

73. Beginning in 1873, Badger was the wealthiest African American in Atlanta for two decades. Tate was third in 1872, behind AME Bishop T. M. D. Ward. He climbed into second place after Ward's departure from the city and remained there until at least 1880. Thornbery, "Development of Black Atlanta," 324; Fulton County Tax Digest, 1880.

74. Fulton County Tax Digest; Carter, *The Black Side.*

75. Hamilton was a very successful contractor. His firm, Hamilton and Son, won the contract for Morris Brown College in 1881. He went on to construct buildings for private citizens and black fraternal organizations. Despite his success, white administrators from Atlanta University rejected his offer to erect additional structures on the campus when the school was looking to expand.

76. Du Bois, *Some Efforts of American Negroes for Their Own Social Betterment,* 23.

77. Fulton County Tax Digest, 1900. Five years later the value of the firm was eighteen hundred dollars.

78. Du Bois, *Some Efforts of American Negroes for Their Own Social Betterment,* 23, 28. The Atlanta Loan and Trust Company may not have been an entirely black-owned concern. It does not appear on the Fulton County Tax Digest under the colored section in 1895, 1900, or 1905. Wesley Redding, worth $4,800 as early as 1895 (97 percent of which was invested in real estate), was apparently a boyhood companion and close associate of James English, president of Fourth National Bank. Mixon notes that Redding was invited to church with English at least once a year. He also argues that Redding was charged with bringing information regarding the African American community's concerns to English and his political allies. It is conceivable that English and the Fourth National Bank backed Redding in the development of the hotel.

79. Rental properties that were black-owned and leased to black tenants were less likely to be the "tenements" built by white contractors that black educators and ministers complained of.

80. E. P. Johnson, second principal of the Mitchell Street School and president of the Evangelical Ministers' Union, was president of the board of trustees of the orphanage. Steele's son, barber Robert Steele, was also a trustee. Carter, *The Black Side; Atlanta Independent,* profile of E. P. Johnson, February 27, 1904.

81. Black Atlantans without the resources of Howard, Rucker, and Herndon did their

part in community investment. Black churches in Atlanta thrived in part because congregations prided themselves on paying the mortgage on church property. Mortgage-burning and praise-giving parties were important celebrations. Once free from debt, the churches were more stable and could more easily concentrate on community development and improvement projects (see chapter 3).

82. Ruth Wright Hayre reports that the young student in question was Richard Robert Wright, her paternal grandfather, who attended a "boxcar school" in Atlanta shortly after the Civil War. Hayre, *Tell Them We Are Rising*, 6–9.

Three. The Black Church in Atlanta

1. Frey, "Shaking the Dry Bones," 25. Kolchin, *American Slavery*, 55–57.

2. Frey, *Water from the Rock*, 24–26.

3. Rawick, *The American Slave, Georgia Narratives*, vol. 13, pt. 3, 189, 129.

4. Rawick, *The American Slave, Georgia Narratives*, vol. 12, pt. 1, 198.

5. Hall, "Religious Symbolism of the Iron Pot," 128.

6. My understanding of slave religion continues to be influenced by the work of Sobel, *Trabelin' On;* Mathews, *Religion in the Old South;* Stuckey, *Slave Culture;* Levine, *Black Culture and Black Consciousness;* and Boles, *Masters and Slaves in the House of the Lord.* For more than three decades, historians have recognized the link between West African cultural traditions and those of enslaved African Americans. Most significantly the profession has moved away from an "either/or" dynamic, instead substituting a more sophisticated analysis of the relationship between African/American cultures. Sylvia Frey's analysis of the dialectical process involved in the transmission of the Christian faith suggests that Africans' beliefs and practices both altered and were altered by white evangelical traditions.

7. Pearson, *Designs against Charleston;* Blassingame, *Black New Orleans*, 6, 13–14.

8. Blassingame, "Before the Ghetto," 463–88.

9. Eighth U.S. Census, 1860, Fulton County .

10. Thornbery, "Development of Black Atlanta," 158, 161, 185; City Directory, 1900. See Jackson and Patterson, "Brief History of Selected Black Churches," 31–52.

11. Big Bethel AME Church pamphlet, June 27, 1990, Big Bethel AME Church file (hereafter BBAME file) and Friendship Baptist Church Centennial Celebration Pamphlet, April 1962, FBC file, Atlanta University Archives.

12. Wheat Street, originally Mt. Pleasant, Baptist, was the largest black Baptist church in the city by the turn of the nineteenth century and was one of the most activist Atlanta churches of the twentieth century. Men and women of some wealth and high status were members of Wheat Street, including Mrs. Caroline Badger, grocers Peter Eskridge, Thomas Goosby, Columbus King, and Willis Murphy. Wheat Street, like Bethel and Friendship, sponsored mutual aid societies and missions to tend to the black poor. The loss, by fire, of most of the nineteenth-century records limits discussion of Wheat Street Baptist Church. I have chosen Friendship Baptist to represent the Baptist contribution in Atlanta because of its pre–Civil War history, its role in helping to build

other congregations, and the consistency of leadership. Three men served as ministers at Friendship Baptist from 1862 to 1962: Frank Quarles (1862–81), E. R. Carter (1881–1943), and Maynard Jackson (1943–62).

13. Bethel AME Church Pamphlet, June 27, 1990, BBAME file. No surviving list of parishioners for Bethel AME exists. Some of Atlanta's nineteen free people of color may have accompanied slaves to Bethel's worship services.

14. Ibid.; Thornbery, "Development of Black Atlanta," 139. The AME church was nearly destroyed by fire during the siege of Atlanta.

15. Du Bois, *Some Efforts of American Negroes for Their Own Social Betterment*, 9.

16. Thornbery, "Development of Black Atlanta," 147, 157. Bethel AME did experience congregational infighting in the post–Civil War period. The transfer and appointment of ministers by the regional/national office often sparked controversy within the congregation.

17. FBC Records, June 13, 1848, FBC file.

18. FBC Records, September 1858, FBC file.

19. The FBC records list twenty-nine members of the African Church as of January 1859. Several more slaves requested dismission over the remainder of that year, a process that continued through 1864.

20. Carter, *Biographical Sketches of Our Pulpit*, 28–30.

21. FBC Records, February 21, 1864, FBC file.

22. AMA Archives, Georgia, 1867.

23. McMath, *Southern Pilgrimage*, 21–22.

24. First Congregational Church of Atlanta Records (hereafter FCC Records), box 65, drawer 188, Georgia Department of Archives and History.

25. McMath, *Southern Pilgrimage*, 22.

26. Thornbery, "Development of Black Atlanta," 181. Thornbery notes that First Congregational accepted white ministers appointed by the AMA until the church became financially independent in 1894. The Congregational church at the national level was slow to endorse the idea of black ministers. See Jones, *Soldiers of Light and Love*.

27. FBC Records, November 4, 1865, FBC file.

28. FBC Records, March 3, April 7, and May 5, 1866, FBC file. African American congregants made two inquiries to the church committee that had been assigned to consider a separate colored branch of the church in 1864. The committee ignored both inquiries. It is likely that these were early requests for dismission from First Baptist Church.

29. FBC Records, May 5, 1866, and Friendship Baptist Church Centennial Celebration Pamphlet, April 1962, FBC file.

30. FBC Records, November 1865, FBC file.

31. Frederick Ayers to W. E. Whiting, November 21, 1865, AMA Archives, Georgia; Thornbery, "Development of Black Atlanta," 141.

32. FBC Records, June 20, 1866, FBC file.

33. FBC Centennial Celebration Pamphlet, April 1962, FBC file; Thornbery, "Development of Black Atlanta," 141. Quarles's successor, E. R. Carter, made debt reduction a priority of his ministry. The church, according to Carter's *The Black Side*, was solvent and had expanded its worth considerably by 1894.

34. Big Bethel AME Church Pamphlet, June 27, 1990, BBAME file. Woods left Bethel to form a church in the Summerhill area sometime in 1866. He was pastor at Woods' Chapel until 1869 when the Conference relocated him. He returned to serve Woods' Chapel in the 1870s.

35. Bacote, *Story of Atlanta University*, 186, 210.

36. Jackson and Patterson, "Brief History of Selected Black Churches in Atlanta," 38.

37. This may account for the differences in wealth between AME and Baptist ministers in the city. Independent Baptist congregations were responsible for the salary of their ministers. AME ministers and bishops received stipends from the national organizations as well as contributions from the local congregations.

38. Levine, *Black Culture and Black Consciousness*, 140.

39. Montgomery, *Under Their Own Vine and Fig Tree*, 97–101.

40. Levine, *Black Culture and Black Consciousness*, 136–89; Mathews, *Religion in the Old South*, 185–236; Hurston, *The Sanctified Church*, 79–107; and Stuckey, *The Slave Culture*, 3–97. Levine discusses the transformation and decline of slave spirituals in the decades after the Civil War. He also details the rise of gospel song as rooted in spirituals.

41. Blassingame, *Slave Community*, 147, 148.

42. Johnson, *Black Savannah*, 34.

43. Hurston, *The Sanctified Church*, 91, 79–81.

44. Mathews, *Religion in the Old South*, 198–99.

45. Jones, *Soldiers of Light and Love*, 141–42, 154–55.

46. Washington, *Frustrated Fellowship*, 108–12.

47. Washington, *Frustrated Fellowship*, 110.

48. Penn and Bowen, eds., *United Negro*, 585.

49. "American Missionary," September 14, 1870 (qtd. in Jones, *Soldiers of Light and Love*, 155).

50. For an excellent discussion of the politics of disunion within the Baptist church, see Washington, *Frustrated Fellowship*. See also Jones, *Soldiers of Light and Love*, and Clarence Walker, *Rock in a Weary Land*. On the failure of the Methodist Episcopal church to recapture black congregations from either the AME or ME South church, see Montgomery in *Under Their Own Vine and Fig Tree* where he addresses the black desire for independent denominations.

51. Payne, *Recollections of Seventy Years*, 253–54 cited in Stuckey, *Slave Culture*, 93. Also see Walker, *Rock in a Weary Land*. Walker notes that the AME church was opposed to "Loud singing, shouting and gesticulations."

52. Stuckey, *Slave Culture*, 94–95.

53. First Congregational was the only black Congregational church in Atlanta from 1875 to 1900. The Congregationalists, the Episcopalians (who formed two black congregations from 1885 to 1900), the Presbyterians (two congregations in 1880), and the Lutherans (who had no black congregations) were not very successful in developing a following among African Americans in Georgia; none had more than three thousand members in the state. See Dittmer, *Black Georgia in the Progressive Era*.

54. FCC Records.

55. Proctor, *Between Black and White*, 49–53.

56. Ibid., 84–85.

57. Ibid., 51–52.

58. Proctor had been part of a quartet of black students at Yale. The group traveled around New England singing slave spirituals in local churches. The income helped the four pay their way through graduate school (*Between Black and White*, 41–42).

59. FCC Records.

60. Pioneering scholars of African American history August Meier and Elliot Rudwick documented the use of boycott as a political tool to challenge Jim Crow in some twenty-five cities in the South from 1900 to 1906. Meier and Rudwick argue that ministers were essential to the process of developing boycotts in most of the cities, noting that the southern white media and politicians "often pictured" black clergy "as the provocateurs of the boycotts." Though I disagree with their analysis of the role of Henry McNeal Turner in the Atlanta "boycott" of 1903/1904, their presentation of boycotts as evidence of black resistance to "a philosophy of accommodation" is convincing ("The Boycott Movement against Jim Crow Streetcars in the South, 1900–1906," 769).

61. Sobel, *Trabelin' On*, 199–200.

62. Raboteau, *Slave Religion*, 71–72, 84; Sobel, *Trabelin' On*, 197–200; Stuckey, *Slave Culture*, 11–12.

63. City Council Records, March 5, 1852, R (Rough Sections):77.

64. Du Bois, *Some Efforts of American Negroes for Their Own Social Betterment*, 52 and BBAME file, church pamphlet, 12.

65. The Independent Order of Odd Fellows has a tangled history with respect to the "legitimacy" of African American Lodges. Black Odd Fellows belong to the Grand United Order of Odd Fellows (hereafter GUOOF) and are not recognized by the white Independent Order of Odd Fellows (hereafter IOOF). The link between the tradition of secret societies in West African cultures and the appeal of these organizations to African Americans is addressed in chapter 5.

66. Carter, *The Black Side*, 50–52; Du Bois, *Some Efforts of American Negroes for Their Own Social Betterment*, 3, 16.

67. In 1895 the Methodist Episcopal Church (ME as opposed to AME) organized the Epworth League to try to address the social needs of Christian youths. Its stated purpose was to provide "legitimate entertainment and sport in the church for boys and girls, where the company may be select and within the sacred suggestiveness of the church itself, rather than run the risk attendant upon these same young people seeking entertainment promiscuously." The league had a thriving chapter among black Methodist Episcopal congregations in Atlanta. Dr. I. Garland Penn, assistant general secretary of its "colored chapters," was based in Atlanta and credited with encouraging a "refined culture" among the "colored people" (Hartshorn and Penniman, eds., *An Era of Progress and Promise*, 529–30).

68. E. R. Carter Papers, Financial Records, 90–004–01–002, Atlanta Fulton County Public Library, Auburn Avenue Branch.

69. Carter, *The Black Side*, 43–44. Davis, *A Clashing of the Soul*, 145–47. Davis notes the existence of the black Abyssinian Library, "a reading room" that had been founded

in 1880 but was destroyed by fire two years later. Over the protests of members of the local black elite, including John Hope and W. E. B. Du Bois, African Americans were barred from the Carnegie Library, which opened in Atlanta in 1902. The 1894 WCTU library represented an effort on the part of African Americans to provide services to their own community.

70. "In Tribute to the Generous," chapter 10 of *Between Black and White*, details Proctor's efforts to raise money for expansion. He notes that he received twenty-five hundred dollars from "colored people" of other denominations and five thousand dollars from white citizens of Atlanta (*Between Black and White*, 117–120).

71. *Some Efforts of American Negroes for Their Own Social Betterment*, 11.

72. Ibid., 51.

73. FCC Records, box 65, drawer 188.

74. In addition, Proctor devoted much time to the YMCA (colored). First Congregational also offered some support to the Carrie Steele Logan Orphanage.

75. The Men and Religion Forward Movement was part of national Progressive-era reform efforts. Founded in New York City by businessmen concerned with the moral and religious reformation of their city, the movement spread down the eastern seaboard, arriving in Atlanta after the turn of the century. See Gail Bederman, " 'The Women Have Had Charge of the Church Work Long Enough.' "

76. FCC Records, July 31, 1912, box 65, drawer 188. Neill, "The Week They Tore Old Manhattan Street Down," 84–90. McEwen, "First Congregational Church, Atlanta," 129–42.

77. Du Bois, *Some Efforts of American Negroes for Their Own Social Betterment*, 11. Du Bois's perspective on black benevolent societies was complicated. He clearly understood their cultural distinctiveness, linking them to a "communism" born on the "floor of the African jungle." He was also deeply concerned with the "Negro's" march toward "civilization" and "the pressing need of . . . rescue and reformation among Negroes," specifically, "benevolence in its broadest and best sense, and not as pure alms-giving." Like Proctor's, Du Bois's acceptance of the "degradation of the race" seems to have colored his analysis of charity work among poorer African Americans.

78. Roger Lane, *William Dorsey's Philadelphia and Ours*, 246.

Four. Community Action and Resistance

1. Du Bois, *Black Reconstruction in America*, 637–69.

2. Ibid., 638.

3. Foner, *Reconstruction*, 96.

4. Patton, "The Black Community of Augusta and the Struggle for Ware High School," 45; Johnson, *Black Savannah*, 126–29. Johnson reports that schools for black children were "an open secret" in Savannah, where, for the most part, officials ignored the violation of the law in the 1840s.

5. Edmund Asa Ware Papers, Report to the American Missionary Association, 20–B-1–A, pt. 1, Atlanta University Archives. Tate and Daniel continued to teach after the

arrival of the AMA. AMA teacher Rose Hunt noted the assistance of two colored men in the night school. Another teacher later complained that despite their willingness to work, they were not qualified to be AMA teachers. Jennifer Lund Smith identifies Tate's teaching partner as Grandsion Daniels, rather than as Granithan Daniel, in her essay "The Ties that Bind: Educated African American Women in Post-Emancipation Atlanta."

6. Rabinowitz, *Race Relations in the Urban South*, 157.

7. Foner, *Reconstruction*, 98.

8. Ware Papers, Report to the American Missionary Association, 20–B-1–A, pt. 1.

9. AMA Papers, letter from Barnum to Hunt, January 27, 1866.

10. Annual Report of the Board of Education, August 31, 1873 (hereafter Board of Education Reports), Atlanta Fulton Public Library, Main Branch.

11. Du Bois, *Black Reconstruction*, 638.

12. Ibid., 645.

13. Drago, *Black Politicians and Reconstruction in Georgia*, 98. James Porter was expelled from the Georgia state legislature along with other black legislators in September 1868. The 1868 legislature was reinstated in December 1869 by an act of the U.S. Congress. See chapter 6, "Citizenship Denied."

14. Drago characterizes black politicians as politically conservative, "accepting" racial discrimination during much of the period. However, I find no evidence of such conservatism. The Republican legislature reconstructed the municipal code in Atlanta to permit ward-specific elections to the city council, giving the black community, for a brief time, electoral clout in the city. The council became the vehicle through which the community attempted, continually, to exercise agency in the fight for education.

15. State Commissioner of Schools Gustavus J. Orr shared the perspective of the Atlanta school board, noting that "white people pay twenty-nine thirtieths of the taxes" while black children benefited. Complaints about the "numbers and poverty of the colored people [who] constitute a great incumbrance [sic]" on the resources of the state repeatedly surface in the state school commissioner's reports. This fiction would become commonplace in discussions of southern public education from the end of the Civil War to the beginning of the Civil Rights movement. In his discussion of public funding for segregated black schools, James Anderson makes the case that black taxpayers did pay considerably more than one-thirtieth of the cost of their children's education through taxes. In actuality, as the accumulation of real property increased, black taxpayers were double taxed for public education. Under the system of separate and distinctly unequal, black taxpayers paid into a pool of public funds, the bulk of which went to finance white schools while black schools received the remainder. In addition, African Americans privately contributed more money to black schools to help supplement the insufficient funds provided by the state. See the Fourth and Fifth Annual Reports of the State School Commissioner, Atlanta Fulton Public Library, 29, 89, respectively (*The Education of Blacks in the South, 1860–1935*, 154–56).

16. Records of the Proceedings of the Board of Education of the City of Atlanta, Georgia, vol. 1, Report of the Committee on Public Schools to the City Council of Atlanta, Georgia, 1869, 11, Atlanta Board of Education.

17. Board of Education Minutes, September 26, 1872 and November 19, 1872, 1:74, 77.

18. Ibid., 320, 323.

19. Board of Education Report, August 31, 1873, 36; Board of Education Minutes, December 16, 1872, 1:78.

20. City Council Records, May 15, 1874, 8:74.

21. Board of Education Minutes, August 22, 1874, 1:124–28

22. Board of Education Minutes, April 24, 1873, 1:87; Smith, "The Ties that Bind," 97.

23. City Council Records, March 19, 1877, 8:369, 470. The council advanced the board six thousand dollars, a far cry from the requested thirty-five thousand. Smith, "The Tie that Binds," 99.

24. Board of Education Minutes, August 22, 1874, 1:122.

25. The school board purchased the Summer Hill School in 1877, leaving only Storrs under private control.

26. See Du Bois, *Black Reconstruction,* chapter 15.

27. Though, as I have been arguing, the developing commitment to uplift ideology was grafted onto a primary dedication to racial solidarity rooted in their recent experiences of slavery, black educators were not entirely able to escape the individualist leanings of this philosophy. Trained to become the teachers and leaders of their race, to self-identify as "the better class," some blacks chose to pursue other avenues of employment as well as to distance themselves from communities engaged in the uplift project. Glenda Gilmore, who also roots much of the black community activism of this period in "their lived experiences in slavery," recognizes that some blacks "embraced bourgeois individualism" and rejected a life of service to the race (*Gender and Jim Crow,* chapter 4). I would argue that the tendency to reject both the ideology of uplift and community-based activism grew as greater numbers of blacks gained access to education and their material wealth increased. Addressing the ideology of progress and uplift imbedded in the education for blacks, Stephanie Shaw argues that students were able to overcome the "tension inherent in balancing their individual advantages against perceived community responsibilities" because they were able to "transcend" the very slight class and status differences that defined the black community in the last quarter of the nineteenth century. (*What a Woman Ought to Be and to Do,* chapter 3).

28. *Iola Leroy, or Shadows Uplifted,* 219. Frances Ellen Watkins Harper authored what Frances Smith Foster has suggested was "the first best-selling novel by an Afro-American writer prior to the twentieth century." Born free in Baltimore, Maryland in the 1820s, Harper moved to Philadelphia where she became a protégée of abolitionist and Underground Railroad chronicler William Still. The first black female teacher at Union Seminary in Wilberforce, Ohio, Harper championed civil and political rights for blacks and women. See Frances Smith Foster's introduction to the 1988 Oxford University Press edition of *Iola Leroy.*

29. Both James Anderson and Stephanie Shaw discuss the efforts of educators, northern missionaries, and local teachers to instill a sense of moral and social leadership in their students. The goal, as Shaw points out, was to create generations of men and women who would by example lead their race in the acculturation of Victorian values and in the

battle for their civil rights (Anderson, *The Education of Blacks in the South;* Shaw, *What a Woman Ought to Be and to Do*). See also Davis, *A Clashing of the Soul,* 89–90 and Du Bois, *The Souls of Black Folk,* 82–83.

30. Rouse, *Lugenia Burns Hope,* 28–29. In 1898, Lugenia Burns Hope moved to Atlanta from Chicago where she had engaged in social work with the Kings Daughters and the Silver Cross Club. She applied her considerable social work skills to addressing the problems of vice and crime as well as those of inadequate housing, waste and sewage removal, and lack of recreational facilities for children in Black Atlanta. The Neighborhood Union was founded in 1908 with, as Rouse explains, very ambitious goals, including improving sanitation services, improving neighborhood interaction, and providing lectures and services to instill "habits of cleanliness" and "promote child welfare." See chapter 4, as well as Hunter, *"To 'Joy My Freedom."*

31. Davis, *Henry Grady's New South,* 82.

32. Board of Education Minutes, August 23, 1877, 1:241.

33. Board of Education Minutes, July 26, 1877, and August 27, 1877, 1:240, 244.

34. Board of Education Minutes, October 9 and 25, 1877, 1:251–52. Smith identifies Indiana Clark and Ella Townsley, AU graduates, as "the first black women to teach in the Atlanta public school system." This is correct if Norris and Turner, who were hired by the public school board to serve at Storrs, an AMA affiliated school that served as a public school for blacks, are discounted. Norris's and Turner's employment was a direct result of black community pressure and worthy of note (Smith, "The Ties that Bind," 97).

35. Board of Education Minutes, June 13, 1878, 1:272. Ministers A. Brown, Owen George, R. A. Hall, J. L. Hamilton, W. H. Harrison, A. W. Lowe, and W. H. Tilman were also members of the council. H. Curry, H. Lutton, V. Wares, A. Simms, B. H. Townsley, A. Floyd, J. Perry, Owen Smith, and A. Holmes rounded out the twenty-five.

36. Board of Education Minutes, September 2, 1878, 1:278–79. Both of David Howard's daughters, A. D. Badger and L. E. Badger, were employed as teachers in the Houston Street School in 1895.

37. John Beatie was the white school board member who represented the mostly black third ward. He served twenty years and eventually became president of the school board in 1892. Beatie was a supporter of black public schools and was very active in pressuring the board to provide more facilities for black children in both the 1870s and 1880s. Given the history of the black community's pattern of lobbying, it is likely that his constituents from the third ward made their desires for more public school space for black children a condition of his reelection.

38. Tenth Annual Report for the School Year Ending September 1, 1881, 8, Atlanta Fulton Public Library, Main Branch.

39. Ibid.

40. Eighteenth Annual Report for the School Year Ending January, 31, 1889, 16.

41. *Southern Recorder,* October 2, 1886.

42. Sixteenth Annual Report for the School Year Ending January 1, 1887, 13.

43. Board of Education Minutes, June 29, 1889, 2:60. The African American community tended to accept the gender conventions of the era with regard to salary discrepan-

cies between male and female teachers and principals. Black women who tried to make ends meet on miserly teachers' salaries found their lives proscribed by wage discrimination and were often forced to take second jobs to supplement their income. Many women, including Eva Beatrice Dykes, one of the nation's first black female Ph.D.s, spoke out against the practice of wage discrimination on the basis of gender. Yet, for the most part, the black community focused greater attention on ending discrimination based on race rather than gender. Significantly, the same ideology that stressed black female selflessness in service to the race work of uplift and acculturation also supported the Victorian notion that women could be paid less because they were not male heads of households. In a similar vein, the black community in Atlanta did not challenge the 1883 school board policy prohibiting the employment of married teachers. While the Atlanta school board amended this policy five years later to allow individual married women to serve with specific approval of the board, the black community did not contest the belief that female teachers should resign from the profession upon their marriage (Smith, "The Ties that Bind"). In Atlanta and across the South, blacks did object to the fact that white female educators were paid more than their black peers and they struggled to increase the baseline salaries of all black teachers. For the most part, however, blacks were unable to end wage discrimination on the basis of race for teachers in the nineteenth century. Stephanie Shaw reports that the legal battle to equalize salaries for black teachers was spearheaded by the NAACP with the backing of local black community members in the 1930s and 1940s (*What a Woman Ought to Be and to Do*, 201–2). For a more detailed discussion see Tushnet, *The NAACP's Legal Strategy against Segregated Education.*

44. Thirteenth Annual Report of the Board of Education for the Year Ending January 1, 1885, 12.

45. *Atlanta Independent,* April 13, 1907.

46. "Our City Schools Again," *Atlanta Independent,* January 23, 1904.

47. In early twentieth-century municipal elections, blacks used their votes as leverage in the battle for access to public education. Black leaders let it be known that they would endorse a 1921 school bond issue only if the city would begin construction of a black public high school. The municipal elections of 1921 differed from those of 1903 in that African Americans, voting as a block, had twice previously helped to defeat the measure. School board officials, recognizing the need for the bond issue, finally acceded to black demands for a public high school.

48. Upon relocating to Atlanta the Augusta Institute changed its name first to Atlanta Baptist Seminary (1879), then to Atlanta Baptist College (1897), finally settling on Morehouse College (1913). The school granted the first college degree in 1883.

49. Clark University charged one-dollar monthly tuition in 1880; room and board fees were an additional six to eight dollars. Tuition at Spelman and Atlanta Baptist Seminary also rose to one dollar per month in the 1880s. Atlanta Baptist Seminary charged six to seven dollars per month for board and washing. By 1895, Clark day students above the fourth grade paid $1.50 per month in tuition; board cost $11.50 per month (City Directory, 1880, 1885, 1890, and 1895).

50. Some African American students attending Atlanta's black colleges were indeed

the children of the South's black elite from Savannah and Augusta. David Levering Lewis, reporting on the population at AU when Du Bois arrived in 1897, notes that "the children of white fathers, or of parents whose fathers and grandfathers were white, came to the university from all over the South" (*W. E. B. Du Bois: Biography of a Race*, 213–14). Atlanta's black universities and colleges, like Fisk, Howard, Tuskegee, and Hampton, did serve the educational needs of a variety of African Americans, including the "mulatto elite." Bazoline Usher speaking of her time as an undergraduate at Atlanta University at the turn of the century recalled "girls who were sent there by their white fathers, most of . . . [whom] were able to pay full board." However, these schools also admitted and graduated thousands of black men and women, newly freed slaves, with no white ancestry and no privileged status. Ms. Usher notes that she was "a part-time student" who had to put in two hours of laundry work to help finance her tuition at AU (Ilhe, ed., *Black Women in Higher Education*, 71).

51. Davis, *A Clashing of the Soul*, 90–91. Davis details the increasing divide between John Hope and Booker T. Washington as Hope recognized the extent to which Washington was willing to accommodate the position of white conservatives. A "race man," who, despite his family background and fair complexion, devoted his life to agitating for black equality, Hope aligned himself with Henry Trotter, W. E. B. Du Bois, and Alonzo Herndon in the Niagara movement in an effort to challenge Washington's dominance.

52. Bacote, *The Story of Atlanta University*, 186.

53. Report of the Board of Visitors, *Atlanta Constitution*, July 3, 1871.

54. Ihle, ed., *Black Women in Higher Education*, 63.

55. Penn, *United Negro*, 454.

56. *Baptist Home Mission Monthly*, 1–2 (May 1878–December 1880): 106. Jennifer Lund Smith observes that freed blacks, "sensed both the racial and regional condescension of northern whites, and they were not always comfortable with the values promoted by northern missionaries" ("The Ties that Bind," 95). This view is consistent with Jacqueline Jones's commentary that northern missionary teachers "did not find . . . an eager and compliant audience" among urban blacks (*Soldiers of Light and Love*, 143).

Five. Fraternity, Community, and Status

1. *The Idea of Fraternity in America*, 62.

2. This term is borrowed from Evelyn Brooks Higginbotham's *Righteous Discontent*. Brooks Higginbotham argues that black Baptist women used traditional methods of political protest to fight against Jim Crow and also engaged in and promoted social and cultural transformation in an atttempt to subvert the ideology of racism.

3. Du Bois, *The College-Bred Negro*, 57.

4. White, *Too Heavy a Load*, 67–72.

5. Penn, *United Negro*, 449.

6. Proctor, "Negro Womanhood," Henry Hugh Proctor Papers, Amistad Research Center, Tulane University, New Orleans, La.

7. Penn, *United Negro*, 437.

8. Ibid., 440.

9. White, *Too Heavy a Load*, 36, 86. White notes that Addie Hunton was extraordinarily active in black progressive work in the first three decades of the twentieth century. In addition to serving as an organizer for the Georgia Federation of Colored Women's Clubs as well as for the National Association of Women's Clubs (NACW), she was also instrumental in the development of the Brooklyn Suffrage League. She also helped organize the NAACP and served as a representative of the AKA sorority. Further, as Christine Ann Lutz notes in her doctoral dissertation on the Hunton family, Addie Hunton wrote for Jesse Max Barber's Atlanta-based *Voice of the Negro* ("The Dizzy Steep to Heaven," 138–39, 146).

10. *United Negro*, 433–35.

11. White, *Too Heavy a Load*, 61. Hunton wrote "Negro Womanhood Defended" as a rather scathing reply to William Hannibal Thomas who, in the 1901 volume *The American Negro, What He Was, What He Is and What He May Become*, condemned "ninety percent of the negro women of America as lascivious by instinct and in bondage to physical pleasure" (qtd. in White, 61).

12. *Spelman Messenger* 22 (April 1906): 2; *Spelman Messenger* 28 (March 1912): 2.

13. Deborah Gray White notes that black clubwomen understood "that the sexual exploitation of black women originated during the slavery era" and more important, they "believed they could overcome their history" through a program of cultural improvement that stressed the need for chastity (*Too Heavy a Load*, 69). Glenda Gilmore, in *Gender and Jim Crow*, also supports this view. Gilmore notes that black women who supported the work of the WCTU advocated adoption of mainstream Victorian values both to protect the image of black women and to aid in their efforts to fight racist exclusion (101–5).

14. Wallace, "Are We Men?" 182.

15. Salvatore, *We All Got History*, 66.

16. McWilliams, *The Idea of Fraternity in America*, 587. McWilliams addressed the history of black fraternal organizations in the final chapter of his work. In a section entitled Sinn Fein (we ourselves), McWilliams explains that "racial community and fraternity" are "rooted in the immediate experiences and feelings of black Americans." He goes on to argue that the commitment to "the black world[,] . . . a setting which is 'home,'" is a response to white racism and oppression. "The very solace and comfort available in black society are inseparably related to feelings of defeat . . . If home is a fortress to which man can repair, in black America it has also been a prison, a 'mark of oppression.'" While much of McWilliams' discussion of fraternity is salient to my discussion, his understanding of black community as primarily a prison is not consistent with contemporary historical analysis.

17. Black Freemasonry in America had its origins with Prince Hall and the founding of the first lodge of black Masons in Boston in 1776. The English Odd Fellows granted the first charter to African Americans in 1843 (Voorhis, *Negro Masonry in the United States*, 3–11).

18. Big Bethel AME Centennial Celebration Flyer, August 29, 1965, and Carter, *The Black Side*, 50–51. The Grand United Order of Odd Fellows would become the largest black fraternal organization in Georgia in the first quarter of the twentieth century. The

size and wealth of the organization made it a lending institution for blacks in the south. See Dittmer, *Black Georgia*, 57.

19. *Atlanta Independent.*

20. For example, local Atlanta Masons contributed to the construction of a Masonic widows' and orphans' home in Americus, Georgia. See Du Bois, *Some Efforts of American Negroes for Their Own Social Betterment*, 52.

21. City Council Records, October 27, 1871, 7:68; April 7 and 24, 1874, 8:55, 64.

22. Fulton County Tax Digest, 1895; Carter, *The Black Side*, 52.

23. Carter, *The Black Side*, 52.

24. Cargile made a good living as an undertaker. The Fulton County Tax Digest lists his taxable property as $1,617 in 1876 and $2,025 in 1885.

25. The Good Samaritans were listed in the 1890 Fulton County Tax Digest as owning fifteen hundred dollars in taxable property.

26. City Council Records, April 2, 1877, 8:474; January 8, February 18, March 14, and March 18, 1878, 9:411, 710–11, 763, 764; January 15, 1883, 10:94; September 6, 1886, 11:519–20.

27. The Independent Order of Red Men, a white fraternal order, had petitioned the Atlanta City Council in 1876, asking to purchase lots in Oakland Cemetery to sell to its members. The request was approved May 1, 1876 (City Council Records, 8:358).

28. Carter, *The Black Side*, 27. Carter states that the building owned by the Good Samaritans was worth thirty thousand dollars. The 1895 Fulton County Tax Digest lists the value of the property at $7,500. Four years later, according to the Atlanta University study, the order had "lost possession" of the building. See Du Bois, *Some Efforts of American Negroes for Their Own Social Betterment*, 52.

29. Du Bois, *Some Efforts of American Negroes for Their Own Social Betterment*, 52.

30. Price, "Friendly Visiting," in Du Bois, ed. *Social and Physical Condition of Negroes in Cities*, 59.

31. Du Bois, *Social and Physical Condition of Negroes in Cities*, 59.

32. Ibid., 58.

33. Ibid., 45.

34. Du Bois, *Some Efforts of American Negroes for Their Own Social Betterment*, 20–21. Also see Henderson, *Atlanta Life Insurance Company*, 1–11.

35. Du Bois, *Some Efforts of American Negroes for Their Own Social Betterment*, 19. There is no other reference to this organization in the sources.

36. Carter, *The Black Side*, 38–43.

37. Henderson, *Atlanta Life Insurance Company*, 13.

38. Ibid., 15. Henderson argues that "blacks believed that regulatory legislation would guarantee that companies carried out their part of the insurance agreement and would place 'the insurer and insured upon mutual grounds'"(14). Du Bois, in his analysis of mutual aid societies, does not dispute the fact that "irresponsible parties" were involved in insurance societies; however, I have found no evidence that suggests members of mutual aid societies were supporters of this legislation. Also see Dittmer, *Black Georgia*, 48–49.

39. Rev. James Arthur Hopkins, cited in Henderson, *Atlanta Life Insurance Company*, 17. White insurance firms apparently recognized the potential profit to be made insuring

African Americans in Georgia. William D. Driskell, secretary and superintendent of the black-owned United Mutual Relief Association of Georgia, reported in the *Atlanta Independent* that agents of "white fraternal and industrial insurance companies" had spread rumors about improper business practices at UMRA in order to lure potential customers. The UMRA regularly published quarterly statements of receipts, disbursements, and assets in the *Atlanta Independent*, and appears to have had a thriving business. The firm reported a year-end balance of $180,775.06 in December 1903.

40. The black newspapers played an important role in supporting the public outreach of the fraternal orders and benevolent societies. Along with advertisements for black-owned businesses and services and chatty news columns with reports of a black matron's most recent gala, local black newspapers—Ben Davis's *Atlanta Independent* and the AME's *Christian Recorder*—advertised upcoming events in the community and printed notices of lodge meetings. In addition, the *Atlanta Independent* regularly carried an ad for a "Colored Baseball Park, Between Barracks Line and Clark University. Owned and controlled exclusively by colored people. A place where you can go and enjoy all occasions."

41. The life of the Huntons is detailed by Christine Ann Lutz in "The Dizzy Steep to Heaven." Adele Logan Alexander offers a brief commentary on the Hunton family in the introduction to a volume that contains Addie W. Hunton and Kathryn M. Johnson's *Two Colored Women* as well as Addie W. Hunton's biography of her husband, William Alphaeus Hunton. Both Lutz and Alexander note that the upheaval of the 1906 riot pushed the Huntons to relocate to the north.

42. Davis reports that Hope delivered an address at the YMCA Colored Department's convention in Atlanta in 1903. Like Hunton (who had balked at the YMCA International Committee's decision to host a meeting in the segregated Kimball House in 1901), Hope was disturbed by the discriminatory practices of the YMCA, though, Davis notes, he "never wavered in his support for[it]" (*A Clashing of the Soul*, 186, 187).

43. "Good Work of YMCA," *Atlanta Independent*, January 20, 1904.

44. *Atlanta Independent*, February 6, 1904. Arguing that the government did have an obligation to provide education for descendents of freed slaves were H. W. B. Wilson, E. W. Kinchen, and D. L. Morgan of Gammon Theological Seminary. Arguing against the government's responsibility to provide for the education of the freedmen's descendants were C. L. Harper, educator W. B. Matthews, and Jas. W. Woodiee of the YMCA. Dr. John Hope, Reverend J. S. Flipper, and political activist H. A. Rucker served as judges.

45. Frederick Douglass Literary Society Announcement, *Atlanta Independent*, February 27, 1904. A. D. Williams, grandfather of M. L. King Jr., gave the benediction at the February 22 gathering.

46. See Hunter, *"To 'Joy My Freedom,"* chapter 8, "Dancing and Carousing the Night Away," 168–86. Atlanta's famous Odd Fellows Hall was not erected in what would become Sweet Auburn Avenue's black business district until 1904. Sweet Auburn blossomed more in the decade after than before the riot.

47. Carter G. Woodson criticized the author of *Secret Societies: A Cultural Study of Fraternalism in the United States* in his review in the *Journal of Negro History* for ignoring the history of black fraternalism. Maurice Wallace, in "Are We Men?: Prince Hall,

Martin Delany, and the Masculine Ideal in Black Freemasonry," argues that the pattern of "academic neglect" concerning black fraternal orders has not changed over time.

48. Du Bois, *Some Efforts of American Negroes for Their Own Social Betterment*, 17.

49. Ibid., 5.

50. Betty Kuyk, "The African Derivation of Black Fraternal Orders in the United States," 581. Writing more than thirty years after Du Bois, sociologist James A. Jackson offered an analysis in the *Crisis* magazine of fraternal societies that foreshadowed Kuyk's presentation of them as evidence of the survival of African culture and centers of masculine leadership training. Jackson argued that secret societies in the era of Jim Crow served a useful function. "Denied the right to vote, to participate in primaries or local caucuses, and without the privilege of participation in other community organizations, where else would the Negro have become trained to meet the demands for political and civic intelligence of a practical sort, as the race pushed forward into national affairs? The Negro political leaders of the 'Early Eighties' and the 'Gay Nineties' were virtually all products of lodge room education" (235). Historian John Dittmer also weighed in on the role of black fraternal organizations, noting "Lodge membership gave blacks a sense of 'belonging,' of 'being somebody.' It provided training in leadership, teamwork, and institutional government for a race excluded from participation in the affairs of the total community" (*Black Georgia*, 59).

51. Brooks Higginbotham, *Righteous Discontent*, 17.

52. Foner, "The Meaning of Freedom in the Age of Emancipation," 458.

53. Hartshorn, *An Era of Progress and Promise*.

54. Ibid., introductory pages.

55. Ibid., 463.

56. Ibid., 58.

57. Ibid., 59.

58. Brooks Higginbotham, *Righteous Discontent*, 187–88. Karen Ferguson, a fellow participant in the University of Houston Black History Workshop, also emphasizes the importance of Brooks Higginbotham's concept of the politics of respectability in her recent work on Atlanta, *Black Politics in New Deal Atlanta*.

59. Du Bois, *The Souls of Black Folk*, 137.

60. Stephanie Shaw, *What a Woman Ought to Be and to Do*, 81. This quote is taken from chapter 3, which begins with a telling epigram: "We are not educating individuals but manufacturing levers"—a phrase that highlights the dual nature of the process of education and acculturation in the postbellum period. Black children, male and female, were to be skilled in trades for improved employment opportunities as well as trained in Christian values and Victorian mores, while at the same time being educated to lift and lead their race in freedom.

Six. Citizenship Denied

1. Drago, *Black Politicians and Reconstruction in Georgia: A Splendid Failure*.

2. Ibid., 48–56. The Georgia Supreme Court also endorsed the right of African Ameri-

cans to hold office in 1869, deciding in favor of Richard White of Chatham County. See Du Bois, *Black Reconstruction*, 470.

3. Aptheker, *A Documentary History of the Negro People in the United States*. This was just one of a series of political conventions of freedmen and -women across the South during Reconstruction. Frank Quarles and James Tate both served as delegates to the convention from Fulton County. See Smith, "The Ties that Bind," n. 15.

4. Drago, *Black Politicians and Reconstruction in Georgia*, 28.

5. Bryant's biographer, Ruth Currie-McDaniel, speaks well of him, describing him as a "carpetbagger of conscience" who began his political life "seemingly on the cutting edge of Radicalism," going "so far as to say that blacks were socially equal." Currie-McDaniel highlights Bryant's efforts to stave off the impact of Blodgett and Bullock's corrupt deal making and racial exclusion in the early 1870s. Yet despite this praise, Currie-McDaniel concedes that Bryant had, by the spring of 1877, "made his peace with the Republican Party's shift" to the "lily-white" strategy that denied patronage, political access, and civil rights to African Americans (*Carpetbagger of Conscience*, 181, 153, 154). Also see Russell Duncan, *Entrepreneur for Equality*, for more on Bullock.

6. Quoted in Drago, *Black Politicians and Reconstruction in Georgia*, 42.

7. Freedmen meeting at the Augusta Convention had passed a resolution endorsing the proposition that lands in possession of freed blacks in the state should not be confiscated except through a direct act of Congress. This resolution stood in opposition to the policy of the Johnson Administration.

8. Turner, Bradley, and Campbell were just three of thirty-seven black delegates elected to serve at the 1867 constitutional convention. Of the three, Henry McNeal Turner would go on to figure most prominently in the story of black political action in Atlanta. In addition to serving two terms in the Georgia legislature, Turner won patronage appointments as postmaster and customs inspector. Frustrated with the Republican Party's failure to protect black civil rights, he left formal politics in 1875, relocating to Pennsylvania. Turner was appointed bishop in the AME Church in 1880 and returned to Morris Brown College in Atlanta where he served as president through the turn of the century. Turner would become increasingly militant as Jim Crow traditions hardened, condemning, for example, the 1883 U.S. Supreme Court decision that overturned the 1875 Civil Rights Act as one that "fathers all the Jim Crow cars into which colored people are huddled . . . [and] made the ballot of the black man a parody, his citizenship a nullity and his freedom a burlesque." In the 1890s and 1900s, he would consistently agitate against segregation in transportation in Atlanta. Bishop Turner would eventually denounce the American flag as "a dirty contemptible rag" and call for blacks to return to Africa (Drago, *Black Politicians and Reconstruction in Georgia*, 157–59). For a complete biography of Turner, see Stephen W. Angell, *Bishop Henry McNeal Turner and African American Religion in the South*. For more information on Tunis Campbell, see Russell Duncan, *Freedom's Shore: Tunis Campbell and the Georgia Freedmen*.

9. Bryant, "We Have No Chance of Justice before the Courts," in *Georgia in Black and White*, ed. John C. Inscoe, 18.

10. John T. Costin's resolution, which was accepted as part of the Judiciary report,

stated that "there shall be no distinction between the classes of persons who compose Grand and Petit Juries" and called for all jurors to be compensated equally for their time. Since the resolution did not specifically state that African Americans had the right to serve as jurors, it allowed white conservatives to justify barring blacks.

11. Drago, 43–44; Sanford, "The Negro in the Political Reconstruction of Georgia," 19. Similarly, conservative forces combined to declare Georgia a white man's country by proposing disfranchisement for blacks in 1907. W. H. Rogers, the lone black representative in office, defended the rights of blacks to vote by arguing that the then proposed Felder-Williams Bill was counter to the Fifteenth Amendment and therefore unconstitutional.

12. Sanford, "The Negro in the Political Reconstruction of Georgia," 22–26. A. A. Bradley was accused of being A. Bradley of New York State who had been tried and convicted of breach of promise for having told a young mulatto woman he would marry her in order to seduce her. Opponents charged that Bradley's felony conviction invalidated his status as a citizen and as a result he could not legally be elected to office. Bradley did not deny the charges but suggested that many white delegates were guilty of similar deeds. Also see Reidy, "Aaron A. Bradley: Voice of Black Labor in the Georgia Lowcountry."

13. Sanford, "The Negro in the Political Reconstruction of Georgia," 38. Twenty-six of twenty-nine elected African American legislators were expelled. Simeon Beard, Edwin Belcher, and Madison Davis, all mulattos, were so fair their race could not be determined and so they escaped expulsion. F. H. Fyall, also a fair mulatto, was expelled with other blacks despite his protestations that he was white. Both Belcher and Davis faced the censure of black voters for their failure to embrace their race. See Foner, *Freedom's Lawmakers,* 14, 15–16, 58, 80.

14. Sanford, "The Negro in the Political Reconstruction of Georgia," 39.

15. *Atlanta Constitution,* July 20, 1871. The editors of the *Constitution* chose to overlook the February 1868 visit of Nathan Bedford Forrest to Atlanta as part of a Ku Klux Klan promotional tour as well as the numerous attacks on black men and women in counties surrounding the city. See Bryant, "We Have No Chance of Justice before the Courts," 23. Also see Du Bois, *Black Reconstruction,* 503–4. Both the Committee on Reconstruction and the Joint Select Committee to Inquire into the Affairs of the Late Insurrectionary States heard testimony involving the legislative expulsion, Ku Klux Klan violence, the Camilla Riot of September 1868, and other violations of the civil rights of African Americans in the state of Georgia.

16. Blassingame, "Before the Ghetto," 463–88. Foner, *Freedom's Lawmakers,* 241–42.

17. *Atlanta Independent,* February 13, 1904; Perry, "The Negro as a Political Factor in Georgia," 10–11, 15–16, 32.

18. Russell and Thornbery, "William Finch of Atlanta," 313–14. The expulsion of black legislators in 1868 enabled Democratic officials in Atlanta to secure a change in the charter allowing for citywide elections that functioned to dilute black voting strength. The reinstatement by the Congress in December 1869 allowed a Republican representative to reverse the earlier decision in time for the 1870 elections.

19. Watts, "Black Political Progress in Atlanta," 274.

20. Bacote, "The Negro in Atlanta Politics," 338–39. The elections of 1895 and 1896 were exceptions. The strength of the Populist Party at the time posed a threat to Democratic rule in the city—the Democrats temporarily suspended the white primary, and black voters proved to be instrumental in helping to defeat Populist candidates in both elections. Once the Populist threat was neutralized, Democrats reinstated the white primary ("The Negro in Atlanta Politics," 338–39).

21. Drago, *Black Politicians and Reconstruction in Georgia,* 43–44.

22. Kousser noted that the 1877 poll tax law, advocated by Confederate General Robert Toombs, had the desired consequence of diminishing the black vote in Georgia. Kousser also noted that the cumulative poll tax law had a detrimental effect upon the state's Populist Party by disfranchising the base of working-class and poor whites, an analysis shared by Michael Perman. See Kousser, *The Shaping of Southern Politics,* 210–11 and Perman, *Struggle for Mastery,* 281–82.

23. Georgia Constitution, 1877. The city of Atlanta instituted a similar law in the city code of 1875. Voters were required to pay all yearly taxes prior to registration. Eugene Watts notes that these requirements were relaxed when city fathers perceived that a large black voting population would serve their purposes. The poll tax law would have been particularly effective in eliminating the black vote in Atlanta. The Fulton County Tax Digest of 1880 notes that there were some 627 African American tax-paying property owners in the city of Atlanta. An additional 485 property owners were defaulters that year, unable to pay their taxes when they were due. Of the total 1,113 property owners, only 31 owned at least one thousand dollars in property.

24. Georgia Laws, 1908, 27, cited in Perry, "The Negro as a Political Factor in Georgia," 20.

25. Earlier efforts to disfranchise the black population (e.g., the 1899 Hardwick Bill) were voted down in the legislature on the grounds that such measures would also reduce the number of whites able to vote. The Hardwick Bill had made both literacy and property ownership requirements for voter registration, rather than just one or the other.

26. Watts, "Black Political Progress in Atlanta," 268–86. Watts notes that the average property value of black politicians in Atlanta was less than one thousand dollars prior to 1890.

27. In 1953, Dr. Rufus E. Clement, Atlanta University president, became the first African American elected to a city office in the twentieth century; he was elected to the Board of Education as the representative from the third ward (Bacote, "The Negro in Atlanta Politics," 349).

28. Watts, "Black Political Progress in Atlanta," 273–79.

29. The ticket was composed of Floyd Crumbly, Lucius Lee, R. S. Lovingood, Charles McHenry, Jack McKinley, Isaac P. Moyer, Willis Murphy, J. W. Palmer, and John D. Render.

30. Finch became a business partner with Danwell Brydie in 1868. Within the same year he became sole proprietor of his tailor shop. While much has been made of Finch's business ownership, he did not excel financially until the 1880s. In 1878, Finch's total

worth was $645: $550 in city property, $40 in livestock, $50 in household goods, and $5 in tools (Fulton County Tax Digest, 1878).

31. Russell and Thornbery, "William Finch of Atlanta," 309.

32. Sources list Graham alternately as a railroad worker and carpenter. Howard Rabinowitz, in *Race Relations in the Urban South*, calls Graham an "obscure 40 year old railroad worker." Russell and Thornbery identify Graham as "an illiterate carpenter." Graham, like other unskilled freedmen, may have tried his hand at a number of day jobs before settling into a chosen profession in the mid-1870s.

33. Carter, *The Black Side*, 180. *Atlanta Independent*, February 13, 1904.

34. Carter, *The Black Side*, 178.

35. "Profile of Jackson McHenry," *Atlanta Independent*, February 6, 1904. In a response to a biting commentary from editor Ben Davis concerning Henry McNeal Turner's failed attempt to organize a boycott against the streetcar company, Turner noted that he "bought a horse and buggy from Mr. Jackson McHenry." E. R. Carter also observed that McHenry was operating a hack shop in his 1894 book, *The Black Side*.

36. Fulton County Tax Digest, 1890, 1895, and 1900.

37. Carter, *The Black Side*, 61–62.

38. *Southern Recorder*, October 8, 1886.

39. Carter, *The Black Side*, 61–62; *Atlanta Independent*, January 23–April 13, 1904; Russell and Thornbery, "William Finch of Atlanta."

40. Carter, *The Black Side*, 246; E. R. Carter Papers. Carter visited Europe at least three times. The experiences of the 1888 visit, his first, were chronicled in *Descriptive Scenes of Europe and the Orient*, published in 1890. A second trip in 1891 took Carter to the Holy Land as well as Germany, Belgium, and Ireland. A third trip after the turn of the century was part of a fund-raising tour to collect donations for the establishment of a home for wayward young black males in the city of Atlanta. The governor of Georgia personally penned letters of introduction for Carter, vouching for his good character and honest intentions.

41. "The Negro and Prohibition in Atlanta, 1885–1887," 57.

42. "The Negro and Prohibition in Atlanta," 41.

43. Ibid., 51.

44. Ibid., 40–41.

45. Ibid., 51.

46. Ibid., 54.

47. Hunter, *"To 'Joy my Freedom,"* 162–64. Hunter notes that some lower-status blacks, recognizing the negative impact that the consumption of alcohol had on finances and family stability, were also prohibitionists.

48. *Southern Recorder*, October 29, 1886.

49. Moore, "The Negro and Prohibition in Atlanta," 47. Russell, *Atlanta, 1847–1890*, 210–11. Russell and Moore offer a different picture of the 1886 municipal elections from that of Clarence Bacote. See Bacote, "The Negro in Atlanta Politics."

50. "The Negro and Prohibition in Atlanta," 45.

51. Quoted in Moore, "The Negro and Prohibition in Atlanta," 45 and 53. The Knights

of Labor were something of a force to be reckoned with in 1880s Atlanta. Melton McLaurin's 1978 book-length treatment, *Knights of Labor in the South*, remains a valuable resource for labor historians who seek to understand working-class white activism in the region. More recently, Kuhn's *Contesting the New South Order* offers a brief account of the four thousand Knights of Labor members who were involved in boycotts and strikes in the city from 1882 to 1890. Russell, in *Atlanta, 1847–1890*, identifies the antiprohibitionist Mutual Aid Brotherhood, active in the elections of the 1880s, as "the political arm of the Knights of Labor" (211).

52. Moore, "The Negro and Prohibition in Atlanta," 55–56; Russell, *Atlanta, 1847–1890*, 212–13.

53. Bacote, "The Negro in Atlanta Politics," 336.

54. Bacote, "The Negro in Atlanta Politics," 335.

55. Russell, *Atlanta, 1847–1890*, 211.

56. Moore, "The Negro and Prohibition in Atlanta," 42. The Young Men's Prohibition Club awarded a one hundred–dollar prize to Carter's First Ward Club for "recording the greatest number of votes against liquor."

57. Mixon, "Politics and Race: Henry A. Rucker and Aldine Chambers during the Era of the Atlanta Riot of 1906," paper presented at the Association of the Study of African American Life and History Conference, October 1, 2000, Washington, D.C.

58. Kuhn, *Contesting the New South Order*, 26. The *Atlanta Constitution* cartoon is reprinted on pages 28–29 of Kuhn's text.

59. Davis, *Henry Grady's New South*, 153–54.

60. Du Bois, *Dusk of Dawn*; Brundage, *Lynching in the New South*; Leon Litwack's essay in Allen, ed., *Without Sanctuary*; Davis, *A Clashing of the Soul*; Hale, *Making Whiteness*.

61. Davis, *Henry Grady's New South*, 159.

62. In 1897, radical racist, white feminist, and journalist Rebecca Felton urged Southern white men to rally to the defense of white womanhood by lynching black rapists. Felton argued that black men, set free by emancipation and made mad by being elevated to a status of political equality with white men, had reverted to their brutal animalistic state, making them a threat to the purity of white women. Her suggested solution to the problem of the black beast that allegedly menaced and raped white women by the hundreds was disfranchisement and lynching. See Williamson, *The Crucible of Race*, and Brundage, *Lynching in the New South*.

63. Davis, *A Clashing of the Soul*, 118.

64. See Du Bois, *The Negro in Business*.

65. Lewis, *W. E. B. Du Bois: The Biography of a Race*, 320–22. Several Black Atlantans attended the July 1905 meeting: Du Bois, one of the chief organizers, businessman Alonzo Herndon and his son Norris, journalist Max Barber (founder of the *Voice of the Negro*), and Gammon Theological Seminary president John Bowen. Lewis notes that John Hope and Atlanta University professor George Towns had planned to attend the meeting but had been detained. Herndon, an earlier supporter of Booker T. Washington, later withdrew from the Niagara movement. Alexa Benson Henderson notes Herndon's absence from the movement in *Atlanta Life Insurance Company*, 37–38, arguing that "there is

no evidence that the criticisms of influential people in Tuskegee or Atlanta dissuaded Herndon from participating further in the Niagara Movement. He may have thought the movement would not be well received in Atlanta." This rather benign reading is countered by Lewis's assertion that Herndon's involvement was at the behest of his wife Adrienne. Adrienne Herndon, who taught French at Atlanta University, may have been more radical on the issue of equal rights than her husband—which would explain her presence at a November 1905 civil rights conference in Atlanta. Her death in 1910, combined with suspected pressure from Washington, may have played a role in Herndon's abandonment of the movement (Donaldson, "Georgia's New Negroes").

66. *Atlanta Independent,* February 10, 1906. Davis, an avid follower of Booker T. Washington, frequently used his newspaper to attack those whom he identified as too radical on race. But while he frequently condemned Hope, Du Bois, Proctor, and others, he shared their commitment to the idea of the moral uplift of the race. Davis also supported Henry McNeal Turner's stand against the 1903 municipal ordinance requiring that streetcars be segregated.

67. Michael Perman, *Struggle for Mastery,* 8.

Seven. The Turn toward Violence

1. Journalist Jesse Max Barber, one of the most prominent men to leave the city, reported in the *Voice of the Negro* that some five thousand blacks fled the city in the wake of the riot. Historian Charles Crowe, in the second portion of his two-part study of the riot, revised this number downwards to one thousand ("Racial Massacre in Atlanta, September 22, 1906," 166, n.172). Barber's tale of being given the option by James W. English of either doing time on the Georgia chain gang or departing from the city as punishment for his bold letter to the *New York World* is related in part 2 of Mixon's "The Atlanta Race Riot of 1906," in Dittmer's *Black Georgia in the Progressive Era,* and in Hunter's *"To 'Joy my Freedom."* Barber himself remains the best source on the subject of his departure from the city and his relocation to Chicago ("Why Mr. Barber Left Atlanta").

2. Much has been made of Sweet Auburn Avenue, aka Black Peachtree. However, the vast majority of the property development on the strip occurred in the second and third decade of the twentieth century. The Rucker Building (1904) and the Odd Fellows Hall (completed 1914) were joined by a host of other black-owned structures in the 1920s. While the move toward Auburn Avenue predates the riot, the violence of 1906 accelerated the rate of black retreat (White, "The Black Sides of Atlanta," 212). Also see Fennel, "A Demographic Study of Black Business."

3. The Georgia system of convict lease was authorized in December 1866 but first acted upon in 1868. Similarly, the legislature voted in September 1908 to end the system of convict lease, effective April 1909. See David C. Berry, "Free Labor He Found Unsatisfactory," 5, 12.

4. Berry, "Free Labor He Found Unsatisfactory," 6–7. Lichtenstein, *Twice the Work of Free Labor,* 118.

5. Berry, "Free Labor He Found Unsatisfactory," 8–9; Mancini, *One Dies, Get Another,* 90–94; Davis, *Henry Grady's New South,* 65, 145–46.

6. Lichtenstein, *Twice the Work of Free Labor,* 116.

7. Annual Reports of the Chief of Police of the City of Atlanta, Georgia, 1897, 1900–1908, Atlanta History Center.

8. Crowe, "Racial Violence and Social Reform," 234–56.

9. Lichtenstein, *Twice the Work of Free Labor,* 113.

10. *Atlanta Independent,* March 2, 1907. Nella, who obviously shared editor Ben Davis's Washingtonian vision, challenged the black elite to devise a solution to the problem of "thousands of men and boys that can not be found" when there was work to be had in Atlanta. "Yet," he continued, "there are those on our street corners every day that will not work for love nor money."

11. Black neighborhoods suffered with issues of lack of access to running water, with municipal garbage dumping in their midst, and with open flow or raw sewage on their streets well after the turn of the century. Though the 1899 death of his son Burghardt was a result of diphtheria, W. E. B. Du Bois would blame both the absence of black doctors and the filth in the streets of Black Atlanta for the loss of his child. See Hunter, *"To 'Joy My Freedom,"* chapter 3.

12. White, "The Black Sides of Atlanta," 208–12.

13. August Meier and Elliot Rudwick, as noted, documented the widespread efforts of blacks in the Jim Crow South to boycott segregated streetcars. In the case of the 1904 streetcar boycott in Atlanta, Meier and Rudwick misreport the actions of McNeal Turner—charging him with helping "to break the boycott by ostentatiously riding on Jim Crow cars," based upon Ben Davis's January 23 editorial, and disregarding Turner's testimony. See "The Boycott Movement Against Jim Crow Streetcars in the South," 769, n. 79. Edmund Drago in *Black Politicians in Georgia* notes that Turner's wife had been a victim of discrimination on streetcars (99). Glenda Gilmore reports that "the better class of Afro-Americans in Atlanta" engaged in the boycott (*Gender and Jim Crow,* 101). Tera Hunter also notes that "an unidentified group of women led a boycott when a streetcar company arrested and imprisoned a black man for refusing to sit in seats designated for his race" (*"To 'Joy My Freedom,"* 99).

14. Dittmer, *Black Georgia in the Progressive Era,* 97–101.

15. Perman, *Struggle for Mastery,* 286–89. Perman, in concert with Williamson, *Crucible of Race,* and Dittmer, *Black Georgia in the Progressive Era,* notes that Smith, as a "gold democrat," had not been in support of Populist style reforms in his early career. Neither had Smith been a radical on the issue of race, falling instead in the category of conservative, as described by Williamson in *Crucible of Race.* As a conservative, Smith did not assume racial equality between blacks and whites, and was comfortable with blacks being relegated to a subservient position through means other than irrational violence. For more discussion of the political career of Hoke Smith, see Dewey W. Grantham, *Hoke Smith and the Politics of the New South.*

16. Perman, *Struggle for Mastery,* 284–85.

17. Dittmer, *Black Georgia in the Progressive Era,* 99.

18. *Atlanta Constitution,* September 2, 1905 (qtd. in Dittmer, *Black Georgia in the Progressive Era,* 100).

19. There was, as noted by Perman and Dittmer, considerable resistance to additional

measures towards disfranchisement. Legislators wrangled for months over the best way to avoid losing white voters while trying to eliminate black ones. The compromise, as addressed in chapter 6, was the addition of a permanent "good character" clause. Nevertheless, Joseph M. Brown, who succeeded Smith in the governor's seat, argued that the 1908 amendment had "discouraged 85,000 white men from registering." See Dittmer, *Black Georgia in the Progressive Era*, 103.

20. Dittmer, *Black Georgia in the Progressive Era*, 101–3; Perman, *Struggle for Mastery*, 292–93.

21. Perman, *Struggle for Mastery*, 17.

22. Of the cases reported in the six months preceding the riot, two were actual rapes and three were attempted. In the remaining seven cases, three "may have been attempts," three were cases of panic or fright on the part of a white woman, and one was an attempted suicide (Baker, *Following the Color Line*, 5).

23. Baker, *Following the Color Line*, 5–9; Mixon, "The Atlanta Riot of 1906," 486–89.

24. "Meeting of Citizens to Suppress Crime," *Atlanta Constitution*, September 1, 1906.

25. Ibid.; Mixon "The Atlanta Riot of 1906," 504.

26. Ibid.

27. "Believes Negro Detectives Would Help," *Atlanta Constitution*, September 4, 1906. Townsley also referred to the African Methodist Episcopal Ministers' Union of Atlanta. He notes they may have produced a resolution concerning the issues at hand.

28. In a public speech, Sheriff Nelms threatened the black community with extreme violence, noting that "the outrages upon white women must stop, if every negro in many miles of Atlanta have [sic] to be killed."

29. "Negro Condemns Crimes," *Atlanta Constitution*, September 4, 1906.

30. *Atlanta Independent*, September 22, 1906.

31. Mixon, "The Atlanta Riot of 1906," 509–11.

32. Editorial, *Atlanta Independent*, September 15 and 22, 1906.

33. Editorial, *Atlanta Independent*, September 22, 1906.

34. Mixon, "The Atlanta Riot of 1906," 505–8.

35. "A Father Begged to Settle Case with Negro," *Atlanta Constitution*, September 22, 1906.

36. A combination grocery store and eatery owned by a Greek family was also destroyed in the riot. The crowd chased a black man into the store near the corner of Walton and Forsyth. Jim Brown, the owner, and his son Eustace were both beaten after they tried to prevent the mob from entering the shop in pursuit. The store was demolished in the ensuing melee.

37. "Chased Negros All Night," *Atlanta Constitution*, September 23, 1906.

38. Williamson, *The Crucible of Race*, 215–20.

39. "Rain Helped Restore Order," *Atlanta Constitution*, September 23, 1906.

40. White, *A Man Called White*, 8.

41. Rouse, *Lugenia Burns Hope*, 42–44.

42. Mrs. Robert C. Thompson, thirty-five years old and pregnant with her first child, witnessed the scene from her front porch. Apparently shocked by the violence, she

suffered a heart attack and died. "Two Blacks Riddled by Posse," *Atlanta Constitution,* September 25, 1906.

43. Baker, *Following the Color Line,* 13–14.

44. Black mortician David Howard later reported many more dead, including several "black" men who were brought to his shop. The "blacks" were actually whites in black face and were secretly buried in the black side of the cemetery. See Mixon, "Atlanta Riot of 1906."

45. "A New Start for the Saloons," *Atlanta Constitution,* September 28, 1906.

46. "Dixon's Play Will Not Come," *Atlanta Constitution,* September 28, 1906.

47. "Twenty Meet Today to Stop Riots," *Atlanta Constitution,* September 25, 1906.

48. The problem of discrimination and violent mistreatment of blacks aboard street-cars was, as noted, an old one. Blacks protested assaults by streetcar personnel and white riders as early as 1875.

49. Committee members included former mayor and police commissioner turned banker James English; L. Q. Rosser, president of the Board of Education; Sam D. Jones, president of the Chamber of Commerce; attorneys W. D. Ellis and Charles T. Hopkins; A. B. Steele, merchant; Forrest Adair, realtor; M. L. Collier, of the Western Atlantic rail-road; and H. Y. McCord, grocer. This impressive association of business and civic leaders served as an advisory group to the mayor.

50. "Committee of Ten Will Aid Officers," *Atlanta Constitution,* September 26, 1906. Some of Atlanta's "best families," including the Candlers and the Woodruffs, contributed to the riot fund.

51. "Mob Violence, Rape—Their Baneful Consequences," *Atlanta Independent,* October 6, 1906.

52. The Mass Meeting of White and Colored Citizens at Wheat Street Baptist Church on Sunday Last Resulted in Much Good," *Atlanta Independent,* October 6, 1906. David Marx was selected as the leader of the first and largest reform synagogue in Atlanta in the 1890s. Historian Steven Hertzberg reports that Marx (whose name was often misspelled "Marks" in city newspapers) oversaw the expansion of Hebrew Benevolent congrega-tion's program of cultural assimilation, designed to make Atlanta's Jews less "foreign" and therefore more acceptable to their southern white peers. In this work, Marx's ide-ology and career parallels that of Henry Huge Proctor and other black elites who advo-cated acculturation as a means of undermining white racism. The Hebrew Benevolent Congregation grew from a Jewish society established in 1860 and went on to facilitate the development of five separate synagogues, designed to meet the needs of new Jewish immigrants, that were incorporated in the city. By 1910, the total Jewish population was four thousand, 2.6 percent of the total population of the city. Marx maintained his com-mitment to racial harmony well after the riot, serving on the Georgia Commission on Interracial Cooperation in the 1920s. See Hertzberg, *Strangers within the Gate City,* and Dinnerstein and Palsson, eds., *Jews in the South.*

53. Baker, *Following the Color Line,* 24; *Atlanta Independent,* October 1906–April 1907.

54. Tagger, "The Atlanta Race Riot of 1906 and the Black Community," 64–67.

55. "Atlanta Happenings," *Atlanta Independent,* April 13, 1907. An arrangement was

made between the civic league and the city "whereby any colored person who is brought before the city police court and who is innocent or deserving and unable to secure counsel may have counsel provided without cost." Individuals in need of this service were to pursue a recommendation from their minister, who would pass it along to Penn, Proctor, or Carter. The words "innocent" and "deserving," in conjunction with a minister's recommendation, suggest that the Atlanta Civic League and the Colored Co-operative were disinterested in providing such services to blacks of the "lower sort" whose innocence was in question.

56. Ben Davis observed the "Mr. Hyde and Dr. Jekyll" character of Clark Howell, editor of the *Atlanta Constitution*. In an editorial in the *Independent* four months after the riot, Davis, who engaged in his own share of attacks on black character, wondered why Howell, who worked with the Civic League and advocated racial harmony, also printed editorials that "engage[d] in the pastime of slandering the Negro" ("The *Atlanta Constitution* and the Negro," *Atlanta Independent*, January 26, 1907).

57. "Two Elements among the Blacks," *Atlanta Independent*, November 3, 1906, reprinted from the *Atlanta Constitution*, October 30, 1906.

58. Hunter, *"To 'Joy My Freedom,"* 104, 137. Also see Rouse, *Lugenia Burns Hope.*

Epilogue

1. Henry Hugh Proctor Papers, letter from J. L. Key Mayor to Henry Proctor, October 4, 1919; letter from Committee of Church Co-operation to Henry Proctor, October 7, 1919; letter from Clark Howell to city editor of *The Eagle*, December 31, 1919.

2. Henry Hugh Proctor Papers, letter from Carrie Steele Orphanage to Henry Proctor, December 18, 1919; letter from Atlanta Mutual Insurance Company to Henry Proctor, December 31, 1919.

3. Proctor, *Between Black and White*, 181.

4. The story of World War I and its impact on Black Atlanta is, of course, beyond the boundaries of my study. However, Tera Hunter offers an insightful discussion of "work or fight" laws in the city in her work. Specifically, she argues that such laws were used to further penalize black women by demanding that they pursue domestic work so as to free up the labor of white women for the war effort. Interestingly, the resistance to such laws was led, on the local level, by longtime community activist Peter James Bryant (*"To 'Joy My Freedom,"* 229–31).

5. Levine, *Black Culture and Black Consciousness*, 139.

BIBLIOGRAPHY

Primary Sources

ARCHIVAL AND MANUSCRIPT COLLECTIONS

American Baptist Historical Society Archives Center, Valley Forge, Pa. Baptist Home Mission Monthly.

American Missionary Association Papers, Georgia. Hamilton College Library, Clinton, N.Y. Microfilm.

Amistad Research Center, Tulane University, New Orleans, La. Henry Hugh Proctor Papers. Adeline Davis Proctor, "Negro Womanhood—Its Present."

Atlanta Fulton Public Library, Auburn Avenue Branch, Atlanta, Ga. Ray Stannard Baker, "A Race Riot and After," *The American Magazine*, April 1907. E. R. Carter Papers.

Atlanta Fulton Public Library, Main Branch, Atlanta, Ga. Annual Reports of the Board of Education, 1873–1912. Annual Reports of the State School Commissioner of Georgia, 1875, 1887–88, 1889–90.

Atlanta Historical Society, Atlanta, Ga. Atlanta City Council Minutes, 1851–1900. Atlanta City Council Records, Vol. 1–12, February 2, 1848–June 22, 1891. Atlanta City Directories. Atlanta City Ordinance Book, 1851–60, 1861–69. Hamleiter's Directory, Map of Atlanta, 1870. G. M. Hopkins, City Atlas of Atlanta, Georgia, 1878.

Atlanta History Center. Annual Reports of the Chief of Police of the City of Atlanta, Georgia, 1897, 1900–1908.

Atlanta University Archives, Woodruff Library, Atlanta, Ga. Frederick Ayer Papers, 1865–67. Big Bethel AME Church file. E. R. Carter, *The Black Side: A Partial History of the Business, Religious, and Educational Side of the Negro in Atlanta, Ga.* Friendship Baptist Church file. History of the Masons file. Carrie Steel Logan file. Edmund Asa Ware Papers, 1867–88.

Day, Caroline Bond. Papers. Peabody Museum, Harvard University, Boston, Mass.

DeKalb County Historical Society, DeKalb County, Ga. Badger Family Papers. Land Lottery 1821 Records.

Georgia Department of Archives and History, Atlanta, Ga. Code of the State of Georgia, 1882. First Baptist Church of Atlanta, Records, 1848–68. Microfilm. First Congregational Church of Atlanta, Records, May 1867–May 1881, July 1912–August 1923. Microfilm. Fulton County, Georgia, Tax Digests, 1880, 1885, 1890, 1895, 1900, 1905. Microfilm.

Record of the Proceedings of the Board of Education of the City of Atlanta, Ga., vol. 1, 1869–88 and vol. 2, 1889–98. Atlanta Board of Education, Atlanta, Ga.

Registers of Signatures of Depositors in Branches of the Freedmen's Savings and Trust Co. Roll 6, Atlanta, Ga., January 15, 1870–July 2, 1874. National Archives. Microfilm Publication #816.

Sholes and Weatherbee. Directory of the City of Atlanta, Georgia, 1881. Atlanta, Georgia, 1861–1901 City Directories. New York State Library, Albany. Microfilm.

WPA Slave Narrative Project. Federal Writers' Project, United States Work Projects Administration (USWPA). Manuscript Division, Library of Congress, Washington, D.C.

NEWSPAPERS

Atlanta Constitution
Atlanta Independent
Atlanta Journal
Savannah Tribune
Southern Recorder

GOVERNMENT DOCUMENTS

U.S. Bureau of the Census. Abstract of the Returns of the Fifth Census. 22d Cong., 1st sess., 1830, Doc. 269. DeKalb County Doc. 263, State of Georgia.

U.S. Bureau of the Census. Compendium of the Sixth Census, 1840. Georgia—Recapitulation of the Aggregate Value, and Produce, and Number of Persons Employed in Mines, Agriculture, Commerce, Manufactures, etc., by Counties.

U.S. Bureau of the Census. Compendium of the Seventh Census, 1850. Georgia—Recapitulation of the Aggregate Value, and Produce, and Number of Persons Employed in Mines, Agriculture, Commerce, Manufactures, etc., by Counties.

U.S. Bureau of the Census. Population Schedules of the U.S. Census Returns of the Seventh Census, 1850, DeKalb County, Georgia. Washington, D.C.: Government Printing Office, 1854. Microfilm.

U.S. Bureau of the Census. Population Schedules of the U.S. Census Returns of the Eighth Census, 1860, Fulton County, Georgia. Washington, D.C.: Government Printing Office, 1864. Microfilm.

U.S. Bureau of the Census. Population Schedules of the U.S. Census Returns of the Ninth Census, 1870, Fulton County, Georgia. Washington, D.C.: Government Printing Office, 1874. Microfilm

Secondary Sources

PUBLISHED BOOKS AND ARTICLES

Alexander, Adele Logan. *Ambiguous Lives: Free Women of Color in Rural Georgia, 1789–1879*. Fayetteville: University of Arkansas Press, 1991.

Allen, James, ed. *Without Sanctuary: Lynching Photography in America.* San Francisco: Twin Palms Publishers, 1999.

Anderson, Benedict. *Imagined Communities: Reflections of the Origin and Spread of Nationalism.* Rev. ed. London: Verso, 1991.

Anderson, James D. *The Education of Blacks in the South, 1860–1935.* Chapel Hill: University of North Carolina Press, 1988.

Angell, Stephen Ward. *Bishop Henry McNeal Turner and African-American Religion in the South.* Knoxville: University of Tennessee Press, 1992.

Aptheker, Herbert, ed. *A Documentary History of the Negro People in the United States.* New York: Citadel Press, 1951.

Bacote, Clarence A. "The Negro in Atlanta Politics." *Phylon* 16 (fall 1955): 333–50.

————. *The Story of Atlanta University: A Century of Service 1865–1965.* Princeton, N.J.: Princeton University Press, 1969.

Baker, Ray Stannard. *Following the Color Line: An Account of Negro Citizenship in the American Democracy.* New York: Doubleday, Page and Company, 1908.

Barber, Jessie Max. "Why Mr. Barber Left Atlanta." *Voice of the Negro* 3 (November 1906): 470–74.

Bederman, Gail. " 'The Women Have Had Charge of the Church Work Long Enough': The Men and Religion Forward Movement of 1911–1912 and the Masculinization of Middle-Class Protestantism." *American Quarterly* 41 (September 1989): 432–65.

Beito, David T. *From Mutual Aid to Welfare State: Fraternal Societies and Social Services, 1890–1967.* Chapel Hill: University of North Carolina Press, 2000.

Berkeley, Kathleen C. " 'Colored Ladies also Contributed': Black Women's Activities from Benevolence to Social Welfare, 1866–1896." In *The Web of Southern Social Relations: Women, Family, and Education,* edited by Walter J. Fraser Jr., R. Frank Saunders Jr., and John L. Wakelyn, 181–203. Athens: University of Georgia Press, 1985.

Berlin, Ira. *Slaves without Masters: The Free Negro in the Antebellum South.* New York: Pantheon Books, 1974.

Berlin, Ira, and Philip D. Morgan, eds. *Cultivation and Culture: Labor and the Shaping of Slave Life in the Americas.* Charlottesville: University Press of Virginia, 1993.

Berry, David C. "Free Labor He Found Unsatisfactory: Convict Lease Labor at the Chattahoochee Brick Company, 1885–1909." *Atlanta History* 36 (winter 1993): 5–15.

Blassingame, John W. "Before the Ghetto: The Making of the Black Community in Savannah, Georgia, 1865–1880." *Journal of Southern History* 6 (summer 1973): 463–88.

————. *Black New Orleans, 1860–1880.* Chicago: University of Chicago Press, 1973.

————. *The Slave Community; Plantation Life in the Antebellum South.* New York: Oxford University Press, 1972.

Boles, John B. *Black Southerners, 1619–1869.* Lexington: University Press of Kentucky, 1983.

————, ed. *Masters and Slaves in the House of the Lord: Race and Religion in the American South, 1740–1870.* Lexington: University of Kentucky, 1988.

Brundage, W. Fitzhugh. *Lynching in the New South: Georgia and Virginia, 1880–1930.* Urbana: University of Illinois Press, 1993.

Carnes, Mark C. *Secret Ritual and Manhood in Victorian America.* New Haven, Conn.: Yale University Press, 1989.

Carter, Dan T. "From the Old South to the New." In *From the Old South to the New: Essays on the Transitional South,* edited by Walter J. Fraser Jr. and Winfred B. Moore Jr., 23–32. Westport, Conn.: Greenwood Press, 1981.

Carter, E. R. *Biographical Sketches of Our Pulpit.* 1888. Reprint, Chicago: Afro-American Press, 1969.

———. *The Black Side: A Partial History of the Business, Religious, and Educational Side of the Negro in Atlanta, Ga.* 1894. Reprint, Freeport, N.Y.: Books for Libraries Press, 1971.

Castel, Albert E. *Decision in the West: The Atlanta Campaign of 1864.* Lawrence: University Press of Kansas, 1992.

Catton, Bruce. *This Hallowed Ground: The Story of the Union Side of the Civil War.* New York: Doubleday, 1956.

Chafe, William H. *Civilities and Civil Rights: Greensboro, North Carolina, and the Black Struggle for Freedom.* New York: Oxford University Press, 1980.

Cimbala, Paul A. *Under the Guardianship of the Nation: The Freedmen's Bureau and the Reconstruction of Georgia, 1865–1870.* Athens: University of Georgia Press, 1997.

Cohen, William. *At Freedom's Edge: Black Mobility and the Southern White Quest for Racial Control, 1861–1915.* Baton Rouge: Louisiana State University Press, 1991.

Collins, Randall. *Weberian Sociological Theory.* New York: Cambridge University Press, 1986.

Coulter, E. Merton. *A Short History of Georgia.* Chapel Hill: University of North Carolina Press, 1933.

Crowe, Charles. "Racial Massacre in Atlanta, September 22, 1906." *Journal of Negro History* 54 (April 1969): 150–73.

———. "Racial Violence and Social Reform: Origins of the Atlanta Race Riot of 1906." *Journal of Negro History* 53 (July 1968): 234–56.

Currie-McDaniel, Ruth. *Carpetbagger of Conscience: A Biography of John Emory Bryant.* New York: Fordham University Press, 1999.

Davis, Harold E. *Henry Grady's New South: Atlanta, a Brave and Beautiful City.* Tuscaloosa: University of Alabama Press, 1990.

Davis, Leroy. *A Clashing of the Soul: John Hope and the Dilemma of African American Leadership and Black Higher Education in the Early Twentieth Century.* Athens: University of Georgia Press, 1998.

Day, Caroline Bond. *A Study of Some Negro-White Families in the United States.* Cambridge, Mass.: Peabody Museum of Harvard University, 1932.

Dinnerstein, Leonard, and Mary Dale Palsson, eds. *Jews in the South.* Baton Rouge: Louisiana State University Press, 1973.

Dittmer, John. *Black Georgia in the Progressive Era, 1900–1920.* Urbana: University of Illinois Press, 1977.

Drago, Edmund L.. *Black Politicians and Reconstruction in Georgia: A Splendid Failure.* 1982. Reprint, Athens: University of Georgia Press, 1992.

————. "How Sherman's March through Georgia Affected the Slaves." *Georgia Historical Quarterly* 57 (1973): 361–75.

Du Bois, W. E. B. *Black Reconstruction in America: An Essay toward a History of the Part which Black Folk Played in the Attempt to Reconstruct Democracy in America, 1860–1880.* 1935. Reprint, New York: Atheneum, 1976.

————. *Dusk of Dawn: An Essay toward an Autobiography of a Race Concept.* New York: Harcourt, Brace and Company, 1940.

————. *Souls of Black Folks: Essays and Sketches,* 1903. Reprint, Greenwich, Conn.: Fawcett Publications, 1961.

————, ed. *The College-Bred Negro: Report of a Social Study Made under the Direction of Atlanta University, Together with the Proceedings of the Fifth Conference for the Study of the Negro Problems.* Atlanta University Publication 5. Atlanta: Atlanta University Press, 1900.

————, ed. *Mortality among Negroes in Cities: Proceedings of the Conference for Investigations of City Problems.* Atlanta University Publication 1. Atlanta: Atlanta University Press, 1896.

————, ed. *The Negro Artisan: A Social Study Made under the Direction of Atlanta University by the Seventh Atlanta Conference.* Atlanta University Publication 7. Atlanta: Atlanta University Press, 1902.

————, ed. *The Negro Common School: Report of a Social Study Made under the Direction of Atlanta University, Together with the Proceedings of the Sixth Conference for the Study of the Negro Problems.* Atlanta University Publication 6. Atlanta: Atlanta University Press, 1901.

————, ed. *The Negro in Business: Report of a Social Study Made under the Direction of Atlanta University, Together with the Proceedings of the Fourth Conference for the Study of the Negro Problems.* Atlanta University Publication 4. Atlanta: Atlanta University Press, 1899.

————, ed. *Social and Physical Condition of Negroes in Cities: Report of an Investigation under the Direction of Atlanta University and Proceedings of the Second Conference for the Study of Problems Concerning Negro City Life.* Atlanta University Publications 2. Atlanta: Atlanta University Press, 1897.

————, ed. *Some Efforts of American Negroes for Their Own Social Betterment: Report of an Investigation under the Direction of Atlanta University, Together with the Proceedings of the Third Conference for the Study of the Negro Problems.* Atlanta University Publication 3. Atlanta: Atlanta University Press, 1898.

Duncan, Russell. *Entrepreneur for Equality: Governor Rufus Bullock, Commerce, and Race in post–Civil War Georgia.* Athens: University of Georgia Press, 1994.

————. *Freedom's Shore: Tunis Campbell and the Georgia Freedmen.* Athens: University of Georgia Press, 1986.

Dvorak, Katherine L. *An African American Exodus: The Segregation of the Southern Churches.* Brooklyn, N.Y.: Carlson Publishing, 1991.

Egerton, Douglas R. *He Shall Go out Free: The Lives of Denmark Vesey.* Madison: University of Wisconsin Press, 1999.

Engerman, Stanley M. "Concluding Reflections." In *Working toward Freedom: Slave Society and Domestic Economy in the American South,* edited by Larry E. Hudson Jr., 243–44. Rochester, N.Y.: University of Rochester Press, 1994.

Engerman, Stanley M., and Robert William Fogel. *Time on the Cross: The Economics of American Negro Slavery.* Boston: Little, Brown, 1974.

Ferguson, Karen. *Black Politics in New Deal Atlanta.* Chapel Hill: University of North Carolina Press, 2002.

Fields, Barbara Jeanne. *Slavery and Freedom on the Middle Ground: Maryland during the Nineteenth Century.* New Haven, Conn.: Yale University Press, 1985.

———. "Slavery, Race and Ideology in the United States of America." *New Left Review* 181 (May/June 1990): 95–118.

Fleming, Walter L. "The Freedmen's Savings Bank." Parts 1 and 2. *Yale Review* 14 (May/August 1906): 40–67, 134–46.

Flipper, Henry Ossian. *The Colored Cadet at West Point.* New York: Arno Press, 1969.

Foner, Eric. *Freedom's Lawmakers: A Directory of Black Officeholders during Reconstruction.* Rev. ed. New York: Oxford University Press, 1993.

———. "The Meaning of Freedom in the Age of Emancipation." *Journal of American History* 81 (September 1994): 435–60.

———. *Reconstruction: America's Unfinished Revolution, 1863–1877.* New York: Harper and Row, 1988.

———. "Reconstruction Revisited." *Reviews in American History* 10 (December 1982): 82–100.

Foner, Philip S., and George E. Walker, eds. *Proceedings of the Black National and State Conventions, 1865–1900.* Philadelphia: Temple University Press, 1986.

Frazier, Thomas R., ed. *Afro-American History: Primary Sources.* New York: Harcourt, Brace and World, 1970.

Frey, Sylvia R. "Shaking the Dry Bones: The Dialectic of Conversion." In *Black and White Cultural Interaction in the Antebellum South,* edited by Ted Ownby, 23–44. Jackson: University Press of Mississippi, 1993.

———. *Water from the Rock: Black Resistance in a Revolutionary Age.* Princeton, N. J.: Princeton University Press, 1991.

Gaines, Kevin K. *Uplifting the Race: Black Leadership, Politics, and Culture in the Twentieth Century.* Chapel Hill: University of North Carolina Press, 1996.

Garrett, Franklin M. *Atlanta and Environs: A Chronicle of Its People and Events.* 2 vols. Athens: University of Georgia Press, 1982.

Gatewood, Willard B. *Aristocrats of Color: The Black Elite, 1880–1920.* Bloomington: Indiana University Press, 1990.

Genovese, Eugene D. *Roll, Jordan, Roll: The World the Slaves Made.* New York: Pantheon Books, 1974.

Gilmore, Glenda Elizabeth. *Gender and Jim Crow: Women and the Politics of White*

Supremacy in North Carolina, 1896–1920. Chapel Hill: University of North Carolina Press, 1996.

Gould, Stephen Jay. *The Mismeasure of Man*. Rev. and exp. New York: Norton, 1996.

Grantham, Dewey W. *Hoke Smith and the Politics of the New South*. Baton Rouge: Louisiana State University Press, 1958.

Gutman, Herbert. *The Black Family in Slavery and Freedom, 1750–1925*. New York: Pantheon Books, 1976.

Hahn, Steven. "The Yeomanry of the Nonplantation South: Upper Piedmont Georgia, 1850–1860." In *Class, Conflict, and Consensus: Antebellum Southern Community Studies*, edited by Orville Burton and Robert C. McMath, 29–45. Westport, Conn.: Greenwood Press, 1982.

Hale, Grace Elizabeth. *Making Whiteness: The Culture of Segregation in the South, 1890–1940*. New York: Pantheon, 1998.

Hall, Robert. "The Religious Symbolism of the Iron Pot: The Plausibility of a Congo-Angola Origin." *Western Journal of Black Studies* 13 (spring 1989): 125–29.

Harper, Frances Ellen Watkins. *Iola Leroy, or Shadows Uplifted*. 1893. Reprint, New York: Oxford University Press, 1988.

Harris, J. William. *Plain Folk and Gentry in a Slave Society: White Liberty and Black Slavery in Augusta's Hinterlands*. Baton Rouge: Louisiana State University Press, 1998.

———. "Work and the Family in Black Atlanta, 1880." *Journal of Social History* 9 (spring 1976): 319–30.

Hartshorn, W. N., and George W. Penniman, eds. *An Era of Progress and Promise, 1863–1910: The Religious, Moral, and Educational Development of the American Negro since His Emancipation*. Boston: Priscilla Publishing Company, 1910.

Hayre, Ruth Wright, and Alexis Moore. *Tell Them We Are Rising: A Memoir of Faith in Education*. New York: John Wiley and Sons, Inc., 1997.

Henderson, Alexa Benson. *Atlanta Life Insurance Company: Guardian of Black Economic Dignity*. Tuscaloosa: University of Alabama Press, 1990.

Hertzberg, Steven. *Strangers within the Gate City: The Jews of Atlanta, 1845–1915*. Philadelphia: Jewish Publication Society of America, 1978.

Higginbotham, Evelyn Brooks. "African American Women's History and the Metalanguage of Race." *Signs* 17 (winter 1992): 251–74.

———. *Righteous Discontent: The Women's Movement in the Black Baptist Church, 1880–1920*. Cambridge: Harvard University Press, 1993.

Holt, Thomas. *Black over White: Negro Political Leadership in South Carolina during Reconstruction*. Urbana: University of Illinois Press, 1977.

Hopkins, Richard, "Occupational and Geographic Mobility in Atlanta, 1870–1896." *Journal of Southern History* 34 (May 1968): 200–213.

Horne, Gerald. *Black Liberation/Red Scare: Ben Davis and the Communist Party*. Newark: University of Delaware Press, 1993.

Hornsby, Anne R. "The Accumulation of Wealth by Black Georgians, 1890–1915." *Journal of Negro History* 74 (spring 1989): 11–30.

Hudson, Larry E., Jr. " 'All that Cash': Work and Status in the Slave Quarters." In *Working toward Freedom: Slave Society and Domestic Economy in the American South*, edited by Larry E. Hudson Jr., 77–94. Rochester, N.Y.: University of Rochester Press, 1994.

Hunter, Henry Reid. *The Development of the Public Secondary Schools of Atlanta Georgia, 1845–1937*. 1937. Reprint, Atlanta: Office of School System Historian, 1974.

Hunter, Tera W., "Domination and Resistance: The Politics of Wage Household Labor in New South Atlanta." *Labor History* 34 (spring/summer 1993): 205–20.

———. *"To 'Joy My Freedom": Southern Black Women's Lives and Labors after the Civil War*. Cambridge: Harvard University Press, 1997.

Hunton, Addie W. *William Alphaeus Hunton: A Pioneer Prophet of Young Men*. 1971. Reprint, New York: G. K. Hall and Co., 1997.

Hunton, Addie W., and Kathryn M. Johnson. *Two Colored Women with the American Expedition Forces*. 1920. Reprint, New York: G. K. Hall and Co., 1997.

Hurston, Zora Neale. *The Sanctified Church*. Berkeley, Calif.: Turtle Island, 1981.

Ilhe, Elizabeth L., ed. *Black Women in Higher Education: An Anthology of Essays, Studies, and Documents*. New York: Garland, 1992.

Inscoe, John C., ed. *Georgia in Black and White: Explorations in the Race Relations of a Southern State, 1865–1950*. Athens: University of Georgia Press, 1994.

Jackson, James. "Fraternal Societies Aid Race Progress." *The Crisis* 45 (July 1938): 235–44.

Jackson, Roswell, and Rosalyn Patterson. "A Brief History of Selected Black Churches in Atlanta, Georgia." *Journal of Negro History* 74 (spring 1989): 32–52.

Jaynes, Gerald David. *Branches without Roots: Genesis of the Black Working Class in the American South, 1862–1882*. New York: Oxford University Press, 1986.

Johnson, Michael P., and James Roark. *Black Masters: A Free Family of Color in the Old South*. New York: W. W. Norton, 1984.

Johnson, Whittington B. *Black Savannah: 1788–1864*. Fayetteville: University of Arkansas Press, 1996.

Jones, Jacqueline. *The Dispossessed: America's Underclasses from the Civil War to the Present*. New York: Basic Books, 1992.

———. *Soldiers of Light and Love: Northern Teachers and Georgia Blacks, 1865–1873*. Chapel Hill: University of North Carolina Press, 1980.

Jones, Norrece T. *Born a Child of Freedom, Yet a Slave: Mechanisms of Control and Strategies of Resistance in Anetebellum South Carolina*. Middletown, Conn.: Wesleyan University Press, 1989.

Katz, Michael B., ed. *The "Underclass" Debate: Views from History*. Princeton, N.J.: Princeton University Press, 1993.

King, Wilma. *Stolen Childhood: Slave Youth in Nineteenth-Century America*. Bloomington: Indiana University Press, 1995.

Kolchin, Peter. *American Slavery: 1619–1877*. New York: Hill and Wang, 1993.

Kousser, J. Morgan. *The Shaping of Southern Politics: Suffrage Restriction and the*

Establishment of the One-Party South, 1880–1910. New Haven, Conn.: Yale University Press, 1974.

Kuhn, Clifford M. *Contesting the New South Order: The 1914–1915 Strike at Atlanta's Fulton Mills.* Chapel Hill: University of North Carolina Press, 2001.

Kuyk, Betty M. "The African Derivation of Black Fraternal Orders in the United States." *Society for Comparative Study of Society and History* 25 (October 1983): 559–92.

Lane, Roger. *William Dorsey's Philadelphia and Ours: On the Past and Future of the Black City in America.* New York: Oxford University Press, 1991.

Levine, Lawrence. *Black Culture and Black Consciousness: Afro-American Folk Thought from Slavery to Freedom.* New York: Oxford University Press, 1977.

Lewis, David Levering. *W. E. B. Du Bois: Biography of a Race, 1868–1919.* New York: Henry Holt, 1993.

———. *W. E. B. Du Bois: The Fight for Equality and the American Century, 1919–1963.* New York: Henry Holt, 2000.

Lewis, Earl. "Connecting Memory, Self, and the Power of Place in African American Urban History." In *The New African American Urban History,* edited by Kenneth W. Goings and Raymond A. Mohl, 116–41. Thousand Oaks, Calif.: Sage Publications, 1996.

Lichtenstein, Alex. *Twice the Work of Free Labor: The Political Economy of Convict Labor in the New South.* New York: Verso, 1996.

Mancini, Matthew J. *One Dies, Get Another: Convict Leasing in the American South, 1866–1928.* Columbia: University of South Carolina Press, 1996.

Mathews, Donald G. *Religion in the Old South.* Chicago: University of Chicago Press, 1977.

Matthews, John. "Black Newspapermen and the Black Community in Georgia, 1890–1930." *Georgia Historical Quarterly* 68 (fall 1984): 356–81.

McEwen, Homer C. "First Congregational Church, Atlanta: For the Good of Man and the Glory of God." *Atlanta Historical Society Bulletin* 21 (spring 1977): 129–42.

McLaurin, Melton Alonza. *The Knights of Labor in the South.* Westport, Conn.: Greenwood Press, 1978.

McLeod, Jonathan W. *Workers and Workplace Dynamics in Reconstruction-Era Atlanta: A Case Study.* Afro-American Culture and Society, vol. 10. Los Angeles: Center for Afro-American Studies, University of California, 1989.

McMath, Robert C., ed. *A Southern Pilgrimage: Central Congregational Church of Atlanta, Georgia, 1882–1982.* Atlanta: Central Congregational Church, 1982.

McWilliams, Wilson Carey. *The Idea of Fraternity in America.* Berkeley: University of California Press, 1973.

Meier, August, and David Lewis. "History of the Negro Upper Class in Atlanta, Georgia, 1890–1958." *Journal of Negro Education* 28 (spring 1959): 128–39.

Meier, August, and Elliot Rudwick. "The Boycott Movement against Jim Crow Streetcars in the South, 1900–1906." *Journal of American History* 55 (March 1969): 756–75.

Mjagkij, Nina. *Light in the Darkness: African Americans and the YMCA, 1852–1946.* Lexington: University Press of Kentucky, 1994.

Mohr, Clarence L. *On the Threshold of Freedom: Masters and Slaves in Civil War Georgia.* Athens: University of Georgia Press, 1986.

Montgomery, William E. *Under Their Own Vine and Fig Tree: The African-American Church in the South, 1865–1900.* Baton Rouge: Louisiana State University Press, 1993.

Moore, John Hammond. "The Negro and Prohibition in Atlanta, 1885–1887." *South Atlantic Quarterly* 69 (winter 1970): 38–57.

Morgan, Edmund S. *American Slavery, American Freedom: The Ordeal of Colonial Virginia.* New York: W. W. Norton, 1975.

Neill, Nancy. "The Week They Tore Old Manhattan Street Down." *Business Atlanta* (June 1984): 84–90.

Osthaus, Carl R. *Freedmen, Philanthropy, and Fraud: A History of the Freedmen's Savings Bank.* Urbana: University of Illinois Press, 1976.

Painter, Nell Irvin. "Soul Murder and Slavery: Toward a Fully Loaded Cost Accounting." In *U.S. History as Women's History,* edited by Linda Kerber et al., 125–46. Chapel Hill: University of North Carolina Press, 1995.

Patton, June O. "The Black Community of Augusta and the Struggle for Ware High School, 1880–1899." In *New Perspectives on Black Educational History,* edited by James D. Anderson and Vincent P. Franklin, 61–96. New York: G. K. Hall and Company, 1978.

Pearson, Edward A., ed. *Designs against Charleston: The Trial Record of the Denmark Vesey Slave Conspiracy of 1822.* Chapel Hill: University of North Carolina Press, 1999.

Penn, I. Garland and J. W. E. Bowen, eds. *The United Negro: His Problems and His Progress.* 1902. Reprint, New York: Negro Universities Press, 1969.

Perman, Michael. *Struggle for Mastery: Disfranchisement in the South, 1888–1908.* Chapel Hill: University of North Carolina Press, 2001.

Phillips, Ulrich Bonnell. *American Negro Slavery: A Survey of the Supply, Employment, and Control of Negro Labor as Determined by the Plantation Regime.* 1918. Reprint, Gloucester, Mass.: P. Smith, 1959.

Pomerantz, Gary M. *Where Peachtree Meets Sweet Auburn: The Saga of Two Families and the Making of Atlanta.* New York: Scribner, 1996.

Poole, Jason. "On Borrowed Ground: Free African-American Life in Charleston, South Carolina, 1810–61." *Essays in History* 36 (1994): 1–33.

Proctor, Henry Hugh. *Between Black and White: Autobiographical Sketches.* 1925. Reprint, Freeport, New York: Black Heritage Library Collection Books, 1971.

Rabinowitz, Howard N. *Race Relations in the Urban South 1865–1890.*Urbana: University of Illinois Press, 1980.

Raboteau, Albert J. *Slave Religion: The "Invisible Institution" in the Antebellum South.* New York: Oxford University Press, 1978.

Ransom, Roger L., and Richard Sutch. *One Kind of Freedom: The Economic Consequences of Emancipation.* New York: Cambridge University Press, 1977.

Rawick, George P., ed. *The American Slave: A Composite Autobiography*. Vols. 12–13. 1941. Reprint, Westport, Conn.: Greenwood Publishing Company, 1972.

Reidy, Joseph P. "Aaron A. Bradley: Voice of Black Labor in the Georgia Lowcountry." In *Southern Black Leaders of the Reconstruction Era*, edited by Howard N. Rabinowitz, 281–333. Urbana: University of Illinois Press, 1982.

————. *From Slavery to Agrarian Capitalism in the Cotton Plantation South: Central Georgia, 1800–1880*. Chapel Hill: University of North Carolina Press, 1992.

Robinson, Armistead. "Plans Dat Come from God: Institution Building and the Emergence of Black Leadership in Reconstruction Memphis, 1865–1880." In *Toward a New South? Studies in Post–Civil War Southern Communities*, edited by Orville Vernon Burton and Robert C. McMath Jr., 71–102.Westport, Conn.: Greenwood Press, 1982.

Roediger, David R. *The Wages of Whiteness: Race and the Making of the American Working Class*. London: Verso, 1991.

Rouse, Jacqueline, *Lugenia Burns Hope: Black Southern Reformer*. Athens: University of Georgia Press, 1989.

Russell, James Michael. *Atlanta, 1847–1890: City Building in the Old South and the New*. Baton Rouge: Louisiana State University Press, 1988.

Russell, James Michael, and Jerry Thornbery. "William Finch of Atlanta: The Black Politician as Civic Leader." In *Southern Black Leaders of the Reconstruction Era*, edited by Howard N. Rabinowitz, 309–334. Urbana: University of Illinois Press, 1982.

Salvatore, Nick. *We All Got History: The Memory Books of Amos Webber*. New York: Times Books, 1996.

Schweninger, Loren. *Black Property Owners in the South, 1790–1915*. Urbana: University of Illinois Press, 1997.

Shaw, Stephanie J. *What a Woman Ought to Be and to Do: Black Professional Women Workers during the Jim Crow Era*. Chicago: University of Chicago Press, 1996.

Sherman, William T. *Personal Memoirs of General W. T. Sherman, Written by Himself*. Vol. 2. New York: Charles L. Webster, 1892.

Shultz, Mark R. "Interracial Kinship and the Black Middle Class." In *Georgia in Black and White: Explorations in the Race Relations of a Southern State, 1865–1950*, edited by John C. Inscoe, 141–72. Athens: University of Georgia Press, 1994.

Smith, Jennifer Lund. "The Ties that Bind: Educated African American Women in Post-Emancipation Atlanta." In *Georgia in Black and White: Explorations in the Race Relations of a Southern State, 1865–1950*, edited by John C. Inscoe, 91–105. Athens: University of Georgia Press, 1994.

Smith, John Robert. "Notes and Documents of the Day of Atlanta's Big Fire." *Atlanta Historical Journal* 24 (fall 1980): 58–66.

Sobel, Mechal. *Trabelin' On: The Slave Journey to an Afro-Baptist Faith*. Westport, Conn.: Greenwood Press, 1979.

Stampp, Kenneth M. *The Peculiar Institution: Slavery in the Antebellum South*. New York: Knopf, 1956.

Stevenson, Brenda E. *Life in Black and White: Family and Community in the Slave South.* New York: Oxford University Press, 1996.

Stuckey, Sterling. *Slave Culture: Nationalist Theory and the Foundations of Black America.* New York: Oxford University Press, 1987.

Sweat, Edward. "Free Blacks in Antebellum Atlanta." *Atlanta Historical Bulletin* 21 (winter 1977): 64–71.

Thomas, William Hannibal. *The American Negro, What He Was, What He Is, and What He May Become: A Critical and Practical Discussion.* New York: Macmillan and Company, 1901.

Tushnet, Mark V. *The NAACP's Legal Strategy against Segregated Education, 1925–1950.* Chapel Hill: University of North Carolina Press, 1987.

Voorhis, Harold V. B. *Negro Masonry in the United States.* New York: H. Emerson, 1940.

Walker, Clarence E. *Deromanticizing Black History: Critical Essays and Reappraisals.* Knoxville: University of Tennessee Press, 1991.

———. *A Rock in a Weary Land: The African Methodist Episcopal Church during the Civil War and Reconstruction.* Baton Rouge: Louisiana State University Press, 1982.

Walker, Juliet E. K. *History of Black Business in America: Capitalism, Race, Entrepreneurship.* New York: Macmillan Library Reference, 1998.

Wallace, Maurice. "Are We Men?: Prince Hall, Martin Delany, and the Masculine Ideal in Black Freemasonry, 1775–1865." In *National Imaginaries, American Identities: The Cultural Work of American Iconography,* edited by Larry J. Reynolds and Gordon Hutner, 182–210. Princeton, N.J.: Princeton University Press, 2000.

Wallis, Don, ed. *All We Had Was Each Other: The Black Community of Madison, Indiana: An Oral History of the Black Community of Madison, Indiana.* Bloomington: Indiana University Press, 1990.

Washington, James Melvin. *Frustrated Fellowship: The Black Baptist Quest for Social Power.* Macon, Ga.: Mercer University Press, 1986.

Watts, Eugene J. "Black Political Progress in Atlanta." *Journal of Negro History* 59 (1974): 268–86.

Weber, Max. *On Charisma and Institution Building: Selected Papers.* Translated by S. N. Eisenstadt. Chicago: University of Chicago Press, 1968.

Weber, Max. *The Theory of Social and Economic Organization.* Translated by A. M. Henderson and Talcott Parsons, revised and edited by Talcott Parsons. New York: Oxford University Press, 1986.

White, Dana F. "The Black Sides of Atlanta: A Geography of Expansion and Containment, 1870–1975." *Atlanta Historical Journal* 26 (summer/fall 1982): 199–225.

White, Deborah Gray. *Ar'n't I a Woman? Female Slaves in the Plantation South.* New York: W. W. Norton, 1985.

———. *Too Heavy a Load: Black Women in Defense of Themselves, 1894–1994.* New York: W. W. Norton, 1999.

White, Walter F. *A Man Called White: The Autobiography of Walter White.* New York: Viking Press, 1948.

Williamson, Joel. *The Crucible of Race: Black/White Relations in the American South since Emancipation.* New York: Oxford University Press, 1984.

Winant, Howard. *Racial Conditions: Politics, Theory, Comparisons.* Minneapolis: University of Minnesota Press, 1994.

Wright, C. T. "The Development of Public Schools for Blacks in Atlanta, 1872–1900." *Atlanta Historical Society Bulletin* 21 (spring 1977): 115–28.

Wright, George C. *Life behind a Veil: Blacks in Louisville, Kentucky, 1865–1930.* Baton Rouge: Louisiana State University Press, 1985.

DISSERTATIONS AND THESES

Benson, Alexa Wynell. "Race Relations in Atlanta, as Seen in a Critical Analysis of the City Council Proceedings and Other Related Works, 1865–1877." M.A. thesis, Atlanta University, 1966.

Collier Thomas, Bettye. "Race Relations in Atlanta, from 1877 through 1890, as Seen in a Critical Analysis of the Atlanta City Council Proceedings and Other Related Works." M.A. thesis, Atlanta University, 1966.

Fennel, Dwight. "A Demographic Study of Black Business, 1905–1908, with Respect to the Race Riot of 1906." M.A. Thesis, Atlanta University, 1977.

Hahn, Stephen Howard. "The Roots of Southern Populism: Yeoman Farmers and the Transformation of Georgia's Upper Piedmont, 1850–1890." Ph.D. diss., Yale University, 1979.

Hunter, Tera W. "Household Workers in the Making: Afro-American Women in Atlanta and the New South, 1861 to 1920." Ph.D. diss., Yale University, 1990.

Lane, Theodore Maxwell. "The Black Reconstructionist in Georgia: 1865–1877." M.A. thesis, Atlanta University, 1966.

Lutz, Christine Ann. "The Dizzy Steep to Heaven: The Hunton Family, 1850–1970." Ph.D. diss., Georgia State University, 2001.

Mixon, Greg L. "The Atlanta Riot of 1906." Ph.D. diss., University of Cincinnati, 1989.

Perry, Geraldine Jiggitts. "The Negro as a Political Factor in Georgia, 1896–1912." M.A. thesis, Atlanta University, 1947.

Porter, Michael Leroy. "Black Atlanta: An Interdisciplinary Study of Blacks on the East Side of Atlanta, 1890–1930." Ph.D. diss., Emory University, 1974.

Sanford, Paul Laurence. "The Negro in the Political Reconstruction of Georgia, 1865–1872." M.A. Thesis, Atlanta University, 1947.

Tagger, Barbara A. "The Atlanta Race Riot of 1906 and the Black Community." M.A. thesis, Atlanta University, 1984.

Thornbery, John Jerry. "The Development of Black Atlanta, 1865–1885." Ph.D. diss., University of Maryland, 1977.

UNPUBLISHED PAPERS

Donaldson, Bobby J. "Georgia's New Negroes: The 1906 Equal Rights Convention." Paper presented at the Association for the Study of African American Life and History Conference, Washington, D.C., September 30, 2000.

Maclachlan, Gretchen Ehrmann. "Black Women's Work in Atlanta, 1880–1910: Labor Market and Life Cycle Issues." Paper presented at the third annual Southern Conference on Women's History, Rice University, Houston, Texas, June 3, 1994.

INDEX